A Crisis for the American Press

BOOKS BY JOHN HOHENBERG

The Pulitzer Prize Story (an anthology)
The Professional Journalist (a textbook, in its 4th edition)
Foreign Correspondence: The Great Reporters and Their Times
The New Front Page (an anthology)
*Between Two Worlds: Policy, Press and Public Opinion in Asian-American
    Relations*
The News Media: A Journalist Looks at His Profession
Free Press / Free People: The Best Cause
New Era in the Pacific: An Adventure in Public Diplomacy
The Pulitzer Prizes (a history)

A
CRISIS FOR
THE
AMERICAN PRESS

JOHN HOHENBERG

COLUMBIA UNIVERSITY PRESS

NEW YORK   1978

John Hohenberg was a working newspaperman for 25 years in New York, Washington, and abroad. He has taught at Columbia, the University of Tennessee, the University of Kansas, and the Chinese University of Hong Kong. He won the 1974 award of the Society of Professional Journalists / Sigma Delta Chi for distinguished teaching in journalism, and two other prizes of the Society for two of his ten books. In 1976 he won a Pulitzer Prize Special Award for his services to American journalism.

Library of Congress Cataloging in Publication Data

Hohenberg, John.
    A crisis for the American press.

    Includes index.
    1. American newspapers. 2. Government and the press—United States. I. Title.
PN4867.H58   071'.3   78.9631
ISBN 0-231-04578-6

Columbia University Press
New York—Guildford, Surrey

CONTENTS

PREFACE

A POWERFUL and influential segment of the American public has developed strong doubts about its press, both as to reliability and judgment. While this has happened before in the history of the republic, the separation has seldom been so pronounced. Nor has it lasted so long.

The gap between press and people is not easy to define. In all probability, it parallels to a very large degree the sense of alienation and resentment that exists between many prime movers in government and the most influential part of the press. As our institutions have declined to public esteem, the differences between them have intensified.

Even though the purely local small city and rural dailies and weeklies have been least affected by public displeasure, they are nonetheless well aware of it. And so is television, which is generally far more timid than the press in dealing with the issues of the day.

Certainly, there have been many times in our history as a nation when the press merited public disapproval. But it is hard for journalists to understand why this should be so today in view of the substantial accomplishments of numerous newspapers, both large and small, in the general area of public service. Yet, short of a thunderclap of a national emergency that brings everybody together, I doubt that much can be done about the low standing of the press in public opinion for the time being.

When public trust in government declines and deeply affects the faith of millions of people in its principles and practices, the press is the institution that is least likely to profit from the resultant disillusionment. Nor is the damage likely to be repaired very soon.

Of all the charges that are flung against the American press with varying degrees of anger and scorn, the worst is disbelief both in what it publishes and in the rectitude of its intentions. This is also the most difficult to answer. For if a measured and detailed response is offered, then the press is held to be guilty once again of the most familiar of its faults, an extreme sensitivity to criticism. And if there is no response, why then, of course, the press is arrogant, self-seeking, and undoubtedly guilty as charged.

It cannot be denied, least of all by a practicing journalist of mellow years, that the press has faults. They are many and grievous in character. As the least regulated of our institutions, the press is often prone to claim more privileges than it merits. Its self-righteousness is legendary. Its insensitivity to individual suffering, depicted in glaring headlines, pictures, and stories, is sometimes beyond belief. It is the first to attack others but invariably resents outside scrutiny of its own deeds or misdeeds. Although it is the champion of free enterprise, its own business affairs are increasingly restricted by the dominance of a relatively few large corporations. Its profits, for the most part, have soared to record highs; yet, many newspapers are printing less news and are charging more for it. Worse still, some of the oldest are demonstrably out of touch with both their subscribers and the mainstream of American life.

In consequence, one should not wonder at the continued public indifference when appeals are made to defend the freedom of the press—that is, to defend the privileged position of the press in the United States. Strangely enough, the press itself hasn't done a great deal to defend itself although it is under serious and increasing attack in this country, as is the theory of challenge and conflict under which it operates at its best.

Inside and outside government, efforts have been made for well-nigh two decades to contain both the scope of the press's operations and the more sensitive news it distributes. Pressure, intimidation, court actions involving huge costs and even prison terms for offenders have been invoked in these incessant antipress campaigns. In such a situation, the public's lack of interest in the fate of its press may one day be crucial.

The two basic declared motives of this assault on the First Amendment have been to protect national security and to uphold the right of fair trial—objectives that the press shares. The undeclared objectives, usually disguised under a flow of reassuring rhetoric, have been somewhat less than high-minded—particularly in the Democratic administration of Lyndon Baines Johnson and the Republican administration of Richard Milhous Nixon. Both detested the press, but for different reasons.

Among intellectuals, steeped in hostility toward the press since the era of Upton Sinclair, the general conclusion is that whatever happens to the press is the press's own fault. Many business people, led by lawyers, find it easy to agree with this thesis of wholesale damnation. And courts in many parts of the land are acting upon it.

Despite all the warning signs, the attitude of numerous professional journalists is puzzling. Except in extreme cases, such as the Pentagon Papers and Watergate, they don't really like to band together for any reason. And so they procrastinate. They argue that newspapers are better than they ever have been, that the public will come around. They take comfort in record profits as well as in the new-found status and wealth of the more prominent ones among them.

This is the easy way out. It is typical of a comfort-loving land, of a pleasure-loving people who hate to confront an unpleasant issue until they are forced to do so. We hear it so often in our daily lives: "Oh, it's not worth worrying about now. It will keep until tomorrow." Alas, we have not yet learned, from bitter experience with other grave social problems, that it can be very costly to wait until tomorrow.

The reality is that the tangible damage to the news media in the United States already runs into the millions of dollars in legal fees expended in self-defense. The intangible cost may be even greater. Some responsible editors have conceded privately that they are much more careful now in what they undertake, what they permit their staffs to report, and the extent of their interpretation and editorializing.

There is little sense in applying soothing syrup in such a situation. It is futile to say, as so many do, that the problems of the press are temporary, that the First Amendment will always prevail in the land of the free and the home of the brave. It is pleasant to take refuge in Miltonian philosophy, which contemplates the eventual triumph of truth over falsehood, but it won't help much now.

For one thing, there is nothing temporary about this problem. It is a gathering crisis. For another, should public indifference turn to outright hostility, the rights of the press could be twisted out of all recognition by either legislative sanctions or the courts, or both.

I undertook this book only after a great deal of thought and soul-searching. Like most Americans, I have been extremely reluctant to believe that the press has anything to fear in a society that is, for all its imperfections, the most open and liberal-minded on earth. However, after testing my ideas and my tentative conclusions during many fruitful discussions at the University of Tennessee, the University of Kansas, and my own alma mater, Columbia University, I decided to proceed.

I am most grateful to the Gannett Foundation for a grant arranged through the good offices of the University of Tennessee, which enabled me to complete my research and much of my writing. My thanks also go to Dean Donald G. Hileman of the University of Tennessee's College of Communications and to Dr. Dozier Cade, the director of journalism studies, for their interest and encouragement. I am indebted, as well, to Dean Del Brinkman of the William Allen White School of Journalism at the University of Kansas, and to my Kansas colleagues, Professors John B. Bremner and Calder Pickett, for designing a course in which I could range over the entire field of journalism's problems. The discussions with my students at Tennessee and Kansas were both stimulating and helpful.

As for Columbia University's Graduate School of Journalism, to which I owe so much, it was a happy occasion when I was able to participate in a seminar there in late 1977 on "The Next 25 Years in Journalism" in honor of the 25th anniversary of the Class of 1952 (and my own 50th). If the discussion of my central thesis by those who attended was both intense and critical, that was in the Columbia tradition and I welcomed the examination.

Necessarily, I absolve all who assisted me in the preparation of this book of responsibility for what appears here.

There have been many false alarms over fancied dangers to the freedom of the press in the United States. At one time, when I was a student at Columbia, there were so many exaggerated crises that they became the subject of innocent merriment on Morningside Heights. And later, as a young newspaperman caught up in the organization of the Newspaper Guild, I was as indignant as my fellow-reporters over attempts to depict us as threats to a free press because we sought to improve our lot. But even in the pit of the Great Depression, most of us in the newsrooms of the land had faith in our country and our own future, and in Franklin Roosevelt and the New Deal (it was the publishers mainly who put their trust in Herbert Hoover and Alf M. Landon).

Today, circumstances are vastly different. Our people are no longer as secure in their faith about our national destiny. Among our youth, confidence has waned for many in the rightness of our democratic principles and our championship of freedom in the world. Our trust in the rectitude of our public officials and the credibility of our government is appallingly weak. How could it be otherwise with an ex-Attorney General of the United States who has done time in prison, an ex-Vice President and ex-director of the Central Intelligence Agency who are on record with pleas of no contest to criminal charges, and an ex-President who was forced to resign after a vote for impeachment by the House Judiciary Committee and who was spared further prosecution by a Presidential pardon?

The passions and recriminations aroused by such circumstances as these cannot easily be surmounted. They will inevitably contribute to the domestic tensions that arise from an increasingly desperate search for security in a world where security no longer exists for anybody. If there is sufficient public clamor, unthinking people willingly yield some of their freedoms in the hope of being more secure. And while as a nation we have not yet reached so critical a stage, I do believe that there are clear and present dangers that affect this country, its liberties and—necessarily—its free press. That is why this book has been written.

Aquebogue, N.Y.   JOHN HOHENBERG
June 1978

A Crisis for the American Press

You say that freedom of utterance is not for time of stress, and I reply with the sad truth that only in time of stress is freedom of utterance in danger. No one questions it in calm days because it is not needed. And the reverse is true also; only when free utterance is suppressed is it needed, and when it is needed it is most vital to justice. Peace is good. But if you are interested in peace through force and without free discussion, that is to say, free utterance decently and in order–your interest in justice is slight. And peace without justice is tyranny, no matter how you may sugar-coat it with expediency. This state today is in more danger from suppression than from violence, because in the end, suppression leads to violence. . . .

—From an editorial, "To an Anxious Friend," written by William Allen White in the Emporia (Kansas) *Gazette* on July 27, 1922.

ONE

A QUESTION OF CONFIDENCE

1. *The View from Clinton, Tenn.*

DEEP IN the lush green hill country of east Tennessee, people take their news the same way they take their liquor—hard, straight, and with a bit of a jolt to it. And the weekly Clinton *Courier News* gives it to them.

You won't find anything fancy or stylish about the *Courier News*, except maybe the boss's red, white, and blue letterheads. But then, people make allowances for the boss, Horace V. Wells, Jr., a tough-minded Democrat who has been working hard-shell Republican territory for the better part of five decades.

People still remember that when the school integration crisis burst upon the South with the United States Supreme Court decision of 1954, Wells stood up for the law even though he didn't like it. Nor did he let the fierce resentment of his neighbors sway him. Even after the bombing of the beautiful new Clinton High School, a terrorist act that sent a tremor of fear through much of the nation, the *Courier News* continued on its unpopular course.

"I'm not running a popularity contest," Wells often said. "I'm running a newspaper and I want to do what's right." For his courage, he won the Elijah P. Lovejoy award of Southern Illinois University in 1957—a rare honor for a weekly editor in the Tennessee hill country. Even those of his neighbors who disagreed

1

with him on so emotional an issue were just a little bit proud of him because he showed guts.

It was in the pit of the Great Depression, in 1933, that Wells came to Clinton, an unremarkable small town set down against the rugged beauty of the wooded countryside. He was a graduate of Vanderbilt (1928), and had had five years' experience on the Nashville *Tennessean*, rising to state news editor at the time he quit.

Starting up as a stranger in a locked-in community at that time called for both foolhardiness and faith. People thought, perhaps, that Wells showed a bit of both when he took over the weekly Clinton *Courier*. After awhile, he bought the Anderson County *News* and combined it with his own paper, renaming it the *Courier News*.

"I began belonging to everything for which there was no pay and I guess I worked around the clock a lot of times," he once said. Maybe that helped. But mostly it was Wells's own efforts that caused his paper to prosper and made him a respected figure in the land. Now that he is past seventy years of age, you would expect that he could relax serenely into the role of hill country sage. After all, his is one of the more successful among the nation's 7,500 weeklies. He has a paid circulation of 6,500 copies every week in a town of only 4,860, which means that his paper is widely and faithfully read in surrounding Anderson County.

But Wells isn't all that satisfied. He is concerned about the state of mind of his people, as every good editor must be, because he detects a deep current of unrest and dissatisfaction. And he is even more worried about the state of the newspaper business in general.

In good times and bad, even during the hateful turmoil over school integration, nobody in east Tennessee ever questioned Wells's right to put out the kind of paper he wanted his community to read—until recently. Then, like many another editor in the land, he began to feel—almost instinctively at first, and later by watching the polls—that the public's attitude toward newspapers was changing—and not for the better. It didn't seem to have much to do with the *Courier News*, particularly; people had become used to the paper's support of causes and candidates not precisely in the main stream of thought in east Tennessee. The problem seemed to be newspapers—all newspapers.

It would have been easy to blame the decline of prestige for the press on television, with its flashing colors, its close personal identification with many millions of viewers, and its easy-to-accept philosophy of entertainment. But Wells appreciated, as did most of his fellow editors, that the popularity of television was far from the basic reason for the change in public taste. For if that had been the only explanation for the widening differences between press and people, the outside world would have been quite right in concluding that this is a nation of idiots who do not deserve the freedoms guaranteed under the Constitution and who would soon enough fritter all of them away.

In his own small corner of the nation, Wells thoughtfully analyzed the problem. He saw that his principal hill country critics were not by any means his political opponents or personal adversaries. Nor were they the rag-tag and bobtail crew of know-nothings who objected to almost everything.

On the contrary, those who had become the most critical of the press seemed to stem basically from the substantial middle class—the merchants and bankers, professional people, and even a few politicans who would mutter cautious objections long before they had to stand for reelection.

Had Wells sought to shut off criticism to protect his own interests in the community, he could have done so very simply. As a country editor, he could have inveighed against the sins of the big city press and waved the flag against the New York *Times* and the Washington *Post*. But that, to him, would have been both ignoble and dishonest. Instead, he chose to listen. And he listened long and carefully to the people he trusted—and to those who trusted him.

One day, a banker friend of his stated the case against the press briefly, bluntly and forcefully: "I believe newspapers go too far in what they publish. They should have somebody to regulate and control them, just as banks do. And the sooner the better."-Wells was shocked, to put it mildly. If something he had printed in the *Courier News* had upset his friend, he would have understood. But the general indictment of the press of a whole great nation was something he had not expected from so responsible and respected a source.

He thought of quoting the First Amendment but realized it would amount to little more than an affront to his friend's intelligence. The banker was well aware of the First Amendment and the rights of the press that it guaranteed. So Wells asked quietly, "If you want to regulate the press, who would do the regulating? The President? Congress? The local judge? The sheriff?"

The banker shrugged. It didn't matter, he replied. That could be worked out. But the important point was that control—a *little* control—was necessary nowadays for the good of the country. "There's no such thing as a *little* control," Wells replied. "You've seen that happen in other countries. A little control soon leads to a lot of control. And censorship is next. And then . . . "

He let the unspoken thought linger. The banker knew quite well what the editor had implied. Once a free press vanished, all the other rights for which free men had fought for centuries also would quickly disappear.

There was a bit more talk, slow and earnest and yet good-natured in the manner of hill country people. But in the end, the banker was unconvinced that a little regulation of the press would be a dangerous thing. And so, with regret, Wells watched his friend walk away, the argument unresolved.

Horace Wells is not alone. Literally hundreds of editors throughout the nation have had such experiences, either in conversations with subscribers, chance encounters with irate citizens here and there, or in an often stunning attack delivered through the mails. The letters, somehow, seem to hurt the most because many are so angry and so violent in their reproaches.

The puzzling, the uncertain, the frustrating part of such experiences for Wells and his fellow editors is the sense of public unrest with which they must deal. None of them can *really* pinpoint the reasons for the press's comparatively low position in public opinion at a time when its public image should be improving. Nor does there seem to be any consistency behind the suggestions, proposals, and even demands that are being made in various parts of the land for *just a little* control of the press.

In the hill country of Tennessee, as in the great cities across the country, there aren't many who would reasonably expect people, press, and government to be in continual agreement for very long. The notion of such a perpetual honeymoon flies in the face of both the theory and practice of the democratic experience.

But, as many an editorialist has written, a basic faith and trust must exist among the contending elements of such a society if there is to be any unity of purpose. Unfortunately, these qualities have been in short supply for quite a long time, for there has been no real tranquility in the land since the Eisenhower administration. Both government and press, for different reasons, are paying a part of the price for it in public discontent.

Back in the Tennessee hills, Horace Wells can see quite well what is happening, but he doesn't pretend to know what to do about it. And so he puts out the very best *Courier News* that he can every Thursday and hopes for understanding, knowing the newspaper business has need of a great deal more than that.

2. . . . And the View from Manhattan

John Bertram Oakes is scarcely the kind of editor for whom you would want to throw a costume surprise party. In his many years of service for the New York *Times*, he never pretended to be anything he was not and thoroughly mistrusted those who could not meet his own rather elevated standards of conduct.

Not that Oakes was a snob. He was very far from it. But he also was a graduate of Princeton, magna cum laude; a member of Phi Beta Kappa; a Rhodes Scholar at Queens College, Oxford; and the editorial page editor of the New York *Times* for 15 years. Of course it was *possible* to call such a man "just folks." But, as Nicholas Murray Butler once observed rather crossly when someone asked if he could smoke in the Trustees' Room at Columbia University: "Yes. But no one ever does."

In his own reserved manner, Oakes was devoted to newspaper work, although he seldom made much of point of it. The closest he usually came to an encomium was during an occasional university lecture when he told of an early experience at Princeton. As he recalled, he had been considering a particular course and decided to interview the professor before signing up. But after he had mounted several flights of stairs and entered a tiny room high in the recesses of one of Princeton's severely Gothic buildings, he couldn't think of anything to say when he stood in the presence of an elderly bearded scholar. So he mentioned the title of the course and blurted out: "Is it any good?" The professor was dismayed. "Any good? Any good?" he cried. "Why, it's my life's work!"

Newspapering was Oakes's life's work and he was equally concerned by irresponsible comments about it. He himself had always been circumspect in his own conduct, as could be expected of the *Times's* editorial page editor. At one time, when the paper came out for Eisenhower for President and Oakes confessed himself to be for Adlai E. Stevenson, the opposing candidate, he simply took leave of writing political editorials for the duration of the 1952 Presidential campaign. It was, in effect, a "witch's sabbatical."

On an even more celebrated occasion, when the *Times* came out for Daniel Patrick Moynihan in the 1976 Democratic primary election for the U. S. Senate in New York, Oakes dissented in a one-sentence letter to the editor. He had attempted a full-dress discussion, but the *Times* would have none of it. The decision had been made. Accordingly, with characteristic calm and good manners, he retired from the *Times*'s editorial page but agreed to write occasional articles elsewhere in the paper.

What drew public attention to the dispute was both the abrupt manner of Oakes's leave-taking and the fact that the publisher of the paper was his cousin, Arthur Ochs Sulzberger. Whatever Oakes's and Sulzberger's intentions may have been, this was scarcely a squabble that could be confined to the family. Not, at any rate, when best-selling books were being written about the "inside" history of the *Times*.

It follows that what Oakes had to say about the position of newspapers in the United States would also become a matter of public concern. For whatever he wrote under his own name was widely read and remarked upon. His conclusions, summing up a lifetime of experience, were far from reassuring.

When Oakes published his article on "Confidence in the Press,"[1] shortly before leaving the *Times*'s editorial page, this was the position:

—Reporters had been tossed into jail for refusing to reveal the sources of their news on demand of a judge.

—Newspapers had been gagged by the courts.

—Editors had been haled before the bench and their news organizations had been obliged to spend staggering sums to defend their rights, a deterrent to their less courageous associates.

—News sources had been closed off by the courts and by some government agencies as well in a variety of ways.

—The Central Intelligence Agency had disclosed that it had had journalists on its payroll for some time and, while it said the practice had been stopped, it continued to insist on accepting the "voluntary" offerings of journalists.

—The Federal courts, in an unprecedented action, had halted the New York *Times* and Washington *Post* from publishing the Pentagon Papers for 15 days before the U. S. Supreme Court decided that the government had not established its claim of a breach in national security from such publication.

—In successive sessions of Congress, bills had been introduced with the announced intention of saving the nation from a prying press by measures up to and including an Official Secrets Act.

As Oakes was well aware, the press had been under almost continuous attack for more than two decades. Nor were these strictures confined to the courts and the various government agencies. Criticism had pelted the nation's newspapers from the White House and the citadels of business and finance, from universities and the great foundations, from labor unions and religious organizations, from civil rights and women's rights groups, and from every other imaginable source that believed it was either being misrepresented in the press or denied the attention it properly deserved.

And so Oakes took as his text Alexander Hamilton's warning in the Federalist papers (no. 84) against a free press guarantee in the Constitution:

What is the Liberty of the Press? Who can give it any definition which does not leave the utmost latitude for evasion? I hold it to be impracticable; and from this I infer, that its security, whatever fine declarations may be inserted in any Constitution respecting it, must altogether depend on public opinion, and on the general spirit of the people and of the Government.

Oakes began mildly enough with the observation that the press, like the government, had been putting distance between itself and individual citizens at a time when democracy needed it most. Then he developed his theme of lack of confidence in the press as the greatest danger that beset it, writing:

The intimate, almost personal, relationship between newspaper and reader of an earlier day has declined; and the consequent growing alienation of public from press threatens even greater danger to press freedom than specific legislative or judicial restraints about which we are so rightly concerned . . .

Once the public becomes convinced—however wrongly—that the

press does not deserve that First Amendment guarantee which was written into the Constitution as essential to free government, its legal protection will be hollow, as Alexander Hamilton predicted, and its freedom
will become a sham.

He then defended the adversary position of the press toward
government and all other institutions as "the natural position for a
press that takes seriously its responsibility to uncover what is
wrong or corrupt in public life, or with private institutions or
individuals whose activities affect the public interest."

To be sure, he agreed that there was a responsibility for self-
restraint in deciding whether to publish material that might damage national security or individual reputations. But he also emphasized the degree to which the phrase "national security" had
been used in recent years to cover up "error, venality, corruption,
or even a drift toward authoritarianism and personal rule." The
only sensible course, he argued, was to decide each case on its
own merits.

Then came his own assessment of the position of the press:

Freedom of the press in the United States today is under more
serious attack than at any time since the Sedition Act nearly two centuries ago. As the press has assumed the responsibility in recent years of
inquiring into the hidden recesses of government—executive, legislative
and judicial—the reaction on the part of governing authority has been to
attempt to place new and unaccustomed restrictions upon it.

He mentioned in particular the judicial gag order and the
misuse of judicial power to inquire into the sources of the press,
but at the same time warned his editorial colleagues that they
must be more open with the public and more voluntarily accountable. This was his conclusion:

If there comes to be a widespread public conviction that the press
is a closed institution and therefore not to be trusted, or that the press is
willing to defy the national interest or trample on individual rights
merely to sell papers, the First Amendment protections may indeed
crumble before the combined assault of legislatures and the courts.

Horace Wells, in the hill country of east Tennessee, and John
Oakes, in the rather soiled and bedraggled center of Manhattan,

have identified the central problem of the press, each in his own way. Each also has proposed his own solution—Wells's being to put out the best paper he can and Oakes's to encourage a greater sense of what he calls "responsible self-restraint . . . a moral compact between press and people."

While Norman Cousins was editor of the *Saturday Review*, he added still a third element to this set of proposals—a greater degree of fairness in the press. This was the way he stated his proposition:

> The American people are far better informed about the critical opinions of public figures than about the ideas they advocate or support. Denunciation gets the headlines and makes the six o'clock news. Statements based on careful analysis that call for or endorse lines of positive action are seldom defined as hard news by the media. How is the public to be adequately informed if the yardstick for measuring news overvalues the argumentative and undervalues the reasoned? Does a constant diet of downside news have no effect on the human mind? Is the world best described by a dirge?[2]

The immediate reaction of most leading editors and broadcasters is, of course, to deny that there is a crisis. Or if they know that they are not especially beloved either by the public or the government, they contend that it is all just a misunderstanding and, anyway, "We can handle it." And so many of them seek simplistic solutions to an enormously complicated set of adverse circumstances.

Thus, since television and radio have taken over the first telling of the news with mixed results, some editors try with lamentable effect to put out a daily local magazine crammed with jolly little features. Other editors feel that the American people are condemning the press as ancient peoples put to death the bearers of bad news, and therefore they bore their readers with mostly counterfeit or manufactured "good" news.

The wealthier and more powerful papers, having noticed that Sunday papers have generally been able to resist the trend toward declining circulations, are publishing suffocatingly large

Sunday editions every day in the week with predictably soporific results.

Among the remaining family-owned newspapers, which are declining in number year by year, the tendency is to sell out to the prosperous and aggressive newspaper chains. In this way they seek to avoid the estate taxes that would destroy the property if the original owners tried to pass it on to their heirs.

These and other expedients may work for awhile, but few believe they will produce a better feeling toward the press as a whole. Nor is it possible that the central problem can be resolved by the continued technical improvement of the production process, however much it may increase the earning potential of the press.

The upshot has been a strengthening of the policy of challenge and conflict by those editors, mainly of a tough new breed, who deeply believe in the adversary position as a necessity for newspapers of quality and principle. A few have rather timidly gone along with insistent demands for greater public participation in the conduct of newspapers. But the editorial old guard has unflinchingly set itself against such outside influences as voluntary codes of conduct, news councils, public advocates called ombudsmen, and the like. They will be content to die in style across the top of Page 1 but they will never surrender their control of it, come what may.

Small wonder then, amid such confusion, that the American public is somewhat less than enthusiastic over its press!

3. *"Why Don't They Like Us?"*

The editorial mind, as nonjournalists have been wont to observe since the time of Jonathan Swift, is a fearsome and wondrous thing. To be explicit, your average editor seldom knows what he wants until it rests before him on a sheet of copy paper or, perhaps, appears in the opposition papers or on television.

This makes it difficult for all concerned and gives rise to the supposition that the editorial mind is an enigma. It isn't. But its vagaries cause editors of all sizes and shapes and political dispositions to do surprising and unexpected things.

Take, for example, the case of Dick Leonard. He is solid, as becomes the editor of the employee-owned Milwaukee *Journal*. He is talented and hard working, as witness his rise in 20 years from beginning reporter to the top of the editorial hierarchy of his paper. He is a member in good standing of the journalistic establishment, having been president of the Society of Professional Journalists/ Sigma Delta Chi and a member of the Advisory Board on the Pulitzer Prizes.

You would expect such a man to be giving pep talks on the unheralded beauties of journalism to the deserving—and perhaps a few of the undeserving—youth of the land, to be genially side stepping embarrassment and comporting himself as an editorial potentate in general. But one night, while on a speaking tour, it simply didn't turn out that way.

Perhaps Leonard had had a bad day. Or a moment of utter frustration, which happens to even the best of editors. Or maybe he just wanted to stir things up. In any event, he suddenly exclaimed before a professional audience that had been nodding a bit: "Why doesn't the public give us more support? Why don't the American people appreciate the press? Why don't they like us?"[3]

The audience came to rapidly. Leonard didn't pretend to have the answers but he had a lot more questions that he posed in a tough and earnest manner:

We editors always preach fairness, but do we really practice it? Do we undermine our own credibility? Do we permit too much trivia in the news, too much entertainment, too little news of substance? Do we exploit violence for the sake of violence? Are we too distant from our readers?

There was a lot more of this for the rest of the evening, for once such a subject is opened up the newspaper fraternity falls to arguing over past and present policies and dissecting its own faults. There is nothing exceptional about this in journalism. It used to be a favorite pastime when working newspaper people were usually poor and had to gather after work in the the corner saloon for a beer. It still is, now that many are affluent and impeccably middle-class and have acquired more lofty platforms, ranging in importance from fashionable cocktail parties in Georgetown to the imposing lecterns of great universities.

But let an outsider accuse journalists of almost any fault, large or small, and there is an abrupt closing of ranks against the infidel, a snarl of defiance, and a determination to belittle and disabuse the rash critic. This is the line that was taken more than 30 years ago with the publication of a rather mild critique, "A Free and Responsible Press," put together by a distinguished commission under the leadership of Robert M. Hutchins of the University of Chicago. The tactic has been endlessly repeated ever since.

It is really too bad. For the journalist's resentment of outside scrutiny and criticism remains his one salutary weakness that makes all others possible. It only serves to compound the press's difficulties in explaining itself to the public. As Leonard observed on the night of his own critical outburst, "Too few people understand newspapers, their motives and their limitations. And yet, if we can't persuade the public to have more confidence in us, what chance does the free press have?"

Why, indeed, do "they" not like newspapers? Leonard's question, as far as I have been able to determine, didn't break into print at the time it was asked; if it did, belatedly, it scarcely attracted much attention outside the audience to which it was addressed. And yet, it does merit a decent and considerate answer.

It is sheer bravado for grumbling editors to contend, as some have, that the public's critical reaction from so many diverse sources merely proves that the press is doing its job. And it is nothing short of insanity for insensitive ones to continue to brush criticism aside and laugh off the notion that there never can be a day of reckoning for the free press in the United States because of the guarantees of the First Amendment.

Had President Nixon's White House "plumbers" not bungled their assignment and had he been able to use the government's investigative and taxing agencies effectively against the journalists on his "enemies" list, his ferocious campaign against the press might have caused very real damage. Indeed, despite the nonsense that Spiro Agnew spouted about the press during his campaign against the "nattering nabobs," some of the most eminent newspapers in the land toned down their criticism of the administration until it became clear that the Vice President would be forced out of office. As one editor told me at the time: "That guy is important. He could cost us the relicensing of some of our television stations."

It is a mistake, also, for editors to confuse their current critics, who represent some of the strongest and most respected elements in our society, with the ignorant yahoos of the far right who have showered the press with abuse since the evil time of Senator Joseph R. McCarthy, Jr. To the know-nothings, the myth that a substantial part of the press is in tune with a Communist conspiracy against the nation is still very much alive. But, it is one thing to disregard anonymous threatening letters and scatological telephone calls, and quite another to ignore the complaints of a responsible citizenry. For those who worry most about the press today are, by and large, high-minded people.

Some gravely discuss what they consider to be the excesses of the press behind the closed doors of some of our most influential foundations and other affiliated organizations. Others, mainly the leaders of bench and bar, studiously explore various legal avenues that might lead eventually to some kind of limitation on the press. There is discontent, too, in the ranks of elected public officials, but very few who must run for reelection are inclined to pick a fight with the news media on which they must depend for their public exposure. Thus, only the strongest and the bravest are in a position to speak out—but more are doing it now than in years past.

One of these critical documents, produced and published under the name of Walter B. Wriston, chairman of the First National City Bank of New York, was so mordantly fascinating in its implications that it was reproduced in *The Bulletin of the American Society of Newspaper Editors* and given an indifferent answer.[4] It deserves examination here because it is presumably in tune with the views of a major, and perhaps a dominant, segment of the nation's financial and business leadership.

Wriston's thesis was that the press had turned its back on the reporting of American progress and had, instead, fostered the belief that things are growing "progressively and rapidly worse." This was the way he put the case:

> The dominant theme is the new American way of failure. No one wins; we always lose. Jack Armstrong and Tom Swift are dead . . . . Logical argument has given way to sniping. We no longer have great debates. The accusatory has replaced the explanatory.

As if that weren't tough enough, Wriston argued that the policy of accenting the negative in the press erodes optimism, a quality that he called "one of the cornerstones of democracy." And although he swore fealty to the principles of the First Amendment (everybody does), he delivered this solemn warning to the malefactors of the press:

> Power without accountability is an invitation to trouble. History teaches that when any sector of our society grows too powerful it is only a matter of time before that power is curbed. Usually the sector affected, be it business or labor or the police or the press, fails to appreciate why society is reacting against what they perceive to be right and just.

He wound up with what amounted to an endorsement of John Oakes's plea for more self-discipline by the press, but added an implied threat against the First Amendment:

The freedom of all of us rides with the freedom of the press. Nevertheless, its continued freedom and ours will ultimately depend upon the media not exploiting to the fullest their unlimited power. They can and must criticize the government but they cannot replace constitutional authority by assuming that no secrets are valid . . . . In a world in which one government after another abandons democracy, we all must justify our freedom by the use we make of it every day. When freedom is abused until it becomes license, all liberty is put in jeopardy . . . .

Such rebukes from the community of bankers and merchants have been the lot of the press at every critical period in the nation's history, beginning with Tory outcries against the revolutionary colonial press for undermining the sacred principles of business as usual. What makes the Wriston paper something out of the ordinary is the position of the author, the timing of the warning he has given, and the implications of his remarks about the First Amendment.

It may be objected that he does not detail the crimes of the press against the optimistic mood of the nation in specifics, which would invite a telling rebuttal; moreover, he fails to indicate the punishment he has in mind to fit these undefined crimes. What he evidently seeks is the creation of optimism by fiat to offset the Lockheed and other bribery scandals, the illegal campaign contributions that were admitted to by numerous corporations, and other acts of omission and commission that gave business a very bad press.

In such circumstances even that dauntless king of American optimists, George F. Babbitt, might well hesitate to decree optimism in the press by 4 a. m. tomorrow, or whenever the last edition of the morning paper locks up. The jest, however, cannot refute the argument. Wriston is not Babbitt, nor is he Canute. What he sets forth, in his effort to check the messengers with bad news from effectively completing their sorrowful journeys, is an opinion that is held—and strongly held—by other eminent critics of the press. He may well be charged, as he has been, with misrepresenting the position of the press and distorting both American history and jurisprudence, but that will not change his mind or the minds of his associates.

To cite only a small part of the mounting record of complaints against the press by those who advertise in it or, at the very least, influence its advertisers:[5]

James L. Ferguson, chairman and chief executive of General Foods Corporation, has written that some of the business coverage in the press is both clumsy and biased. This was his point:

> The journalist too often sees the business system as boring at best and dangerous at worst. The businessman sees it not only as challenging and exciting but as the engine that makes society go . . . .
> To the journalist, freedom of the press is a sacred thing. To the businessman, freedom of enterprise and commerce are no less sacred, as are the trust and public confidence on which they rest. But the central question here is not who is right and who is wrong, but whether we can permit an adversary relationship to lead to a confrontation.

David J. Mahoney, president of Norton Simon Inc., also has called for the abandonment of the adversary relationship between journalism and business, dropping a veiled threat in the process: "We're not going to suffer silently while being blamed for the sins of the world by self-styled adversaries who substitute trendy distrust for objective standards of accountability."

Far from suffering silently, business people are probably as loud in their declamations against the press as are lawyers, who already have set quite a record decibel rate. Frederic W. West, Jr., president of Bethlehem Steel, concedes that business people sometimes believe journalists are "out to get business." Donald S. McNaughton, chairman of the Prudential Insurance Company, says business and the news media are like "two strange dogs . . . suspicious of each other's intentions." And Lewis F. Powell, Jr., before he became a member of the U. S. Supreme Court, actually charged that the news media were helping destroy the free enterprise system.[6]

The journalistic response has been predictable. Katharine Graham, publisher of the Washington *Post* and thereby an orna-

ment of business in her own right, is willing to listen to complaints
from aggrieved business people but warns industrial leaders not
to expect boosterism from the press. "It's not our business to
build anything up or tear it down," she says.

Ralph Otwell, editor of the Chicago *Sun-Times*, is even more
explicit in his own response:

> The gulf separating business from the press will always exist as long
> as we have a free and democratic society. It is the destiny of a *free
> enterprise* press to be a *free-wheeling* press, spurning the complacency
> that business leaders would enjoy and rejecting the lethargy that public
> officials would encourage. As long as the business community exercises
> the power and control it does over the lives and life styles of Americans,
> there will be that constitutional mandate for the press to stop, look, and
> listen at everything that business does.[7]

This is all very well, being pure and righteous and traditional
in posture, but it does not meet the main point around which
business leaders and others are circling so warily. It remained for
the ever pugnacious John B. Connally, ex-governor of Texas and a
cabinet officer in both Democratic and Republican administrations, to come right out and say it:

> The communications industry today is big business—as big as any in
> America, including some industries that a lot of people contend should
> be broken up . . . . Anyone familiar with publishing and broadcasting
> recognizes the trend toward concentration of influence in a few hands.
> This is plainly evident in the growth of newspaper chains and the de-
> cline in competitive news markets.

What Connally was saying fits neatly into the hypothesis that
"big media" could be subject to antitrust action in the foreseeable
future. He embroidered this thesis, pointing out that this was no
longer the struggling colonial press of John Peter Zenger, but "an
influential power center equivalent to the Presidency, the Congress or the Supreme Court." He went on:

> Many people are wary of the power of the press and the potential
> for abuse . . . I believe many Americans resent the smugness demon-
> strated among some elements of the press to the effect that "it is our job

to get to the bottom of everything, no matter who it hurts. We are the judge, jury and prosecutor, not merely the recorder of human events."

To this view, Kevin Phillips, a conservative, has given his blessing with the observation that recognition of the news media as a collection of "massive business empires" can focus debate "on reducing media concentration to a safer size by traditional legal and economic policy." In other words, to use the title of Phillips's own article on the subject, this means "Busting the Media Trusts." It would be easy, given these conservative outbursts, to postulate a conspiracy theory in which the far right is the villain and the press its destined victim. But conspiracy theories, although very much in fashion nowadays, seldom stand up very well before the rude thrust of facts. For instance, the author of a Congressional proposal for a study of the concentration of American press ownership, along with other basic industries, is a liberal Democrat, Representative Morris K. Udall of Arizona.

True, Messrs. Connally and Udall arrive at compatible positions out of completely different motives, as does Phillips. But all three can declaim, as Udall does, that it is "disturbing" to find more than 70 percent of American circulation of newspapers in the hands of a few group publishers.

While Udall makes the customary liberal genuflection to the First Amendment, and concedes that talk of regulating newspapers is an "area of special caution," that does not deter him from his main point, to wit:

> But the business of publishing is also the business of selling advertising, which no one has contended is exempt from antitrust laws. It is true that one can drive out competition and do great damage to consumers with a newspaper cartel even as with an oil cartel.

Udall's assessment itself isn't so damaging, for it is doubtful if the Congress is prepared right now to plunge into an antitrust investigation of the press and broadcasting industries. Nor can Connally's complaints be taken completely at face value, for at least a part of his argument is politically self-serving. What really hurts the press, as I have determined for myself in numerous interviews, is that so many prominent people in government, past and present, hold the same views or similar ones. This may not be a complete reply to Dick Leonard's question, but it is harmful nonetheless.

James J. Kilpatrick, a conservative by nature and an optimist by disposition, sums up the position when he says, "Newspapers are not loved . . . . It is just as the Book of Common Prayer reminds us: We have done those things which we ought not to have done, and have not done those things which we ought to have done."[8]

But what has the press done that is so terrible? What crimes have been committed by the nation's newspapers that justify such an outcry by the business community and such threats on the floor of the House? It is an old adage that the accuser must come into a court of law with clean hands if he is to make out an effective case against the accused. The same standard of conduct applies to the court of public opinion.

When one examines the record before the Securities and Exchange Commission of American firms accused of paying off foreign officials with bribes to improve business, about 360 companies had reported taking part in such practices by the end of 1977; not one, however, involved a newspaper or, so far as is known, any other news organization.

The world's largest corporation, Exxon, was also the largest accused of foreign payoffs. The SEC charged in a civil complaint that Exxon had paid at least $56.5 million to foreign officials in at least 15 countries. This exceeded the previous record of $38 million by Lockheed.

While it is not a crime in the United States to bribe foreign officials, the SEC's regulations require such disclosures in regular statements filed by companies. And while Exxon argued that the payments were legal political contributions, and made no admission of guilt, it did agree to a permanent injunction against violations of security laws. No newspaper or, so far as is known, any other news organization had to make such a stipulation.

Moreover, in the field of banking, it was no editor or publisher who was obliged to disclose a record of overdrafts of very large sums but the Carter administration's first director of the Office of Management and Budget, Bert Lance, who felt obliged to resign his post. One wonders why Wriston, as an outstanding representative of the banking community, kicked up such a storm about the press and yet was not conspicuous in the ranks of the critics of the Atlanta banker, Bert Lance. Truly, as Wriston said, "We must all justify our freedom by the use we make of it every day." But that also applies to oil companies, airplane companies, and bankers as well as the press.[9]

4. What the Polls Show

Editors have been publishing polls since 1936. In that year the *Literary Digest* poll picked Alf Landon of Kansas to beat President Franklin D. Roosevelt but the Kansan was buried under Roosevelt's victory of 46 states to two. However, despite the development of much more scientific procedures and a generally good record for accuracy (with the exception of the Truman election of 1948 and a few others), the polls have seldom been given high priority in editorial judgment until recently. That was when most of them began showing a marked decline of the press in public favor.

This was one of the key sets of statistics:

At the peak of the Watergate investigation in 1973, when public confidence in most American institutions was at a low ebb, a national poll by the Louis Harris organization showed that among 1,498 adult respondents 41 percent registered a verdict of "great confidence" in the leaders of television news, and the leaders of the press won a similar endorsement from 30 percent.

But four years later, in a poll by the same organization conducted in the same manner, television news fell to a "great confidence" level of only 28 percent and the press plunged to an abysmal 20 percent. Early in 1978, Harris released another poll involving 16 major American institutions that showed "great confidence" in 15 of them had increased for the first time since 1973. But for the 16th, the press, "great confidence" had dropped to 19 percent. Even television news by that time had gone up to 30 percent.

Dr. Bernard Roshco, a journalist turned sociologist, argues that Harris's data show that all institutions have been sliding in public esteem since 1966 and are still far from recovery. For example, medicine rose from 42 percent in 1977 to 55 percent in 1978 but is still far below the 1966 mark of 73 percent who had "great confidence" in its leaders. Moreover, in the 1978 poll, the press still ranked ahead of the leaders of law firms, with only 16 percent in the highest category of public confidence; Congress, with 15 percent; organized labor, with 15 percent, and advertising agencies, with 11 percent.[10]

Curiously, a Roper poll released in 1978 showed that 36 percent of respondents rated newspaper reporters as most believable on the subject of corruption in government, with television commentators in second place with 29 percent. They were rated far above leaders of government, with 14 percent, and leaders of business and education, with only 4 percent each. But that didn't seem to improve the image of the American newspaper.[11]

Probably it is true to some extent that the press's showing is affected by the general public malaise toward most American institutions. But it is also evident that the public looks at its newspapers and its television news in quite different ways, and not always to the disadvantage of the former.

The nature of television' advantage is difficult to pinpoint in any poll, even the TV industry's own Roper poll. For example, in 1976, Roper's respondents showed there was no increase over nine years in the percentage of those who said they received most of their news from TV. It remained at 64 percent. However, the same poll over the same nine-year period showed a 6 percent decline, from 55 to 49 percent, in the number of respondents who said they received most of their news from newspapers. To add to the confusion, 36 percent of respondents said they received *all* their news from TV in 1976.[12]

Without doubt, television has cut into newspaper readership, but to what extent seems to be guesswork. It is clear, however, from the Harris poll, that whatever gains the newspapers made during the Watergate period were temporary.

For those who sought a more promising evaluation of the press's position, the Gallup poll offered scant comfort. In a 1976 survey conducted for Potomac Associates, a private research organization in Washington, D. C., supported in part by the Rockefeller Foundation, Gallup lumped the press and the TV news together in posing this question: "How much trust and confidence do you have in the mass media—such as newspapers, TV, and radio in general—when it comes to reporting the news fully, accurately and fairly?" Unlike Harris, who made public only the score for "great confidence," the Gallup responses were broken down as follows:

A great deal	18%
A fair amount	55%
Not very much	22%
None at all	4%
Don't know	1%

Dr. George Gallup, the dean of American poll-takers, stressed that his question, his approach, and his method differed from Harris's analysis, for Harris had asked only about "great confidence" in the *people* running the press whereas Gallup had covered all the news media.[13]

Gallup commented:

A second look at the figures reveals the rather interesting fact that Harris's figure reporting "a great deal of confidence" in the *people* in charge of running the press comes out exactly the same as our own finding for "a great deal" of trust and confidence in the *mass media*—18 percent.[14]

It didn't seem to help much when the press was linked with television news, in consequence. The public verdict was adverse to both, if only the top figure was considered.

What Potomac Associates did with Gallup's figures, however, is something else again. It constitutes an exercise in the creation of optimism, which heartened a few newspaper editors until they examined the figures closely.

Through a statistical process known as "indexing," a composite score (*not* a percentage) was developed by Potomac as follows from Gallup's original figures:

> A *great deal* was scored at 100 points.
> A *fair amount,* two-thirds of 100 points.
> *Not very much,* one-third of 100 points.
> *None at all,* zero.

When this was applied to Gallup's tabulation, the "indexing" produced this composite score:

A great deal	18
A fair amount	37
Not very much	7
Total	62

Potomac further adapted Gallup's percentages to its own composite scores by making the following arbitrary decision: "Any score above the midpoint of 50 indicates at least a minimum of 'fair amount' of trust and confidence; anything below suggests a lack of trust and confidence, or no trust and confidence at all."

So it turned out that the mass media's composite score of 62 in the Potomac survey was an excellent showing. It was just behind composite scores for trust and confidence in the American people, 70; military leadership, 68; young people, 67; and the American system, 66. The Federal government was considerably lower, with scores ranging from 50 to 55.[15]

The Potomac authors reflected with satisfaction on what they termed a high degree of confidence in the American system, shown by their indexing, and concluded: "One of the bedrocks of a democratic society must be the faith that its members have in themselves as well as in their system overall. Americans, we find, do have faith—in spite of, or perhaps even because of—the trying times they have experienced over the past few years."[16]

There was measured scorn for the conclusion of the Harris survey, which had shown a distinct downward trend in confidence in the American system until 1977: "Our citizens do not go through wild gyrations in their perspectives on key elements of our society."[17]

One critical observation about the Potomac survey was that its findings were not tested by validation, a common statistical method. The validating process tries to demonstrate by a complicated formula that the index does in fact predict what it is supposed to predict.[18] Often, it is successful. But in the absence of any validation for the Potomac study, it appeared to disinterested social scientists that its usefulness for the news media was limited to a comparison with its own findings in former years. Here, at least, there was a crumb of confort for the press. Its standing had gone up two points out of 100 over four years.[19].

Admittedly, the government did better in its comeback in public opinion. Despite a slump in President Carter's personal popularity from the peak at his inauguration, high confidence in the White House itself rose from 18 to 26 percent between 1976 and 1978, the Supreme Court jumped from 22 to 31 percent between 1977 and 1978, the military went from 23 to 31 percent in the same period, and even Congress improved its image from 9 to 15 percent. These were Harris poll results that showed the beginning of a recovery of public confidence in government leadership, although the figures were still far below their 1966 highs.[20]

There have been few surveys in recent years that turned out somewhat more favorably for the press. A poll by the National Opinion Research Center showed in the spring of 1976 that 28 percent of respondents had a "great deal of confidence" in the people running the press but only 18 percent had the same degree of confidence" in the people running television. But it must be emphasized that the NORC poll did not ask about TV news, which led respondents to believe that all TV programming was included.[21]

A different poll, this one by the Roper organization, showed newspaper and TV reporters together had earned a "high opinion" among 18 percent of respondents, fourth highest behind physicians, 36 percent; educators, 20 percent; and bankers, 19 percent. Roper's respondents, moreover, registered a 41 percent verdict of being "well satisfied" with their radio stations, 39 percent with their TV stations, and 34 percent with their newspapers. This was against a high of 54 percent for banking services and 45 percent for physicians and dentists, but a low of 11 percent for "the movies you have around here."

Another Gallup poll turned out to be favorable to newspapers but it was based only on adult preferences (people over 21) rather than the broader base used in most polls. It is common knowledge, of course, that younger people read fewer newspapers on the whole. In any event, Gallup's figures showed that 71 percent of his adult respondents in 1957 were newspaper readers, 54 percent listened to radio news, and 38 percent received their news from TV. By 1973, however, Gallup's data showed TV news had captured 62 percent of adult respondents, newspapers had dropped slightly to 70 percent, and radio news had increased to 59 percent.[23] There is no way of comparing this to Roper's poll showing TV superiority as a newsgiver because Gallup and Roper used entirely different audiences.

In a later survey, Gallup tried to pinpoint some of the main causes of public dissatisfaction with the press. He found that 39 percent agreed and 37 percent partly agreed that newspapers devote too much space to what is wrong with America and not enough to what is right, while only 8 percent disagreed. On the issue of accuracy, 67 percent of the respondents agreed that newspapers are not careful about getting their facts straight, with disagreement from only 9 percent. As for the treatment of controversial issues, the job done by newspapers in presenting both sides was rated excellent by only 8 percent, and 80 percent felt newspapers slanted the news.[24]

These were not very high marks for fairness and accuracy, on which good newspapers expend a great deal of effort. Nor was there much to cheer about in the public's view of press policy, which was basically an endorsement of the Walter Wriston thesis that newspapers should teach faith in the American system. The trouble is that the Founding Fathers did not have that purpose precisely in mind when they wrote the First Amendment.

There is some reason to believe that at least a part of the public's indifferent perception of the press arises from either a lack of knowledge or a lack of understanding of the First Amendment, which states:

Congress shall make no law respecting an establishment of religion, or prohibiting the free exercise thereof; or abridging the freedom of speech, or of the press; or the right of the people peaceably to assemble, and to petition the government for a redress of grievances.

Gallup found that fewer than half the people he polled knew that the guarantee of a free press was in the Constitution, the total being 45 percent. When he asked what part of the Constitution, only 7 percent replied it was in the First Amendment and 12 percent said it was in the Bill of Rights.[25]

This was of a piece with the result of a survey at the University of Texas, in which college students, politicians, teachers, and the general public were asked if they favored a law against slanting the news. The findings: 71 percent of the students favored such a law, as did 52 percent of the general public, 38 percent of the teachers, and 30 percent of the politicians.[26]

Another survey, conducted by the National Assessment of Educational Progress, a federally financed group, found that one-fifth of Americans aged 26 to 35 either denied or were undecided about the right of a newspaper to criticize an elected government official. The poll included 90,000 Americans in various age groups.[27]

Thus, as was pointed out by Bill Monroe of NBC's "Meet the Press," the First Amendment has not been repealed but it is becoming less of a reality. And this, in summation, is the lesson of the polls.

Marquis Childs, the St. Louis *Post-Dispatch's* veteran political correspondent, understated the case when he wrote, at the conclusion of a national study of public attitudes toward newspapers: "If we are to keep an independent press in the last years of this century, we shall all have to do a great deal more than we have done thus far."[28]

But what is to be done? Childs counsels that the press has an obligation to educate the public, "not only in self-interest but for the general good of the nation." Admittedly, newspapers have never been very good at promoting their own public image but there is no evidence to suggest that the American people would be greatly impressed by such a massive campaign of self-promotion. A very large section of the public has long believed that there is too much self-congratulation in the press and too little self-criticism.

Fifty years ago, Walter Lippmann warned, "There is everywhere an increasingly angry disillusionment about the press, a growing sense of being baffled and misled." He concluded that, if the situation couldn't be changed, "some day Congress, in a fit of temper egged on by an outraged public opinion, will operate on the press with an axe."[29]

What Lippmann complained about then was sensationalism and irresponsibility. And although we have a much better press today on the whole, the public is even more dissatisfied with the press than it was in Lippmann's time—if the polls are to be believed. At any rate, whoever has been educating the public in the glories of the press for the last half-century—if anybody—has been somewhat less than effective. For Lippmann's words have a peculiarly apposite ring to them today.

5. *The Issues*

The immigrant peoples of my father's generation, like my father himself, could not have envisaged a situation under which their press, for all its violence and partisanship and other glaring imperfections, could have been threatened with a curtailment of its freedom. They had come from lands where it was impossible to read an honest word about government, or the interests dependent on government, in their daily press; where, for that matter, any small truth or even a semblance of the truth had to be passed along in furtive whispers to trusted neighbors. Criticism of the government was an act of madness or desperation. And newspapers were, in Bismarck's colorful definition, "the reptile press," which crawled on its belly before him.

In the United States, the first sign that the adopted land of these frightened immigrants was truly free came in the appearance of public discussion of the ills of government in the daily newspapers, which could be purchased for a penny or two and read openly anywhere.

Reading the press was, therefore, a prized privilege to a less sophisticated and more trustful generation of Americans. Such is the turn of events in a single lifetime that the press today not only is taken for granted but even television, with its manufactured excitement, does not try to maintain national attention with the news for more than 30 minutes except under extraordinary circumstances.

There is no doubt, as John Oakes pointed out, that the sense of intimacy and dependence on newspapers that was a part of the lives of earlier generations has weakened. Perhaps, in time, it will vanish altogether and that will be a tragedy.

Alexis de Tocqueville discerned one of the principal reasons for its existence almost a century-and-a-half ago when he examined the liberty of the press in America and wrote: "The liberty of writing, like all other liberty, is most formidable when it is a novelty, for a people who have never been accustomed to hear state affairs discussed before them place implicit confidence in the first tribune who presents himself."[30]

In this era, when the great waves of immigration of the late 19th and early 20th centuries have been absorbed and more than 60 million people are attending schools and colleges in the United States, there is no longer any novelty attached to the free press. As for the discussion of affairs of state, or of politics of any other kind, the public is so surfeited with such material that it pays little heed to political developments unless they produce shock, sensation, or dramatic changes in the character of public office. Even worse, interest in the whole democratic process of self-government in America has fallen so low that only 53 percent of the eligible electorate bothered to vote in the 1976 Presidential election and less than half that number cast ballots in some of the state primaries. A Harris poll taken during the campaign showed that 64 percent of the respondents felt that "the people running the country don't care what happens to you," up from 26 percent ten years before. And 63 percent agreed that "what you think doesn't count any more," up from 33 percent in 1971.[31]

It is scarcely surprising, therefore, that confidence in the press has eroded in almost direct proportion to the loss of faith in government itself. Nor is it remarkable in any sense that this has happened in spite of the adversary position toward government that is a dominant feature of many of the strongest and wealthiest newspapers in the land. The public has correctly discerned that these same newspapers over the years have supported the government more than they have opposed it, and this is even more true of the bulk of the American press. The beneficial effect of the

Watergate expose, therefore, has long since worn off for almost all newspapers except, perhaps, the Washington *Post*.

To gauge the strength of the current attacks on the press, one has to go back to the earliest days of the republic. It is true that the circumstances were vastly different, that the infant press was small, weak, brawling and almost entirely given over to political partisanship and biased reporting. But something can be learned from the effect it had on the American public at the time and, in particular, on the Presidency.

The views of so self-proclaimed a friend of the press as Thomas Jefferson, for example, underwent a violent change between the time of the Constitutional Convention and his Presidency. In 1787, he wrote the most persuasive and most quoted of all encomiums for a free press:

The basis of our governments being the opinion of the people, the very first object should be to keep that right; and were it left to me to decide whether we should have a government without newspapers or newspapers without a government, I should not hesitate for a moment to prefer the latter. But I should mean that every man should receive those papers and be capable of reading them.[32]

Sixteen years later, Jefferson was writing in a quite different vein, for he was completely at odds with what he called the Tory press, as was a large section of the American public. This was his latter-day view:

The Federalists, having failed in destroying the freedom of the press by their gag-law, seem to have attacked it in an opposite form, that is by pushing its licentiousness and its lying to such a degree of prostitution as to deprive it of all credit. And the fact is that so abandoned are the Tory presses in this particular that even the least informed of people have learned that nothing in a newspaper is to be believed.

This is a dangerous state of things, and the press ought to be restored to its credibility if possible. The restraints provided by the laws of the states are sufficient for this if applied. And I have therefore long thought that a few prosecutions of the most prominent offenders would have a wholesome effect in restoring the integrity of the presses. Not a general prosecution, for that would look like persecution, but a selected one . . . . [33]

If so great a defender of the rights of man as Jefferson leaned toward a selective prosecution of opposing editors, then it is understandable that less noble politicians would consider these and stronger measures to bring an unruly institution to heel. Just how far President Nixon would have gone if he had been able to deal as he wished with those on his "enemies" list is problematical, but there is little doubt that he was headed in an authoritarian direction.

The position today is that the American press—or at least an important section of it—has been accused of all manner of infractions against the common good. It has been charged with undermining national security, nullifying the process of fair trial, hamstringing the nation's intelligence agencies, damaging the economy with uncritical attacks on business, distorting and otherwise interfering with the proper conduct of foreign policy, slighting religion, unfairly attacking organized labor, and discriminating within its own ranks against women, blacks, and minorities in general.

The indictment is so broad that one is tempted to observe that, if only half of it were true, we would long ago have lapsed into a hopeless state of anarchy at home and would be sprawled in hapless weakness before our foes abroad. Yet, true or not, these are the charges the press must answer in one way or another. And the answers, as yet, have been so unconvincing that defense lawyers cry out against a biased press if they lose their case, hoping a higher court will be sympathetic, and incompetent public officials attack the press as a last resort to try to save themselves. These forays against newspapers have become virtually standard operating procedure in public office—so much so that reporters no longer regard them as news.

It is not of immediate consequences whether there is to be a day of reckoning, and when, or whether, the penalties to be imposed are to be minimal or drastic in nature. This grave prospect will be dealt with in a later section of this book. The more immediate problem is that the American public, in displaying such a debilitating lack of confidence in its press, has created an atmosphere in which punitive actions are possible against all the news media.

Mercifully, we have not reached the stage in which cannons are turned on a newspaper building, as occurred in Baltimore during the War of 1812, or a mob murders an unpopular editor, the fate of Rev. Elijah P. Lovejoy in 1837 in Alton, Ill.[34] Yet, it is worth noting that a ruthless gang was so little worried about the press and its impact on the public that paid killers murdered an investigative reporter, Don Bolles of the Arizona *Republic*, while he was crusading against corruption.° During the Hanafi Muslims' seizure of hostages in Washington, D. C., a reporter for a local radio station was killed. And a few Croatian terrorists were able to coerce the mightiest newspapers in the land into publishing their propaganda demands before releasing the hostages they had seized on a hijacked plane.

These outrages did not seem to make a dent in public apathy. In fact, when a group of public-spirited reporters went to Arizona with the support of their newspapers to try to conclude successfully Bolles's crusade against criminal elements and their political allies, they met with outright hostility. The chief result seemed to be pressure on the news media, particularly television, to tone down the coverage of certain types of news events, such as terrorism, the holding of hostages, and riots. Also, there were many who lectured the press to show "greater responsibility."

°John Harvey Adamson of Phoenix, Ariz., pleaded guilty to second degree murder in the Bolles case in January 1977, after confessing that he planted a bomb beneath Bolles's car in Phoenix on June 2, 1976. Adamson then testified that Max Dunlap, a Phoenix building contractor, had hired him to kill Bolles and that James Robinson, a plumber from nearby Chandler, Ariz., had detonated the bomb in Bolles's car with a radio-control device. Dunlap and Robinson were convicted of first degree murder Nov. 6, 1977, and sentenced on Jan. 10, 1978, to die in the Arizona gas chamber. The sentences were appealed. See Associated Press night report Jan. 10, 1978.

It was just as frustrating as an exchange between James Reston of the New York *Times* and Bill D. Moyers during the Vietnam War while Moyers was the White House press secretary under President Johnson. Reston had accused Moyers of not being able to "establish confidence in the public and private statements made in the name of the President." To which Moyers replied in mingled anger and despair: "You [the press] often see things through a keyhole, you see only a small portion of what we in government see. Yours are the errors of incompleteness."[35]

Just what Moyers saw that Reston did not see at the time was never disclosed, nor did Moyers elaborate on his somewhat dubious thesis after he returned to the ranks of journalism and began taking his own pot-shots at the bureaucrats. All of which is a fairly typical conclusion to most debates over press responsibility or lack of it. The principal news media of the country argue that they *are* responsible, but that their critics are not. Out of that kind of dialogue, nothing is likely to eventuate except greater misunderstanding. And the press now has all of that it can stand.

There is a school of thought, developed mainly by the far right, that the whole press really isn't at fault—that public anger should be directed in the main at the chief culprits, the "Big Seven" that are perceived by their detractors as ultraliberal. These are the New York *Times*, Washington *Post, Time, Newsweek*, and the three networks. They are charged in the conservative lexicon with being mainly responsible for what the American people see, hear, and read. It was a favorite topic of Spiro Agnew's before he came to grief. But even after he left the Vice Presidency in disgrace, the tale of undue "Big Seven" liberal influence on the media remained popular.

There is, naturally, no denying the importance of this imposing combination of newspapers, news magazines, and networks. But they could scarcely determine what the news is for all the American media even if they tried, which they are too sensible to attempt. For one thing, the "Big Seven" syndrome ignores the two major American wire services, Associated Press and United Press International, which do more to determine the "play" (i.e., the importance) of news for both print and broadcast media than any other organizations. The complaint has frequently been made, notably by Norman E. Isaacs, that too many editors let the A M and P M news budget summaries of the wire services influence their estimate of the news. Even more important, the theory of the "Big Seven" overlooks the enormous influence of the press chains, eight of which control about half the daily newspaper circulation in the land and some of the leading television outlets as well. It is scarcely logical to assume that such organizations as Knight-Ridder, Gannett, Chicage *Tribune*-New York *News*, Los Angeles *Times-Newsday*, Dow Jones, Newhouse, Scripps-Howard, and Hearst would let any of the "Big Seven" dominate their thinking. Quite the contrary would normally be the case.

The *Wall Street Journal*, with its 1.5 million daily circulation and its dozen or more printing plants throughout the country, is probably a greater influence on the business community than any of the "Big Seven." Indeed, quite a case could be made out to question the essential liberalism of the "Big Seven," but that is another story entirely. The leaders of the moderate-to-conservative press are just as concerned as the "Big Seven" about stimulating public support for the press.

Warren H. Phillips, president of the *Wall Street Journal* and the parent Dow Jones & Co., has declared the issue to be "whether, by limiting what is published, we are going to let the government deprive the public of much of what it should know." He believes that the crisis of confidence between newspapers and the public "goes much deeper than the occasional ineptitude or excesses—which may be sloppy but are not conspiratorial." He concedes that, in a complex, fast-changing society that is overwhelmed by an abundance of news, it is difficult for readers to avoid the feeling, "You can't get the whole truth out of the press." This is the way Phillips puts the case: "People are so committed, so involved, so agitated in this age of change and controversy that many of them look for newspaper accounts of events to reinforce and agree with their own prejudices. If they don't get that, they feel the press is not credible."[36]

No, the myth of the "Big Seven" won't do. It simply isn't possible to settle on a few scapegoats in this troublesome situation. The entire American press, together with the broadcast media, will be affected by whatever happens—Republican, Democratic, and independent; liberal and conservative, large and small, metropolitan, suburban, and rural.

We have reached the stage in this country at which the concept of an independent press in a democratic society will have to be fought out in the public arena once again, as it has been so many times in the past. The difference is that the press now has fewer defenders in high places than it has had for many years and the broadcast media are in even worse shape. All in all, the news media are in for, at the very least, a bumpy ride.

It is the sheerest folly, under the circumstances, for editiors and commentators to continue to assume that the press is suffering primarily because it is the bearer of so much bad news in trying times. The always plain-spoken James J. Kilpatrick calls that nonsense, which it is. As he puts it: "In our own unscholarly way, we are the chroniclers of history; and history remains as Gibbon long ago defined it—little more than a register of the crimes, follies, and misfortunes of mankind. We have always been the bearer of bad news, but we have not always been unloved."Wes Gallagher, upon his retirement as president of the Associated Press, stated the position accurately when he wrote:

"American citizens either will be the best informed elite in the world or the most confused and disillusioned. It is the press, print and broadcast, which will decide. The responsibility is enormous. If the public is left confused, cynical, and disillusioned, you can rest assured of one thing. A free press will disappear. But the responsibility is far greater than this. If a free press disappears, so will all our other democratic institutions."

The most disturbing aspect of the government's developing strategy in dealing with the press is its similarity to the practices of Britain's Official Secrets Acts. In prosecuting a former CIA agent who used unclassified information in his book about the organization, and in obtaining convictions against two men as spies for Vietnam, the Justice Department argued that government information was "government property" and that anybody who "steals" it is guilty of larceny.* In effect, this duplicates the theory behind the British Official Secrets Acts that anybody who discloses or receives government information without authority is guilty of a crime. To the American Civil Liberties Union, the American policy is "dangerous" because it makes almost anything the government does "an official secret."

Added to this is Chief Justice Warren E. Burger's warning that the First Amendment does not confer "special and extraordinary privileges and status" on the press. It is this philosophy that the court upheld in the Stanford *Daily* case by assenting to the right of police to search newspaper offices and quarters of other innocent persons for evidence of a crime by obtaining a search warrant only. Efforts to secure remedial legislation and assurances of support from Vice President Walter F. Mondale can scarcely ease concern over the main thrust of the Carter administration's dealings with the press.[37] One does not have to read editorial pages to conclude that the history of the American press has taken a grave turn in the last quarter of the 20th century.

---

*The law in question is Sec. 641, Federal Criminal Code, which declares the theft of government property to be a crime. By calling government information "property," a unique interpretation, the government obtained both a larceny and an espionage conviction against Ronald L. Humphrey and David Truong as spies for Vietnam, both of whom have appealed. The government also used the law as the basis for prosecuting Frank Snepp, a former CIA agent, for writing an unauthorized book about the CIA, even though he used only unclassified information.

TWO

THE ADVERSARIES

1. Mr. Carter Comes to Washington

THERE WAS once an amiable theory in the cluttered newsrooms of the land that an incoming President of the United States deserved a honeymoon—a few days, perhaps even a few weeks—to adjust to the splendid miseries of his high office. That generous notion, unhappily, has perished. It fell victim to the vigorous application of the theory of challenge and conflict—the root of adversary journalism.

In this benighted and unchivalrous era, accordingly, the press seldom wastes time on ceremony when it takes on a newly inaugurated President. Nor is there much fuss about past loyalties or other obligations, real or fancied, such as party allegiances or the tradition of good manners on or off the editorial page. It is something Walter Lippmann used to call civility in the news business, which was never present in great quantities. Once the election is over, let the victor beware!

The Washington leadership of the press—or at least a substantial part of it—appears to have determined that a President must understand that he will be tightly and critically examined in all his acts. If current precedent is to be taken at face value, the poor fellow must also be made to realize that, if there are to be cheers, he will be lucky to receive one, one-and-a-half, or two.

Three cheers in recent history have been reserved for the

unceremonious departure of Presidents, Messrs. Johnson and Nixon in particular, and not their accession to high office. For that matter, Gerald Ford was not treated with the generosity he deserved for rescuing the Presidency from the gutter, to which his immediate predecessor had reduced it.

This may be unfair, but fairness in the political process has seldom been an outstanding characteristic of the bulk of the American press. And this, in turn, has served to magnify public disbelief in the self-proclaimed fairness of the press in reporting the news. For it is perfectly obvious that the press has been hard on every President, not excepting the blunt-spoken Washington and the sainted Lincoln, as is its right under the First Amendment. It has been far more prone to report a bump on the head rather than a pat on the back.

However, few newcomers have had to take the heat from the very first full day in office, as was the case with Jimmy Carter of Plains, Georgia.

On the morning after the Carter inaugural, Benjamin Bradlee, the executive editor of the Washington *Post*, was asked on the NBC's "Today" show: "Will there be a honeymoon in the Carter administration or is this an idea whose time has gone?" Bradlee, the director of the *Post's* Watergate expose, gave not a thought to his newspaper's support of Carter during the Presidential campaign. That, after all, was ancient history. Now, he was confronted with the proposition that he, of all journalists, should go easy on an incoming President.

He brushed it off quickly and unsmilingly, saying,

I suspect it's an idea whose time won't come. We're interested in each other now, I think, like a couple of dogs enthusiastically sniffing around each other. But I think things will settle down quite quickly to the kind of relationship that is healthy, adversary.

The simile was not exactly elegant, but it made the point. In Bradlee's view, even though the 39th President of the United

States had not yet settled into the Oval Office of the White House that bleak and chilly January 21, 1977, the press was entitled to issue both a warning and a challenge: "En garde!"

What the bemused millions who watch the "Today" show as they choke down breakfast may have thought of the style of the press that day will never be known. But no d'Artagnan, flashing his sword before the castle of Cardinal Richelieu in 17th-century France, could have struck such a defiant posture with greater determination.

Carter and his oncoming Georgians had been put on notice. The press, or at least the considerable part of it that agreed with Bradlee's philosophy, was to be their adversary. But it was only what the new President and his entourage expected. They had scarcely looked for the press to strew roses in their path as they took command of the richest and strongest country in the world.

In its tolerance and its forbearance, the U. S. has been unique in stubbornly sustaining freedom of the press to an extent that is without parallel in the history of civilization. But then, nowhere else in the world has there ever been an engine of public information as great, wealthy, and powerful as the privately owned American press and the privately owned broadcast industry. To the authoritarian regimes in the world, it is incomprehensible that any government, particularly that of the United States, would permit such liberties to exist. Indeed, as Judge Learned Hand observed, many in other lands have looked upon it as folly.[1]

And now doubts about the rationale behind the free press are increasing at home. Among more thoughtful journalists, there is growing concern that this picturesque and bothersome state of affairs may not last much longer without some checkrein in the fourth decade of the atomic age.

The experienced and talented Richard Reeves, after traveling widely during the 1976 Presidential campaign, wrote:

I found out that antipress feeling was more intense than I had imagined, and I had started out thinking it was probably pretty bad.

After hearing one hostile (and nonideological) question after another about *how* television and the newspapers operated during 1976, I came back convinced that the press will be the next American institution to get the Treatment.[2]

Reeves was not alone in expressing his fears. At the time of the Carter attack, many other journalists were struck by the high standing of the new President in public opinion and the relatively low position of the press. And some wondered: Is it really wise to go all out from the first day as an adversary of a President who is just taking office and is, therefore, bound to be at or near the peak of his popularity? Wouldn't it be better to wait until he does something that is worth criticizing?

There was no thought for such mundane concerns during the discussion between Bradlee and his colleagues on the morning after the Carter inaugural, however. Elizabeth Drew of the *New Yorker* went even further than Bradlee in spelling out the press's position against the new President, saying:

The press, like all American citizens, have gone through some changes in attitudes about their politicans, including their president. Not that it's unfriendly, but that it's a little more skeptical, a little more questioning, and they've learned the consequences of not questioning. This will affect President Carther as it will affect other politicians.

Only Joseph Kraft of the Chicago *Sun-Times* appeared to be disturbed over the thrust of the discussion. He protested quietly, with a deprecating smile to soften his objections,

I think that tensions are winding down in this country. I hope they can wind down between us and the administration, and I think I see some good signs of that. I hope we don't have to have a total adversary relationship.

It didn't bother Bradlee, who said,

I see some signs of the anti-Washington bias that you've heard so much about. I think that's—the Georgians have come up and taken a look at the press and it's not all that bad. I find the parties of the last few days—the Georgians are having quite a good time in this city of evil.

In every discussion of the role of the post-Watergate press, someone always brings up the awkward concept of the journalist as folk hero. During the discussion that morning, it fell to Tom Brokaw, the brassy host of the "Today" program, to broach the subject to his guests in this manner:

> What about this point that Joe [Kraft] raises about the tension between press and government? One of the legacies of your [Bradlee's] paper's coverage of Watergate particularly is that everyone has decided to go out and become a kind of folk hero by finding a scandal. Are we looking too hard for scandals while ignoring the broader policy questions that the country deserves to know about?

Bradlee didn't think so. In fact, he observed rather brusquely that he'd worry much more about his reporters not being "sufficiently investigative." The discussion then drifted off into generalities until Brokaw, no mere TV actor with a fancy hairdo but a seasoned former Washington correspondent, raised the possibility that actual hostility could develop between Carter and the press.

Kraft could no longer contain his concern. He burst out in an aggrieved manner, with a reproachful glance at his colleagues:

> I feel a little bit uncomfortable about this whole line of discussion because it seems to me there's an element of narcissism here. We don't make the news. People that are in the news make the news and we cover it.

The recorder of these remarks, who was listening intently to the discussion, could only mutter under his breath at that point, "Ah, if it were only so!" But the pious and pleasant journalism of the average journalism school seldom carries over into the real world, although it was nice to hear a journalist of Kraft's stature endorse the nobility of it all. Such sentiments are usually left to the professors.

Kraft continued:

> I think that there probably will be a honeymoon, I think that there will not be a lot of controversy, and I think we will be much more low-key, and I hope we'll use this opportunity to cover just the subject. We haven't, because we've been too much impressed by controversy.

Having made these shaky predictions as an apparent gesture of good will, Kraft abruptly changed course. He proceeded to embrace controversy himself, as every self-respecting Washington journalist must or forfeit his good standing in that eminent association of nay-sayers. As the focal point of his own critical view of the new President, he took the inaugural walk along Pennsylvainia Avenue as his text, saying,

> On the other hand, I think that walk yesterday showed that Jimmy Carter is very, very good at manipulating or managing or expressing himself in the symbols he chooses, and we've got to be pretty alert, it seems to me, to penetrate that and describe what it is. To say he's better at walking than talking.

As might have been anticipated, the filmed glorification of the Washington *Post*'s Watergate coverage, "All the President's Men," was mentioned to illustrate the difficulty that reporters now have of separating themselves and their views from the news. It was clear that Kraft's colleagues didn't put much stock in his rather academic view of the journalist's mission. And in the following colloquy, it became evident that Kraft himself had been indulging in journalistic hyperbole, an exercise not unknown even among the better columnists:

> BROKAW: Have we become, have we permitted ourselves to become, folk heroes in one form or another? Is that part of the problem?
> BRADLEE: Yes, it sure is. It sure is. And I think it's a point where we intrude upon the news, and that was the original no-no in journalism.
> KRAFT: Absolutely. And I don't think it is really our fault. I think it's a sort of, it's a desert. I mean, it's the failure of the Congress to assert itself, it's the failure of business, of labor, of those players in the game . . .
> BRADLEE: In the Watergate case, it's the failure of the prosecutors to do jobs that prosecutors should be doing and not journalists.
> BROKAW: Isn't it also the failure of us to have our own defenses up about it as well, though?
> BRADLEE: Well, we're a little guilty about it, that's why we're

talking the way we're talking now. I think our defenses . . . I mean, I spent half my life in the—what I call the Washington *Post* crouch, because you're down there waiting to answer some criticism.

KRAFT: But basically we filled a vacuum and I hope someone else will fill it.[3]

It was appropriate for the discussion to end on that melancholy note. For the historic defense of the earnest American journalist for attacking wrongdoing wherever he finds it is precisely that no one else will do the job, or that government is incapable of doing it, or a combination of both.

On the other hand, since journalists are always in a confounded hurry, they never wait very long to find out if some properly constituted body will carry out its sworn duties. Besides, to take cognizance of reality, there is always the chance that some other journalist will take advantage of the opportunity to fill the vacuum, journalism being the hard-nosed competitive profession that it is. And then where will the self-sacrificing dreamer be in his virtuous but misguided notion that governments in a democratic society have the intestinal fortitude to purge themselves?

In any event, although the televised observations on President Carter's first day in office are not precisely historic, they do merit closer examination than is possible during the verbal scrimmage of a talk show.

The image of reporters as folk heroes, for example, is credible only in a play pen. I remember, with the deepest chagrin, that when I came home at age 17 and proudly announced that I had become a newspaper reporter, my mother burst into tears. And many a reporter of this generation has had a familial reaction no less humbling to the soul.

Except under the most extraordinary circumstances, few reporters who enter an American newsroom for the first time have ever had the slightest illusion that they will be heroes to their city editor, to the less than benign ladies and gentlemen of the copy desk, to the auditors who contemptuously scan their expense accounts, or to their ever critical fellow reporters. Nor is the general public overcome with admiration for the godlike qualities of the legman and his feminine counterpart, by whatever name she may be called. It is scarcely news at this juncture that the journalist for the most part is not beloved of humankind—or even greatly trusted.

There are, of course, exceptions. For if names make news, which is the first thing you learn in a journalism school, it is also true that news makes names. Carl Bernstein and Bob Woodward of the Washington *Post* became the most discussed reporters of this generation after they broke the Watergate scandal. Fame draped them with honors. They achieved instant wealth beyond the alcoholic reveries of the few incorrigible romantics who remain in the newsroom. Still, when Tom Brokaw opened a television interview by saluting Bernstein as a folk hero, the far from modest journalist squirmed in annoyance and firmly declined to be one.[4]

It was, in some ways, a memorable scene. Off in the scruffy journalistic Valhalla where he damns his way through all eternity, the sulphurous H. L. Mencken must have roared with laughter at the spectacle of the millionaire reporter shrinking from the proffered television laurel wreath. Ernie Pyle, who gave his life while covering his beloved "goddam infantry" in World War II, remains the only journalist of my lifetime who became an authentic national hero.

As for the adversary theory of reporting, a more important part of the televised discussion, most Washington-based journalists agree that a certain amount of tension between press and government is necessary in an open society. In fact, most of their academic critics argue that there isn't enough tension, that some of it is artificially created, and that anyway the press is too much a part of the national establishment to do a thorough and credible job of criticizing the government.

Just about the only people who would somehow try to curb

the press's self-assumed role of national watchdog are those who fear that too much digging will undermine public confidence in government. But even they would scarcely argue that the press should become the government's cheering section. Nor would they be likely to forgive the press's many faults if it did less prying.

Secretary of State Dean Acheson, on his last day in office, defined the basis for tension between press and government when he wrote to James Reston of the New York *Times*, "To some extent, your purposes and mine are the same . . . . but in other respects they are antithetical. Your job requires you to pry, and mine requires me to keep secret."[5]

There are many in this nation who sincerely believe it is intolerable that the press should dare to inquire into the secrets of their governmet. To such people, the conduct of the press fairly reeks with arrogance. Perhaps there is something to the position, but it is very wobbly; at best it is a distortion and at worst a total misunderstanding of the purposes of the press.

I know of no journalist who would claim that the First Amendment constitutes blanket authority to interfere with the necessary amount of confidentiality that any government requires to conduct its business. And yet, after the searing lessons of the Vietnam War and Watergate, only a singularly myopic journalist would conclude that the government, without exception, has an inherent right to reach secret decisions that vitally affect the lives of all Americans.

To the eager social scientist who would pursue government-press relations to their source, possibly hoping to find incriminating evidence of irresponsibility or worse on one side or the other, preferably both, the trail is bound to be elusive. This uneasy relationship is not something that can be transcribed from a tape recorder or analyzed word for word. It also cannot be measured by the pound like hamburger or scrutinized under a microscope as if it were a particularly curious bug.

The tensions peculiar to this relationship between press and government are caused in the main by countless pressures and many diverse personalities as well as conflicting purposes. Often there are, as well, warring power centers within the government, which spring leaks of the most bizarre information to try to appeal to public opinion through the press. The proliferation of electronic copying equipment has changed the whole character of intragovernmental operations, for it is simple nowadays for one department or official to embarrass another by slipping an incriminating document to a reporter. In addition, the sharpest rivalries exist among the news media themselves, compounding the difficulties of self-government in a country as large as the United States. That increases competition to find news leaks, despite governmental efforts to dissuade the press from publishing its secrets.

You may say, as so many do, "Make laws! Stop it! Put the culprits who leak official secrets in jail!" The answer is that there are laws to safeguard the national security of the United States, but no court in recent years has found that they have been violated. And no reporter has done time for such a crime. However, since 1970, convictions on political corruption charges have been obtained in the Federal courts against a vice president, six congressmen, a United States Attorney General, 20 judges, 3 governors, 34 state legislators, 28 mayors, and 45 local legislators. And at the outset of 1977, 160 others were awaiting trial, including past and present officials involved in the Korean bribery scandal.[6]

The case for maintaining and strengthening the watchdog function of the press over government, in consequence, is considerably more persuasive than the case for prosecuting reporters for ill-defined crimes.

All this may make the press out to be a devilish inconvenince to the government, as indeed it is on occasion. For when a supposedly beneficent new government program is found by investigative reporters to be riddled with inefficiency and corruption, even the most fair-minded administrator begins to suspect darkly that the press exists for the exclusive purpose of lousing everything up.

Here is the way the point was made by Vermont Royster, the ex-editor of the *Wall Street Journal*:

It is not merely that this freedom [of the press] is irritating to our governors, although there are many examples of that. It is also disturbing at times to philosophers, to men of the law, to the citizenry generally and not least to some of those within the press itself. Not only is the performance of the press criticized, but the very extent of its freedom is questioned, both from within and from without. So it is that the right to speak and to spread abroad whatever one wishes remains to this day a revolutionary idea; that is to say, one which has not yet lost its controversial nature through unquestioned acceptance.[7]

2. *The Adversary Position*

The maintenance of tension between press and government is one thing, the pursuit of an all-out adversary position by the press against the government quite another. There is a considerable distance between the two and it can't be brushed asided by saying that they are a part of th same process, which is true. Civil libertarians who favor the first are troubled by the second. So are some editors of both liberal and conservative casts of mind. They simply do not want to create public misunderstanding, any more than Jimmy Carter, who has demonstrated his devotion to the principles of human rights, wants to be accused of trying to muzzle the press.

The difference between being an adversary and merely maintaining tension with the government lies mainly in the attitude and commitment called for by the adversary principle. A. M. Rosenthal, executive editor of the New York *Times*, defined the attitude with devastating simplicity: "The dream of every newspaperman (is) to blow the whole thing wide open."[8] The commitment involves the difference between preparing for a battle now and then, under the theory of tension, or plunging into a protracted conflict with government, which is what the adversary position is all about. If the challenge is accepted, the conflict is unavoidable.

The adversary theory is based on the journalist's unwritten code of conduct that requires the profession to maintain a healthily skeptical attitude toward everybody in general, and officialdom in particular. Just about the first thing young journalists are told when they are assigned to a government beat at the local level is to preserve their independence and never be obligated to anybody. They well understand that their job requires them to be investigators in addition to serving as reporters of record.

For a newspaper to be an adversary requires something more—a commitment to maintain editorial support for its investigative reporters and to force the issue whenever possible instead of side-stepping it. In the old days it was different. For example not even the tempestuous Joseph Pulitzer, in his conflict with President Theodore Roosevelt over the acquisition of the Panama Canal Zone, would have contemplated anything quite as far-reaching.

Necessarily, it takes a wealthy and powerful paper, with a large and competent staff, to undertake so detailed and permanent a scrutiny of government at all levels. While television has the wealth and power, its efforts in that direction have been feeble since the withdrawal of the best of the broadcast investigators, Daniel Schorr. Newspapers like the Washington *Post* and New York *Times*, however, want more reporters with investigative talents, not fewer. And newspapers like the Chicago *Tribune*, Boston *Globe*, Philadelphia *Inquirer*, *Newsday*, and others have established investigative teams that work on a full-time basis and produce results.

What do they investigate? Almost anything that gives them reason to believe that they will uncover a situation of interest to a large public. Investigative reporters have gone into everything from heroin smuggling to the CIA, the Internal Revenue Service to the defrauding of the cities, the ills of the Federal housing program to the scandals of public welfare funding and Medicaid.

A few specialized papers, like the *Wall Street Journal*, scrutinize the great industrial and financial institutions of the private sector as well as government because they have the people and the facilities to do the job.

In addition, both wire service and news syndicates contribute to the national passion for surveillance when they can. Occasionally, an entire newspaper chain goes adventuring into govermental wrong-doing, as the Scripps-Howard newspapers did when they uncovered a scandal in the ancient Congressional practice of junketing abroad at taxpayers' expense.

Smaller newspapers, too, have made notable contributions. The Lufkin (Texas) *News* won the 1977 Pulitzer Prize gold medal for public service by forcing reforms in the U. S. Marines Corps's training and recruitment programs as a result of its inquiry into the suspicious death of a Marine recruit. The Hutchinson (Kansas) *News* went to court in its successful campaign to bring about a long overdue reapportionment of the Kansas Legislature. The Riverside (Calif.) *Press-Enterprise* showed that a California court was defrauding an Indian tribe of its lands. And the Pecos (Texas) *Independent and Enterprise* broke the Billie Sol Estes scandal, thereby bringing a major fraud against the American government to light.

The government is by no means the only target of the press's able corps of investigators. The Winston-Salem (N. C.) *Journal and Sentinel* stopped a strip mining company from destroying one of the most scenic parts of North Carolina. In North Carolina, too, the Tabor City *Tribune* and the Whiteville *Reporter*, both small weeklies, took on the Ku Klux Klan in their own territory and beat the Klansmen. In Nebraska, the weekly Sun Newspapers of Omaha looked into the finances of the almost sacrosanct charity, Boys Town, with salutary results. And the Milwaukee *Journal* and the Louisville *Courier-Journal* succeeded in forcing a stiffening of laws in their respective states against pollution of land and water.

There is much more of this in the records, of course, but

these instances will serve to show the breadth of the inquiries that
are conducted by the press in every section of the country. To
their credit, forward-looking television and radio stations are beginning to emulate the older news media even though electronic
investigations, for the most part, are somewhat limited.

The outpouring of disclosure and criticism is awesome in
both depth and complexity, especially against government at all
levels. But dissatisfied press critics want still more, for they point
out that a few hundred papers at best can be considered active
proponents of the theory of an adversary relationship with goverment. It is perfectly true that not every newspaper initiates inquiries; in all probability, a majority of the nation's dailies do not
uncover a major scandal over the course of a single year. What
does happen, however, is that virtually all dailies are quick to
publish disclosures of others that have an impact on government.

It was once possible, before public trust in government sank
to low levels, to maintain a fairly even balance between the
charges that were made against a particular office-holder or department and the response of the accused. But nowadays, even if
a newspaper endeavors to be fair, the circumstances make it very
difficult for a response to catch up with an allegation. For if a
disclosure has any impact at all, it is picked up by the wire services, circulated to the nation, and published or broadcast by
thousands of outlets. The response, being less dramatic for the
most part, seldom attracts the same notice.

This may be decidedly unfair but it so, as recent experience
has shown. And this is how less aggressive newspapers and local
broadcast media fit into the pattern.

Such is the formidable power of the American engine of public information with which the government must contend 24
hours a day. It follows that adversary journalism, the elaboration
of the theory of challenge and conflict, has become a matter of
major concern. From President Carter's first day in office, he

could not avoid its impact. Nor could he fail to recognize the changes in the public's perception of the press.[*]

3. How the System Works

Ben Bradlee didn't wait very long to show that he meant what he said about using the adversary system to he fullest. Less than a month after President Carter entered the White House, the Washington *Post* ran a sensational story under Bob Woodward's byline on Friday, February 18, 1977, with the flaring Page 1 headline:

CIA PAID MILLIONS TO JORDAN'S KING HUSSEIN

That same day, Secretary of State Cyrus Vance was on his way to the Mideast to meet King Hussein in connection with the new adminstration's peace initiatives in the area. At the very least, administration sources complained, the story was embarrassing; at worst, they feared it might upset peace hopes. But, of course, nothing of the sort happened as a direct result of Woodward's exclusive. Neither Hussein's associates in the Arab League nor the Israelis appeared to be surprised at the news of the payoffs.

However, the *Post* received a lot of scurrilous mail from self-proclaimed patriots and moralists. The letters included charges that the paper had been "unpatriotic" to run the story, that it had been "in the vilest taste," and that it was "the pinnacle of irresponsible journalism." One writer even warned Bradlee and

---

[*]Before Carter's term was half over, the White House and the Justice Department were trying to close off sources to the press with just as much vigor as the Nixon administration. At one point, the New York *Times* reported (May 14, 1978, p.1) that the Justice Department was investigating some of the *Times*'s sources, as well as those of the Associated Press and Washington *Star*. The government was also reported to be looking for a "test case" to "embarrass a news organization." It wasn't exactly the "open administration" that Carter had promised.

Woodward that they were undermining the republic and called
them "by-line-hungry jerks."

The *Post* ran a defensive editorial, a story that quoted White
House Press Secretary Jody Powell as having said the paper was
"very responsible," and wound up the affair with a quote from
Bradlee, who wondered "how good the brave little king's intelligence is, anyway." For good measure, he added: "And with that
$210 million in aid he gets from us, why does he need a million
dollars in 'walking around' money from the CIA?"

President Carter canceled the CIA's largesse, tried to smooth
over the unpleasantness with the Washington *Post*, and Secretary
Vance apparently succeeded in mollifying the angry Hussein. But
the incident had more impact on the press corps than it did on
diplomacy, in the long run, because it renewed the pros and cons
about the practice of adversary journalism.

In Bradlee's defense, he did everything he could to make
certain that the story, if published, would not affect national security. "I was assured," he said, "that national security was in no
way engaged. I'm not saying if they had told me differently, I
would have done differently."

What he did do was to go with Woodward to the White
House three days before the story was published to talk with Jody
Powell about it. Powell, still relatively new to the big leagues of
journalism, was taken aback when the *Post's* executive editor and
star reporter asked him for guidance—"anything we should know
about." The press secretary stalled, said he'd find out.

The next thing that happened, the voluble Zbigniew Brzezin-
ski, the President's security adviser, was on the phone to Bradlee
threatening that the heavens would fall if the story broke in the
Post. Next morning, as a result, Bradlee and Woodward were
ushered into the Oval Office of the White House where President
Carter himself was waiting for them.

Bradlee began aggressively—he has always thought that a
good attack is the best defense—and the President didn't awe
him in the slightest. He said he had learned in his 29 years as a

journalist that national security had never been a good reason to withhold a story from publication.

The President, however, didn't use national security as an excuse. Instead, as Powell later recalled, he talked about the problem, being careful not to suggest editorial pressure, but "he left no doubt what our preference would be"—to dump the story and not publish it. That, of course, Bradlee refused to do, whereupon the President asked for and received assurance that there would be 24 hours' notice before the story ran.

Next day, Bradlee phoned Powell again and said the piece would be published on Friday, to which the press secretary cracked, "Sounds like a hell of a good Sunday story to me." But the Friday decision held. Although some in journalism thought it wouldn't have mattered much to wait a few days before running the story, mainly to avoid embarrassing the new Secretary of State on his first visit to Hussein, support for Bradlee came from his toughest competitor, the New York *Times's* A. M. Rosenthal, who said: "Almost any time you break a sensitive story there are people who would want to delay it for one reason or another. I don't think it was the *Post's* responsibility to sit down and say, 'How will this affect Hussein? How will this affect Vance?'"

The President's initial reaction was strongly against the *Post* in particular and the press in general, which was unsettling to the Washington press corps because some had taken his campaign pledge of an "open administration" at face value. However, Carter was as zealous as President Kennedy had been at the time of the Bay of Pigs fiasco in defending the secrecy of covert operations—even bad ones. Only the President didn't concede that there was anything improper about the Hussein payments; on the contrary, he called them both proper and legal. But he commented:

It can be extremely damaging to our relationship with other nations, to the potential security of the country even in peacetime, for these kinds of operations which are legitimate and proper to be revealed . . . . We are now in a position where some key intelligence sources are becoming reluctant to talk to us for fear of exposure.

He also told a group of visiting Congressmen at the White House, who speedily informed the Associated Press, that the Washington *Post* had been "irresponsible" for publishing the story. Naturally, the remark caused a flap. But the President, a master at the art of dissimulation, loftily closed the incident by permitting Powell to announce that the *Post*, on second thought, really had been "responsible."

There were post mortems. When such unpleasantness occurs in Washington, there always are. Admiral Stansfield Turner, the President's newly named director of the Central Intelligence Agancy, testified before a Senate committee that he favored criminal penalties to halt government officials from leaking national security secrets.

The Washington *Post*, which didn't need a diagram to see that its role in the Hussein matter was involved, at once interviewed Vice President Walter Frederick Mondale. The Vice President, loftily denying that he had discussed the matter with the President, backed away form the proposed imposition of criminal penalties. He did, however, suggest that it might be proper to impose "civil penalties" on government officials who leak secrets. This is governmentese for firing those who embarrass the regime in the press.

Carter supported Mondale at his next press conference, March 9, 1977, and rejected Admiral Turner's demand for criminal penalties, saying

My own interest would be to minimize the use of any criminal penalties for disclosure of information. There are other penalties that can be used without criminal charges and I think that Vice President Mondale drew that distinction.

I don't know yet what procedure we will follow. My own hope would be that we would prevent the disclosure of intelligence or information that might be damaging to our national security rather than trying to control the problem by the imposition of legal criminal penalties.

The President decided to try the milder course first. He drafted an executive order that called upon all government officials to sign a pledge of secrecy before they were given access to classified materials. For those who violated the secrecy pledge, the order ordained, but was not limited to, such punishment as reprimand, suspension without pay, removal, or "other sanction in accordance with applicable law and agency regulations."

From the point of view of security-conscious government officials, this was a necessary and patriotic thing to do. From the point of view of the press, it was difficult to criticize. But while the draft order was being circulated for proposed changes, a highly classified State Department cable about the Panama Canal treaties negotiations was made public by one of the champions of the conservative cause, Senator Robert Dole, the Kansas Republican who had been President Ford's running mate in the 1976 campaign.

Dole, who was leading the fight against Senate confirmation of the treaties, wouldn't say who gave him the cable. It had been sent by the American embassy in Panama to someone in the State Department and gave warning that a Panamanian negotiator was interpreting the treaties as a denial of the right of the United States to intervene militarily in defense of the canal. This, Dole pointed out, was exactly the opposite of the interpretation the Senate had been given by the State Department.

Carter administration forces in the Senate tore into Dole for breaking national security wide open, a rather tiresome claim in the absence of supporting evidence—to which Dole replied, with rhetoric that could have been used by any journalist in a similar position: "We should have learned from Watergate that we can never again allow a 'national security' classification to be used in such a way as to mislead the American people or to cover up politically embarrassing realities."

There were published reports that the government was "investigating" to find out whether Dole could be punished, but when the Kansan showed fight the State Department hastily backed off and said it had never even considered such action.[9] In any event, it was scarcely possible on Constitutional grounds to punish a member of the Congress for acts committed in the course of his official duties. Thus, the new Carter information code had a gaping hole ripped in its strongest protective element before it even was adopted. And it was not done by the liberal-minded press, but by the most conservative of Senators, who incidentally had denounced the New York *Times* for publishing the Pentagon Papers. He won the battle against secrecy but lost the effort to block the Panama Canal treaties.

President Carter has never sought to disguise his ambivalent feelings about the press. As long ago as 1971, at the time of the controversy about the Pentagon Papers, he was quoted as being willing to support a proposed law that would make newspapers criminally liable for publishing classified material that affects national security. The story originated July 9, 1971, in the Atlanta *Constitution*, being published on Page 1 under the byline of Bill Shipp, the paper's political editor. The headline was blunt:

CARTER FAVORS 'SECRETS' LAW

There was no equivocation in the text, either. It took the form of an interview in which Carter, then the governor of Georgia, said he had discussed the possibility of a "secrets" law with Senator Edmund Muskie for about an hour by telephone. It was just after the Supreme Court's decision in the Pentagon Papers case, which was the basis for the discussion. While Carter maintained that he had no objection to the New York *Times*'s publication of the material because it "didn't contain anything new," he was quoted as saying that "direct quotations from classified documents" and even certain declassified materials should be barred from publication by law. The report went on:

He [Carter] said he and Muskie agreed that newspapers should be held liable for publishing any classified information detrimental to the security of the country. Carter . . . said he also proposed that a special category of classification be affixed to certain documents that would never be made public.[10]

James Hoge, editor of the Chicago *Sun-Times*, asked Carter on July 11, 1976, about the story when both were on NBC's "Meet the Press" show just before the Democratic National Convention in New York. It would scarcely have been politic at that time for the former Georgia governor to have come out for a partial censorship of the press, but he did not deny the *Constitution's* story. What he did say was this:

> My preference is that the press be open. I personally feel that the Pentagon Papers should have been revealed by the New York *Times* and I would do everything I could to protect the right of the press to conceal its sources of information and let the responsibility of the press be its major check on how it acted as it deals with sensitive material or with matters that might affect our own country. I would have the strongest possible commitment as President to protect the independence and the autonomy and the right of the press to speak freely, and I favor strong "Sunshine Laws". . . . So everything I do as President will be designed, within the bounds of rationality, to open up the deliberations of the government to the people through the press.[11]

Despite Carter's pledge of open dealings with the press, those who followed him on the campaign trail in 1976 were under no illusions about the resentment in his camp toward some elements of the press. Nor did Powell, his press secretary then and later in the White House, refrain from the most heated arguments with correspondents whom he believed wrong. Sometimes his language was brushed with a touch of the gutter, in James Cagney's phrase, as occurred on the less than glorious occasion when the press secretary referred to "a couple of assholes of the press."

In effect, both the Carter camp and the reporters who were assigned to it slipped insensibly into an adversary position long before the election. The so-called off-the-record meetings between Carter and the correspondents, which were designed to create better feeling, seldom did so. And sometimes, as one correspondent put it, Carter talked about the press "as though he were wounded and bewildered."[12]

Another correspondent, NBC's Judy Woodruff, who had covered Carter while he was governor of Georgia, recalled a painful postelection scene at Faye's Restaurant in Americus, Georgia. The President-elect, his wife, Rosalynn, and their daughter, Amy, were dining there and several reporters joined them.

Before long an argument developed, as usual. Tempers bubbled over. Voices rose. Carter accused the reporters of being inaccurate in some of their predictions about cabinet appointments, which didn't sit very well with them. Few reporters like to be told they are wrong, particularly under such circumstances. Miss Woodruff continued: "He [Carter] got into a back and forth about it. He thought most reporting was accurate but a lot of the speculative reporting was unnecessary and why did we have to stick our necks out? Some reporters defended their stories—it got pretty lively."[13]

The public finally caught a rare glimpse of this combative side of the incoming President on the day after his narrow victory over President Ford. At a news conference on St. Simon's Island, Georgia, Carter told of what he called his "real concern about news coverage" during the campaign. As he explained it:

I felt that the comparison between the treatment of Mr. Ford, particularly on the evening news programs, and myself was just deference shown to the Presidency and the White House. It was a crippling thing . . . something we didn't know how to deal with. Every time I made a mistake, it was the news, and Mr. Ford's news was that he came into the Rose Garden and signed a bill, and he was in charge of things, very authoritative, very sure of himself—no problems, no squabbles, no mistakes.

And that was a period when it looked like everything was going against us, in spite of everything we did, and I have a feeling that, had it not been for the [television] debates, I would have lost.[14]

From that day until the inauguration, a substantial part of the press did a lot of plain and fancy brooding about the new President. In a sense, it was a frustrating time. For the President-elect couldn't very well be criticized for inaction when he had no power to do anything. And he couldn't make a great deal of news, the life blood of the press, until he actually entered the White House.

Not having any large complaints, the press, as is its perverse nature, settled for a lot of small ones. For example, it was said and written that Carter was still a mysterious figure but few pointed out that most politicians from Georgia *would* be mysteries to official Washington. Also, many an editorialist and columnist muttered darkly that nobody knew what to expect of the new President, which also was scarcely news, since he himself hadn't made up his mind yet either about his policies or priorities.

Charles Seib, the Washington *Post's* columnist on the news business, expressed impatience with all concerned—the press, for having done a sloppy job of campaign coverage, and the new President for having made too many promises he couldn't keep. As Seib put it:

> Carter made it clear that he thinks he got less than a fair deal from the press, and the press is going to be laying for him. He made too many promises that are going to be checked. But that's healthy. I think the sooner we get into the adversary relationship, the better . . . . After the inauguration, I think we'll go lie-hunting. I think any politician who says, "I'll never lie to you," has a real problem or a short career.[15]

James Hoge, who established his toughness by making it to the top at the Chicago *Sun-Times*, put the case for moderation to his colleagues. He reminded them that an activist President was taking office, that the public was not exactly enthusiastic about the press, and it was time to take stock. The first reason he gave was based on Carter's view on press regulation, to wit: "Even though he has inveighed against secrecy in government, he has also favored laws to punish newspapers that publish classified material harmful to national security."

The times, Hoge went on, were calmer than the Johnson and Nixon years but public mistrust remained high because of the abuses and coverups in both these administrations. "The taint," he wrote, "has stained not only the makers of news, but the carriers as well. Thus not only Carter has a problem. So does the press."

Yes, he recalled, Carter had promised to run an open administration with frequent press conferences (two a month), telephone interviews with the public, fireside chats, and other public relations trappings. Given the circumstances of other administrations of the immediate past, there was cause for concern whether these admirable objectives would be carried out, but, he suggested, "Let us start by giving Carter the benefit of the doubt."

Like every editor writing about an incoming President, Hoge couldn't resist the usual lecture against attempting to manipulate the news media, knowing full well that the process of manipulation already was under way. As for the adversary role of the press, he was far less belligerent than Bradlee and offered these observations:

> Still giving Carter the benefit of the doubt, what then should be expected of the press? After what we have been through, it would be negligent not to have the press's eye cocked, on the alert for renewed abuses. But perhaps we can exercise restraining judgment and not run off to war before any shots are fired. And perhaps we can avoid the debilitating exercise of fighting the last war.

What Hoge proposed was "a more sophisticated, tempered conception of its [the press's] adversary role . . . a balancing act, believing in government while maintaining its skepticism."[16]

Others were less diplomatic. Sam Donaldson of ABC said, "As long as things go fairly well, there will be an open policy. When they don't I think you are going to see the same problems in the press room we've had before." And Jeff Nesmith of the Philadelphia *Bulletin* rumbled, "Life is a great big Monopoly game to Carter and every piece has to fit in its place—including the press."[17] Summing it all up, one long-time Washington correspondent wrote anonymously, "Carter is not at all enamored of the press corps and tolerates them as a necessary nuisance."[18]

All through the buildup of Cabinet appointments, Senate reactions, and attendant speculation, this journalistic queasiness
over the adversary position continued. It couldn't help but contribute to public uncertainty. But Carter, being in no position to
take a strong line on anything, wisely held his peace and took the
press's small arms fire without a rejoinder.

He knew perfectly well that he had to try to reassure the
nation, regardless of what was said and written about him. And,
beginning with Inauguration Day, he did it with unexpected flair
and grace that temporarily disarmed some of his worst critics. As
Franklin Roosevelt had demonstrated almost fifty years before, it
is very difficult for a querulous—or even a hostile—press to hate
someone who knows how to bring color and excitement to the
drab monotony of government-as-usual. It wasn't in the Sermon
on the Mount, but a born-again Christian could have written:
"Blessed are the newsmakers, for they shall inherit both Page 1
and the network evening news programs."

To be sure, after Carter's walk along Pennsylvania Avenue
with his wife and daughter, there was the usual editorial sniffing,
the familiar columnar sneers about "grandstanding," "press-agen-
try," and "government by gimmick." But nothing could conceal
the delight of the television people over all the pretty postcard
pictures Carter had given them that Inaugural Day, or the satisfaction of newspaper correspondents who had been granted the
rarest of all journalistic boons—a good story. For one day, at
least, there wasn't a Presidential adversary who didn't let his
guard down, consciously or not.

To the nonjournalist, this reaction may seem overstated, even
childish. perhaps, but it is honest. When there is enough news to
keep journalists busy, they seldom worry about much else. And if
this is one of the grossest weaknesses of the press (and even more
so for television), it is at least a foible that the public is usually
willing to forgive. For if there was criticism of the massive coverage of the Pennsylvania Avenue walk, it was buried under the
torrent of approving correspondence and telephoning that inun-

dated the White House. That day, Jimmy Carter was one up on the press.

The Carter news conferences were another surprise. Not even Carter's partisans had expected much from him in the sharp give-and-take with the reporters. During the campaign, he had seldom been able to give a direct and newsworthy answer to a decent question. In addition, he had shown an abysmal fear of offending potential voters or influential groups, which made his early news conferences bland to the point of distaste. Getting him to take a position, many thought, had been like trying to put melted butter on a knife. So the Washington press corps didn't expect much.

Again, Carter confounded his critics. He came across as if he had been President for years. He demonstrated a totally unexpected talent, from his first news conference on, for fielding a variety of questions with candor, unfailing courtesy, literacy, grace, and total humor. He could be cross on occasion, but he was not rude; evasive when he had to be, but usually with an explanation.

Although the press corps by no means faltered in pursuing its adversary role, many of its members were clearly dazzled. The President, from whom so little had been expected, was suddenly pronounced a master of the news conference. Younger journalists compared him to President Kennedy, older ones to Franklin Roosevelt. Not even the woodenheads of the far left and far right could think of anything nasty to say about the Presidential style.

Through his performance, rather than through anything he said or did, he had won a very large measure of respect from the press. He capitalized on it by waging an unexampled postelection campaign with the deliberate intent of boosting his standing in the opinion polls. But here, he didn't trust to the whims of the press; instead, he used television, home-town crowd-pleasing tactics, a telethon, and fireside chats.

Carter had come into the Presidency with a popularity rating of 66 percent, which he managed to maintain in large part for the first few months thereafter.[19] James Reston in the New York *Times* gave this estimate of his position at that time:

> He has some problems with the press. He talks on the record when-ever he likes to anybody who takes his fancy, forgetting the vicious competitive nature of the press. More important, and unusual, he speaks in sentences, thinking between commas, without a subject or predicate out of place, and is responsive to questions. Also, he is unfailingly cour-teous. After Nixon and Ford, all this paradoxical stuttering precision leaves the press in a state of admiring bewilderment. . . . Nobody knows quite where he is going, but it is clear after the last couple of weeks that he is leading the parade.[20]

Unhappily, Carter's favorable status was subject to change. The brief period of calm in the nation's capital proved all too deceptive. For when the press gave massive coverage to the Ha-nafi Muslim outbreak in Washington, there was an ominous—and upsetting—reaction from the President's friend and major politi-cal supporter, Andrew Young.

Young, at that stage, had only lately taken over as the United States ambassador to the United Nations and was making pro-nouncements on almost anything about which he was asked by the press. In response to a press query about the Hanafi siege, he proposed that the reporting of violent demonstrations should be regulated by law. He obviously disapproved of the way the press had handled the riotous blacks. What he suggested was a ruling by the United States Supreme Court to "clarify" the First Amendment and thus prevent both the press and television from "creating a climate of violence." It was the closest anybody in authority had come to advocating press censorship since the dark-est days of World War II.

Mere editorial displeasure couldn't brush off Young's objec-tions. Nor could they be played down because he had made them in an emotional outburst at a news conference in Sacramento, Calif. Even though he later confessed he had been "reacting rather emotionally," and backed down, the incident concerned the press. The reason was President Carter's reaction, for Young was then in high favor at the White House and by far the most influential black spokesman in the administration.

Although the President said he "has no desire to seek legislation or to otherwise impose a solution," he did not disavow the seriousness of Young's comments. Instead, he pointed to the "complexity of the problem" and suggested that the way the press covered "hostage situations" merited both "discussion and sober consideration."[21]

Whith this view, the press had to agree—but only to a point. Stuart H. Loory, managing editor of the Chicago *Sun-Times*, said, "The press must start thinking more about the ways people like terrorists are using us. We have become part of the story." But as for judicial censorship of the news, the *Sun-Times* took strong objection, protesting, "Who would administer a law like that? A national news censor? Do you really want somebody to shut off your news?"[22]

There were objections on many another editorial page, as well. But the public was completely unconcerned. Eventually, a few news organization took mild precautionary measures on the coverage of violence and terrorism. But these were, in the main, cosmetic changes that did not really affect the central issue— giving the news as it happens with all the attendant risks.

If the press was able to deny all but the shadow of a honeymoon to President Carter, he nevertheless came through the opening stages of his administration in good shape. He lost one major appointee, Theodore Sorenson, whom he had nominated for director of the CIA and who withdrew in the face of senatorial opposition. But the nucleus of the "Georgia Mafia," the underpinning of the new White House staff, came through intact— Bert Lance at the Office of Management and Budget, Hamilton Jordan as Presidential assistant, and Jody Powell as press secretary.

Very soon the press realized that this new President would be no ordinary adversary. He was a cool fighter, strong and determined, and a politician of consummate ability. If there was any

certainty about the future, it was that his administration would
provide a time of testing for both the Presidency and the press.

4. The Lance Affair

Bert Lance, a genial Georgia banker with a broad smile and a
big hello, was the strongest member of President Carter's official
family when the new administration took office. He was the President's close friend, confidant and adviser, the administration's
trusted ambassador to the business world. Nobody seemed to be
more secure than the flamboyant six-foot-four-inch, 245-pound
financier. At 45 years of age, he seemed to be riding along on top
of the world.

Thomas Bertram Lance was not born to power. He came out
of small-town Georgia, as did Jimmy Carter, and grew up in a
deeply religious family with strong academic ties. His father was
the president of a small Methodist college, Young Harris, located
in the Georgia town of the same name. Lance did not find aca-
deme so attractive, however. He left the University of Georgia in
his senior year, married a classmate, LaBelle David, and both
returned to their native Calhoun where he became a teller in
LaBelle's grandfather's bank, the Calhoun First National Bank.

Lance moved so fast that Calhoun couldn't keep up with
him. Within no more than a dozen years, he was president of the
Calhoun bank and well on his way to his first million dollars. He
and LaBelle lived like royalty, promoted the bank with fast deals
and glamorous parties, and soon became known as comers in
Georgian society. The big break in his fortunes came in 1966
when he met a peanut farmer from Plains, Jimmy Carter, and
supported him in his unsuccessful run for governor. In 1970,
when Carter ran again and made it to the State House, Lance
became his highway director and financial counselor.

That gave the small town banker big ideas. Four years later,
with a lavish display of pomp and free spending, Lance decided

to try to succeed Carter as governor. But in spite of a lot of campaigning by airplane and the expenditure of almost a million dollars, he finished a poor third in a three-man contest for the Democratic nomination for governor.

It didn't seem to matter. Despite his political failure, Lance was now such a big name in banking that the respected National Bank of Georgia made him its president. He cut loose in Atlanta in spectacular style, moving LaBelle and their children into a 40-room mansion that was reputed to have cost a half million dollars and racing around the southeastern United States in the private airplane the bank had placed at his disposal. He seemed to be accountable to no one. Most of the Georgians of wealth and power were his friends. He would have forty or fifty to breakfast, a hundred or more to dinner, and think nothing of it. He lived like a maharajah.

Whatever he did, wherever he went, Lance never forgot Jimmy Carter. He was Carter's money man, arranging for a loan of $1 million and a line of banking credit for the peanut business that at one time amounted to close to $4 million. The two could not have been better friends.

It was understandable, therefore, that as Carter plunged ahead in his campaign for the Presidency, Lance supported him all the way. There was no doubt, after Carter's victory, that his friend would become a major figure in the new administration. Everybody expected it. So, when the call came two weeks after election day, Lance responded with enthusiasm. He had managed finances in Calhoun and Atlanta. Now he would handle the budget of the United States.

Before President Carter's inauguration, the Senate Governmental Affairs Committee on Jan. 18 recommended Lance's confirmation as director of the Office of Management and Budget with injudicious speed. Not even the Republicans bothered to investigate. And on Inauguration day, Jan. 20, 1977, the Senate voted the smiling Georgian back-slapper into his high office without any real examination of his background.

The press did ask a few questions that month, but it was done *sotto voce*. The Associated Press recalled that Lance had been investigated for possible election law violation in his 1974 gubernatorial campaign. The New York *Times* reported that an inquiry into Lance's financial affairs had been abruptly halted the day before his nomination and that Federal examiners had criticized the way ran the Calhoun bank.

But it was ho-hum stuff. It never hit Page 1. And there was no immediate follow-up. The reporters themselves weren't greatly interested, being much more attracted to the splendid show that Jimmy Carter was putting on in the White House at the outset of his Presidency. As for the editors, most of them were of the same mind as William F. Thomas of the Los Angeles *Times*, who said he didn't want to be a "quick on the trigger hip-shooter."

Despite that, the Lance story wouldn't go away. There was a piece in New York's spritely weekly, the *Village Voice*, that Lance's family had run up rather large bank overdrafts. This appeared in February, less than a month after the banker's confirmation, but nobody paid much attention to it. The respected financial magazine, *Forbes*, with more than half million circulation, went after Lance in the same month with an investigation of what it called questionable practices at the National Bank of Georgia. Still, no action.

The first story that attracted national attention was in *Time's* May 23 issue, in which Lance's somewhat disorderly personal financial dealings were explored. Now the big Georgian became news. The Washington *Post* and the New York *Times* led the pack as summer began with almost daily pieces about Lance's business dealings, his bank loans, and his overdrafts. The news weeklies, *Time* and *Newsweek*, kept pace. And the Philadelphia *Inquirer* of the Knight-Ridder chain, the Chicago *Tribune* and the New York *Daily News*, the Marshall Field-owned Chicago *Sun-Times* and *Daily News*, and the Los Angeles *Times* also joined in the inquiry.

Much of their information had been available to the Senate Governmental Affairs Committee; some of it, indeed, was in its own files and had been ignored at the confirmation hearing. Other data were readily gathered through the Securities and Exchange Commission and additional government sources of banking records. It was no big deal to investigate the background of someone who had lived so long and so prominently in the public eye as Thomas Bertram Lance. But nobody made a crusade out of the story until William Safire, the only conservative New York *Times* columnist since Arthur Krock, dubbed it "Lancegate" and demanded that Congress show the same investigative zeal in this case as they had in the Watergate inquiry. Safire, a former Nixon speech writer, went on to break some exclusive angles that the *Times's* own reporters had missed.*

The White House was appalled. Hamilton Jordan, the President's top assistant, was struck well-nigh speechless because reporters suggested that Lance might be unfit to remain as budget director. Jody Powell, the press secretary who had never actually worked in the news business, became edgy, defensive, and even abusive toward reporters who continued to dig into Lance's tangled affairs. In the worst Ron Ziegler manner, he called one story "trashy," another "nauseating," and continually used barnyard terminology to belittle new disclosures in the Lance case. The press, he seemed to be saying, just didn't understand: Bert Lance was from *Georgia* and he was the President's *close friend*. Things came to such a pass that the veteran John Osborne, of the *New Republic*, told Powell, "You and your people are just about ready to go over the wall on this Lance thing."

President Carter himself intensified the inquiry when he asked the Senate Governmental Affairs Committee on July 13 to extend the Dec. 31 deadline for Lance's divestiture of $3.2 million worth of stock of the National Bank of Georgia. The Pres-

*For his investigation of the Lance case, Safire won a Pulitzer Prize in 1978.

ident pleaded that the stock had declined so much in value that Lance stood to lose more than $1 million if he had to sell out by the deadline. Once again, Lance made such a plausible and sympathetic witness that, as one Senator put it, the committee gave him its "Good Housekeeping seal of approval" on July 25.

Senator Abraham A. Ribicoff, the Connecticut Democrat who was chairman of the committee, and Senator Charles H. Percy, the Illinois Republican who was the leading minority member, professed to be completely satisfied with Lance's explanations. "You have been smeared from one end of the country to the other, in my opinion unjustly," Senator Ribicoff told Lance on July 25. "We can imagine what this has done to you and your family." On the NBC "Today" show next morning, he was quoted as criticizing the news media: "The name of the game today is 'get everybody.' " To clinch matters for the committee, Senator Percy said he was "completely satisfied" with Lance's explanation and moved to drop the inquiry.

But the press continued to ask awkward questions. On August 18, the Carter administration answered by issuing what appeared on the surface to be a very favorable report into Lance's banking practices and other affairs. The author was the Comptroller of the Currency, John G. Heimann, who had been in office only a short time, but he produced a remarkably complete 403-page document.

Its fundamental conclusion was that there was no evidence in the Lance case that "warrants the prosecution of any individuals." However, the report also pointed out that Lance's large bank loans, and the circumstances under which they were arranged, raise questions "as to what constitutes acceptable banking practice." It suggested that the banking laws might be inadequate.

The President brushed aside the questions and seized upon the basic conclusion, exclaiming, "Bert, I'm proud of you!" He extolled his friend on national television as a man of "complete integrity," proclaimed "complete confidence" in him, and sent him back to the Office of Management and Budget with his standing in the administration intact. Lance agreed modestly that the report constituted a "very favorable view" of his work as a banker. And a White House insider cried out happily, "This thing is 90 per cent behind us now." Another remarked that the final judgment had been made: "Bert not only can survive. He has survived."

But the White House reckoned without the fine print in the Comptroller's report and the enterprise of the Washington press corps. The new disclosures became more difficult to answer as they piled up. The Associated Press on August 26 charged that Lance had pledged stock as part of collateral for a $2.6 million New York bank loan, and then violated the agreement by using the interest on the stock as partial collateral for his Chicago bank loan. The New York *Times* accused him of not fully disclosing his financial affairs before the Senate committee. The Washington *Post* said the Comptroller was pressing an inquiry into the bank overdrafts by Lance and members of his family. And it became general knowledge that an investigation of the Calhoun bank had been closed by the United States Attorney handling the case on the day before the formal announcement of Lance's governmental appointment.

The budget director, far from being exonerated, was in deeper trouble than ever. Despite the President's expression of confidence in him, he was now being investigated by the Comptroller, two committees in the Senate, one in the House, the Internal Revenue Service, and the Securities and Exchange Commission.

For a third time, the Senate Governmental Affairs Committee was obliged to take up the Lance case under highly dramatic circumstances. Bill L. Campbell, an imprisoned embezzler who had once worked for Lance's bank in Calhoun, had attempted to implicate the budget director in his crime and persuaded the two leading members of the Senate committee to listen to him. Senators Ribicoff and Percy thought the matter of sufficient importance to see President Carter at the White House over the Labor Day holiday.

Then, the press having been primed in advance by senatorial aides, both senators announced at a press briefing that they had urged the President to ask for Lance's resignation. It was quite a turnaround, the committee having decided only a little more than a month before that the budget director had been unjustly smeared by the press. But now, the senators were smarting under criticism of their own ineptitude in the case and were trying ot recover their dignity, if not their prestige and their credibility. The Governmental Affairs Committee called new hearings in the Lance case. This time, it was to be for keeps.

Before the committee hearings opened, there was a flurry in the nation's capital over rumors that the President's advisers had urged him to seek Lance's resignation, that the President had refused, that Lance himself had determined to stay on and fight every charge, and that the budget director would quit voluntarily once he had been given a chance to exonerate himself before the nation. To all these stories, and worse, Lance had but one reply: That he would not resign. His demeanor remained calm and un-ruffled. He continued to see the President at the White House. They even played tennis together, thus spreading the impression that Carter meant to stand by his friend—the good ole boy from Georgia.

The polls, however, delivered a clear warning to the President that he had overreached himself. A special Gallup Poll, commissioned by *Newsweek*, showed that 67 percent of respondents believed Lance should resign, 21 percent thought he should stay and 12 percent had no opinion. The President suffered, too, for the same poll showed that 54 percent of respondents believed he had protected Lance "too much," 35 percent thought he had handled the case properly, and 11 percent had no opinion. A Harris poll, taken at about the same time, gave the President a 40 percent negative rating for his handling of the Lance affair, only 30 percent said they approved and the rest had no opinion. Even worse, the President's own rating took a sharp drop in the Harris poll, with only 44 percent saying that they approved of the way he was handling the Presidency.

For a poll-conscious President, and Jimmy Carter was by far the most sensitive Chief Executive in this respect since John F. Kennedy, those figures meant trouble. In addition, his own private pollster, Patrick Caddell, whose position in the White House approximated that of a soothsayer, was reputed to have given a strong warning of the danger Lance represented to pending White House programs before Congress.

The mood of the press was just as bleak. James Reston of the New York *Times*, probably the most sympathetic of the major columnists toward the Carter White House, warned that the President was staking his prestige on a dubious case and added, "Also, the relations between the White House and the press have been poisoned by statements on behalf of the President that misled the press, and press reports that dramatized the controversy and infuriated the President and his aides."

An even stronger view came from mid-America, where Dolph C. Simons Jr., of the Lawrence (Kansas) *Journal-World* wrote after a visit to the White House:

> There are not many in Washington who occupy the middle ground relative to Lance, his banking habits, the role of the press and the image of the Carter adminstration.
>
> For those inside the White House, it is a "we" and "they" situation with top administration officals making no attempt to hide their antagonism toward the press, their desire to keep the press from finding out anything it can and an almost fanatical mood that the press and those in the White House are enemies.
>
> Those who follow this line of reasoning think it is the press's fault that Lance now is in trouble. If it were not for the press, they reason, Lance would not be faced with the Senate hearing, his banking practices would not have been questioned and his family would not have suffered its recent embarrassment. It doesn't matter that Lance may have run his banks in a questionable manner, but rather, it is wrong for the press to have reported it.

Lance himself came roaring out of his Georgetown home just before his make-or-break testimony in September before the Senate Governmental Operations Committee and accused the press of trying to destroy him with innuendo and hearsay. To reporters, he protested:

If you can take allegations and innuendoes and hearsay and everything else, the words of a convicted felon, and all those other things, and put them in the paper and show them on television and then say that's fact . . . . And then, without having a chance to refute that and have my day in court, and be faced with the charge that because of that my effectiveness has been damaged and crippled, then we're in sad shape in this country.

The tension was increased by an incredible performance by Jody Powell, who had become almost fanatical in his defense of Lance. In a miserable reminder of the "dirty tricks" and "enemies list" routines of the Nixon White House, Powell phoned several reporters to try to plant a story that Senator Percy, Lance's foremost critic, had accepted rides in a private Bell & Howell airplane without paying for them. The Chicago *Sun-Times*, one of the papers that received the Powell foul tip, disclosed that it was baseless. Whereupon Powell, his rather flimsy cover blown, apologized to Percy publicly and called his action a "dumb mistake." It was somewhat worse than that, for even President Carter was appalled; for the time being, the credibility of the White House Press Office took a disastrous tumble.

Thus, the stage was set for the final act of the drama— Lance's testimony before the Senate Governmental Operations Committee on September 15, 16 and 17. The big Georgian, with the help of Clark Clifford, a distinguished Washington lawyer and veteran Democratic trouble-shooter, put on a virtuoso performance. He admitted nothing, denied everything, and even carried the attack directly to the members of the committee. All this without raising his voice, showing the slightest emotion, or dropping for even one moment his concerned, polite, even deferential

manner. The White House reported mail results had turned in
Lance's favor. The mood among the Georgia Mafia became eu-
phoric. Even the President agreed that his friend had done very
well.

From widespread predictions that Lance was through before
the hearings began, the reporters began hedging their bets. Most
of them reported that Lance now had a chance to ride out the
storm, that the White House might still manage to save him if
public opinion continued in his favor. It was rather typical, all in
all, of the weathervane character of press opinion.

In reality, nothing had changed. None of the serious charges
against Lance's management of his personal and banking affairs
could be withdrawn. True, no one had been able to raise a question against his competence to run the government budget office
or his integrity as a government servant. It was his qualification
for the post that was at last under scrutiny, a procedure that
should have taken place when he first came up for confirmation.

Lance's defenses were simple and basic. On the question of
overdrafts by himself and members of his family in the Calhoun
bank, he argued that this was a routine procedure in country
banks and some others, that he always had had sufficient money in
other accounts to cover the overdrafts and that his personal overdrafts had never approached the $450,000 listed by the Comp-
troller of the Currency for the whole Lance family. In that total,
he testified, were overdrafts by his wife and nine relatives who
dealt with the Calhoun bank.

He defended his use of the Atlanta bank's airplane on extensive travel as a public relations gimmick for the bank's benefit. He
pointed out that he had been given the right to use the airplane in
any way he saw fit and had not, therefore, accounted for any of
these trips in his personal income tax returns. He applied this
defense to all of the 1,300 trips he had taken for the Atlanta bank
in 1975 and 1976, some to football games, others to take friends
to Carter campaign rallies, and a few to transport his family to
various places.

As for the charge of posting the same collateral for two different bank loans, one from a New York bank and another for a
Chicago bank, he contended this was merely an argument with
the New York bank and nothing more. It was his opinion, Lance
said, that he had a perfect right to use the interest from the bank
stock he put up as collateral for the New York loan in order to
secure the Chicago loan. When the New York bank disagreed, he
added that he simply paid off the New York loan and regained his
stock.

The figure of Lance that emerged from the three days of
relentless pounding by his critics was that of a gallant underdog
whose own financial position had been severely damaged by his
government service. At his original confirmation hearing in January, he had testified he had $7.9 million in assets, liabilities of $5.3
million, and a net worth of $2.6 million. But he owed $400,000
annually to cover interest on his bank loans and his investment
income had been sharply reduced by a slump in the price of the
Georgia bank stock. As a result, his financial condition was such
that he put up his Atlanta mansion for sale.

There is little doubt, even at the end, that Lance did not
want to resign. Nor did President Carter want to force the issue,
although all the evidence indicates that he had come to the conclusion even before the third Senate hearing that Lance would
have to go. An Associated Press poll taken directly after the hearing concluded showed that 38 percent of respondents wanted
Lance to resign, 35 percent wanted him to stay and 27 percent
had no opinion. If the President had had any doubts before, that
poll should have ended them.

Early in the week after the Senate hearing, the comings and
goings at the White House intensified. Hamilton Jordan traveled
to Sea Island, Ga., where Lance and his wife were resting, and
suggested that a resignation now was necessary. Still, Lance continued to resist, mainly because his wife believed he should not
give in. But at last, after seeing the President at the White House,
both the Lances surrendered to the inevitable. The letter of resig-

nation was drafted. A tearful President went on national television Sept. 21, concluding, "Bert Lance is my friend . . . a good and honorable man . . . . Nothing that I have heard or read has shaken my belief in Bert's ability or his integrity."

So it ended. Lance had resisted other demands for his resignation, from the *Wall Street Journal* and *Business Week*, the New York *Times* and Washington *Post* and *Newsday*, from the Los Angeles *Times* and numerous other newspapers, from Senators Ribicoff and Percy of the Senate Governmental Operations Committee, even from the majority leader of the Senate, Robert C. Byrd of West Virginia. But when he saw that the President was wounded and ready to part with him, he gave in.

There were many, particularly in the South, who took the position that Lance had been hounded out of office by a virulent and hypercritical press. President Carter was careful not to associate himself with that point of view, which would have made his position more difficult than it already had become. In announcing Lance's resignation the President knew that he would be asked about the role of the press and replied that he thought the newspapers, with some exceptions, had been fair. It scarcely would have been possible for him to say much else.

Without doubt, if the Lance case had not broken wide open during the August dog days when there is precious little news in Washington as a rule, it would not have gotten the big play it did either in the press or television. There also is no question, as the President said, that some overeager reporters rushed into print with unsubstantiated stories that proved to be half truths or no truths at all. In an investigative position of this kind, such bloopers are almost inevitable as outdistanced reporters, or reporters late on the job, try to play catch-up out of sheer desperation. The news business remains the most sharply competitive of all.

Some press critics contended that the Washington press corps, having played a strong role in the overthrow of Richard Nixon, sought to demonstrate evenhandedness against the Democrats as well. The assumption has little support among seasoned professionals. This is not the way the news business works. The story's the thing—and Lance, whether Carter objected or not, was the centerpiece of the story.

The uncontestable point about the press's performance in the Lance case, after all the objections have been considered, is that the nation's newspapers investigated Lance's qualifications as the country's chief budget officer after the doyens of the Senate had failed. One may damn the press as a bunch of busybodies or sensation seekers, but that is the bottom line in the Lance matter. Had the press not conducted the inquiry, nothing would have happened.

This is not to depict the Lance case as another Watergate, or contend that Jimmy Carter's loyalty to his friend is to be equated with Nixon's desperate stonwalling. But the painful reality is that, once Bert Lance was obliged to resign, the Carter administration's credibility suffered and there was a thinning of the swan's down of morality with which the President customarily deflected criticism.

Lance never did get over the notion that he had been persecuted by the press. Even after the Securities and Exchange Commission ordered him to cease acting secretly with Arab bankers to take over certain American banks, he thought his plight was the press's fault. And in an appearance before the American Society of Newspaper Editors, he warned that press censorship could be the eventual outcome. It didn't help him much, for he now was recognized as a Carter liability.

Still the President's loss was not the press's gain. It was virtually the unanimous judgment of the Washington press corps that newspapers, on the whole, did not benefit from their role in the Lance inquiry. And with this assessment most impartial persons had to agree. In this scandal, almost everybody lost.

It was not really Lance's fault, however, that the President's difficulties began to mount with his departure. Through inexperience and over-eagerness to achieve, the Carter administration had taken on so many major obligations from the beginning that it could not possibly make progress on all of them. In fact, mistakes and miscalculations began to cost the President some of the support he had mustered in his successful drive for the White House. The blacks were disenchanted because he had not been able to reduce unemployment substantially in his first year. The Jewish community was outraged by his insistence on a Palenstinian presence in any Mideast settlement and his criticism of Israel. Conservatives attacked him for the Panama Canal Treaties. Some liberals didn't like his energy program. The Senate had its doubts about his Salt II negotiations with the Russians and the House was so cool to the notion of major tax revision that he had to cut his program.

So, like most new Presidents, his standing in the polls nosedived toward the end of his first year and the Washington columnists, both on the left and right, began calling him a one-term President.

In the Harris poll, from a 75 percent approval rating when he took office in January 1977, he sank during the spring of 1978 to 41 percent. A Gallup poll in the spring of 1978 gave him only 39 percent and an AP–NBC News poll showed only 33 percent of the people surveyed gave him an excellent or good rating. The New York *Times*-CBS News poll put his 17-month rating at 38 percent.

That augured trouble in the 1978 Congressional elections and the columnists made it even worse. Rowland Evans and Robert Novak called the President "the political incompetent of 1977." Pat Buchanan, a former Nixon speech-writer, reported jubilantly, "Carter is being talked of as a one-term President." On the same day, the liberal Tom Wicker wrote in the New York *Times*, "People . . . are beginning to ask each other openly, 'Is Jimmy Carter a one-term President?' " The Washington *Post's* David S. Broder adopted an I-told-you-so stance, writing, "The criticisms being shouted now are no different from those catalogued in this space last June."

The veteran editor, Thomas Griffith, observed caustically in *Time* magazine, "Prescription for reading Potomac journalism:

When they're all warmly agreed about something, discount 20 percent for atmospheric distortion."

But that didn't help Jimmy Carter. Even his veracity was soon called into question in the case of Richard Helms of the CIA, and the reportorial litmus test was applied to the celebrated Presidential pledge, "I will never lie to you." The issue was whether the President had or had not consulted with Attorney General Griffin Bell over the prosecution of Helms, former director of the CIA, for alleged false testimony before Congress on CIA intervention in Chile's internal affairs.

Carter said on Sept. 29, 1977, at a broadcast news conference, that Bell "has not consulted with me, nor given me any advice on the Helms question." But on Nov. 1. after the government had agreed to let Helms off with a suspended sentence and a fine if he pleaded no contest to charges that he failed to testify fully and accurately, Bell said he had indeed consulted with the President on the Helms case on July 25. In fact, the Attorney General went on, the President had "authorized us to determine the feasibility" of striking a plea bargain with Helms.

After the deal was consummated and a Federal judge was found who let the ex-CIA chief off with a $2,000 fine and a lecture, even the mild and impartial Frank Cormier of the AP wrote: "Bell's account is, on its face, difficult to square with Carter's September pronouncement." The White House press office ventured several explanations, but only the faithful took much stock in them.

Bell didn't help either his own credibility or that of the Carter administration thereafter when he called on newspapers to "cease and desist" from publishing articles based on information that had been leaked to reporters. The Attorney General made the observation after a spate of news accounts, based on leaks, about his investigation of various U. S. corporations accused of paying bribes overseas. "Cease and desist and allow me to do my role as Attorney General," Bell said to the press. "If there are others who want to run the Justice Department, let them try to be Attorney General."

Within a few weeks, Bell was in trouble again with the press and so was his boss, this time over the dismissal of a Republican U. S. Attorney in Philadelphia, David Marston, at a time when he was investigating some Democratic politicians in the state. President Carter admitted at a press conference that one of the politicians, Rep. Joshua Eilberg of Philadelphia, had telephoned to request Marston's removal; however, the President contended that he had not known about the Eilberg part of the investigation at the time he took Eilberg's call. Subsequently, an equivocal answer the President gave to a Justice Department official obliged him to defend himself at a press conference on January 29, 1978, against an implication that he had known about the Eilberg inquiry at the time of the Eilberg phone call.

Others among Carter's people had their troubles with the press, too, notably Hamilton Jordan, his No. 1 political adviser. It was bad enough when Jordan was accused of making an impolite remark to the Egyptian ambassador's wife at a formal dinner. It was even worse when he was reported to have spewed a drink on a woman in a Washington singles bar. Some sense of the mingled anger and frustration of the Carter White House became evident when the press office issued a 30-page denial of the latter incident.

Then, Dr. Peter Bourne had to resign as the President's drug policy adviser for issuing a phony prescription and the press reported some at the White House smoked marijuana and sniffed cocaine. The President rebuked his press secretary, Jody Powell, for calling such stories "witch hunts" and demanded obedience to the drug laws. Such was the adversary process in the Carter administration.[23]

5. Power and the Press

The strongest manifestation of the power of the press in the United States is that it has managed to retain its freedom for more than 200 years. And this was accomplished despite foreign wars, a great Civil War, riots, panics, depressions, strikes, boycotts, the

ravages of inflation and unemployment, and other associated ca-
lamities that have torn at the unity of this great land.

That, however, scarcely implies that there is approximate
equality between the power of the press and the power of the
institutions and individuals, beginning with the Presidency and
the rest of the government, against which it is arrayed. Demonstrably, such a condition could obtain only in the very rarest of
cases, when the whole weight of public opinion is arrayed on the
side of the press. And that doesn't happen very often.

This is one of the misleading aspects of adversary journalism.
The very nature of the term and the manner in which it is used
implies a contest between equals. And such is not always the case,
as the following tale of two newspapers demonstrates:

The End of the *World*

There is a modest plaque at the edge of City Hall Park in
Manhattan, half hidden by a rude and riotous growth of ivy, that
indicates the spot some distance off where the New York *World*
once lived in fancied security under its shiny golden dome. Few
passersby notice the plaque today; even fewer stop to read the
brief bronzed accolade to the *World's* greatness and meditate on
the meaning of its disappearance from the city that it served with
such distinction.

On the site of the golden dome itself at the approach to the
Brooklyn Bridge, traffic rattles and snarls over the blackened
roadway in never-ending confusion and pedestrians wait impa-
tiently for the changing of signal lights to scuttle from one curb-
stone to another—a harsh and shattering dirge for a forgotten
newspaper. Nobody cares, nobody even asks a question; it is just
as if the *World*, under its golden dome, had been a sometime
thing.

And yet the *World*—Joseph Pulitzer's *World*—was often
called a mighty force in its time. Its power was thought to be so
great that it was both courted and feared by the elect of the land.
This was the paper that brought the Statue of Liberty to America

and set it on its pedestal in New York harbor with pennies contributed by school children and nickels and dimes that flowed
from the poor folk on New York's Lower East Side. Along with
William Randolph Hearst's New York *Journal*, it was blamed—
perhaps more than it merited—for bringing on the Spanish-
American War. When it charged that there had been graft and
malfeasance in public office in connection with the acquisition of
the Panama Canal site (the key editorial was entitled, "Who Got
the $40,000,000?"), President Theodore Roosevelt tried unsucess-
fully to prosecute it and throw its blind and unrepentant owner in
jail.

The *World* persisted despite that, both nationally and locally,
to exercise all the power it possessed, to challenge what it considered to be the forces of evil, to plunge into conflict with exultant
editorial cries. Its campaigns broke the authority of the Ku Klux
Klan, exposed the peonage evil in Florida's convict labor camps,
battered away at Tammany Hall's misrule of New York City, and
contributed to the overthrow of the jaunty, debonair Tammany
mayor, Jimmy Walker.

Walter Lippmann, the preeminent journalist of his time, gave
the *World's* editorial page much of its character and prestige.
Herbert Bayard Swope, whom a rival editor called "a giant
among pygmies," was its executive editor and directed its most
successful crusades. Charles Michelson, its distinguished chief
Washington correspondent, obtained an exclusive interview with
President Wilson at a time when such feats were rare and not
capable of emulation by almost anybody, including book critics.

Among the *World's* critics and columnists were the elite of
the city's journalists, some of whom shared the rarified honor of
membership with George S. Kaufman and Dorothy Parker in the
Hotel Algonquin's Round Table—Heywood Broun, Franklin
Pierce Adams (FPA), Alexander Woollcott, Allan Nevins, Deems
Taylor, Frank Sullivan, and Corey Ford. Among its staff members, at one time or another, were John L. Balderston, the author
of *Berkeley Square*; William Bolitho, the essayist; Sam Spewack,
the playwright; and Laurence Stallings, the book critic who

joined with Maxwell Anderson to write *What Price Glory?*, the best antiwar play of its time.

Surely, on the basis of its record and the people who created it each day, the *World* was a newspaper that deserved to live, that constituted a national resource, that merited the kind of public support on which the free press is founded. Yes, the paper *did* have a fiercely devoted public, but it was never very large; some called it the best-loved newspaper in New York, others the "newspaperman's newspaper." Despite that, despite its power, its crusading zeal, its glamor, it failed.[24]

Even in its greatest days, the *World* was never able to rally the support that would have enabled it to challenge the dominance of the New York *Times* in the class market and the mass appeal of the New York *Daily News*, the first and greatest of the tabloids. The *World* reached 404,000 circulation in 1925, plunged to 285,000 in 1926 when it went from 2¢ to 3¢ a copy and was unable to recoup in 1927 with the restoration of the 2¢ price. When it died on February 27, 1931, it had only 313,000 circulation, as against the New York *Times*'s 417,000, and both were smaller than the *Daily News*. The *Evening World's* 270,000 in 1931 lagged behind the *Evening Journal* and the *Sun* and the *Sunday World's* 492,000 was exceeded by both the *Times* and Hearst's New York *American*.

The circulation pattern was duplicated in the loss of advertising and profits. In 1922, the *World* showed a profit of $500,000, but by 1925 that was cut in half. With the drop in circulation and the flight of advertisers, the *World's* loss amounted to $1,677,625 in 1930. No wonder, therefore, that old J. P.'s heirs were glad to sell out to Scripps-Howard Newspapers for $5 million in 1931 with the resultant merger of the *World* papers with the Scripps's *Telegram*.

Joseph Pulitzer's declaration of principle, which was lashed to the *World's* masthead, survived the *World* and still may be read in the St. Louis *Post-Dispatch*:

Always fight for progress and reform, never tolerate injustice or corruption, always fight demagogues of all parties, never belong to any party, always oppose privileged classes and public plunderers, never lack sympathy for the poor, always remain devoted to the public welfare, never be satisfied with simply printing the news, always be drastically independent, never be afraid to attack wrong either by predatory plutocracy or predatory poverty.

Old J. P. meant it. And so did Herbert Bayard Swope and his gang of roughneck reporters who did his investigating. But in the despairing New York City of the depression era, not enough people were willing to support such a newspaper. In consequence, the modest plaque at the edge of City Hall Park is a reminder that the power of a newspaper is a fragile thing at best, no matter how right and deserving it may be. And nobility of purpose is no guarantee of immortality in print, any more than it is among humankind itself. For the *World*, "drastic independence" became its epitaph.[25]

The Rise of the *Post*

The newspaper that is almost universally regarded today as the very incarnation of the power of the press is the Washington *Post*. Its performance during the Watergate scandal has evoked praise in scholarly commencement addresses and at thousands of movie box offices throughout the land in theaters where *All the President's Men* has been shown. In current history, at least, its position is secure. The New York *Times*, after what it called "weeks of research," has contributed the incidental information that $100 million already has been made out of Watergate books, movies, and legal fees, including some $3.5 million in royalties for Messrs. Woodward and Bernstein on their two books to date.[26] It is a different position, all in all, in which the austere *Times* finds itself, considering that it has held the national leadership of the press virtually unchallenged for many years.

Watergate was by no means the first major expose in the Washington *Post*'s history and it has not been the last. But it was one of the most remarkable in American journalism because the paper stood alone for months in supporting an investigation into what the Nixon administration called "a third-rate burglary" at

Democratic National Headquarters in the Watergate complex on June 17, 1972. The rest of the news media, including the elite of the Washington press corps, accepted the assessment of the White House press secretary, Ron Ziegler. That left the field to the two young and virtually untested reporters, Woodward and Bernstein.

In answer to criticism of the *Post's* position, Katharine Graham, its publisher, simply said, "We are not a national cheerleader." And she backed the investigation without question, which is what publishers are supposed to do but don't always find very convenient.

Mrs. Graham is the daughter of the financier, Eugene Meyer, the first president of the World Bank, who purchased the paper in 1933, and the widow of its publisher, Philip Graham, who committed suicide in 1963. Upon assuming control after her husband's death the last thing she thought of doing was to manage the paper in such a way that she would become known and admired throughout the land as the counterpart of Joseph Pulitzer.

At first, Mrs. Graham was timid and self-effacing; she exhibited about as much assurance as a junior reporter covering his first fire. However, it was her good fortune to have the respect and confidence of two hard-boiled editors, Ben Bradlee and Howard Simons, who ran the paper. From them, she learned very quickly what it meant to follow the Pulitzer principle of never being satisfied with merely printing the news.

In 1971, when her paper was involved in the Pentagon Papers case with the New York *Times*, she learned something else about the power of the press—that it can be very costly to maintain. Legal actions before the Supreme Court and the cost of legal defenses to ward off an attack on the license renewals of her two Florida TV stations amounted to more than $1 million.[27] While she could not prove it, she always suspected that the licensing matter was an outgrowth of the *Post's* adversary position toward the government.

Despite that, she played an major role in Watergate. Someone with less faith might not have been quite so forbearing when the young reporters, Woodward and Bernstein, were leading the *Post* ever deeper into the cover-up trail left by a tottering White House group. Mrs. Graham did wonder, as well she might, when all those other righteous and powerful newspapers in the land would come to the *Post*'s support.

One of her most difficult periods came when John N. Mitchell, the former Attorney General, warned Bernstein that "Katie Graham's gonna get her tit caught in a big fat wringer" if the *Post* published allegations against him in the Watergate coverup. Next morning, all she did was to sweetly ask the reporter if he had any more messages for her. The story was published—the first in a long sequence that led at last to Mitchell's incarceration in an Alabama prison. Mitchell was the first Attorney General of the United States in history to go behind bars.

There was another bad time for Mrs. Graham. It was during the Watergate trials before Federal Judge John N. Sirica when she asked plaintively, "Is it all going to come out? I mean, are we ever going to know about all of this?" After Woodward replied frankly that he wasn't sure, she was depressed, but only for a moment. "Never?" she asked. "Don't tell me that."[28]

It was not until August 9, 1974, when President Nixon resigned and Vice President Ford replaced him, that the *Post* was at last vindicated. The exposure of the "third-rate burglary" and the White House coverup had taken more than two years.

The consequences continued to be felt throughout the Presidential campaign of 1976 and thereafter. Former Governor Ronald Reagan of California, who so narrowly lost the Republican nomination to President Ford, has always believed that Ford's pardon of Nixon in the Watergate case was the main reason for Jimmy Carter's election. And few of the Democratic professionals would dispute him.

The Washington *Post* stood at the very apex of American journalism. It was a heady time for Mrs. Graham, her editors and managers, and Messrs. Woodward and Bernstein, the latter retiring from the daily grind at the age of 32. As other exposes thundered into the paper's headlines, it became must reading in the nation's capital, at the United Nations, and in the world's great chanceries from London and Moscow to Tokyo and Peking.

To uncritical eyes, it all seemed like a grand testimonial to the power of the American press and to the results that could be expected where a free press contended against wrongdoing in high places. It was enought to make skeptics want to salute the flag, repeat the Pledge of Allegiance every morning and equate the "Washington Post March" with "The Star-Spangled Banner."

The point is that, without detracting from the Washington *Post*'s performance, everything went just right for the paper when the Watergate case reached its most critical stage. Between the middle of March and the middle of April 1974, the whole thing began to come apart. Judge Sirica broke through the "stonewalling" of the original Watergate defendants with his persistent questioning. And James W. McCord, Jr., one of the defendants, wrote his celebrated accusatory letter.

Was this, too, attributable to the power of the press? In part, perhaps. For it can be argued that if the Washington *Post* had not made its own damaging disclosures, Sirica might not have begun asking questions. But suppose it hadn't happened that way. Suppose that a less virtuous judge than Sirica, of whom there are one or two, had presided over the Watergate trials. Suppose, further, that the judge had decided to challenge the *Post* by haling Woodward and Bernstein before him and demanding that they identify the source of their allegations.

Since neither they nor their editors have publicly identified to this day their supersource, known to them as "Deep Throat," it is obvious that they would have refused. Then, following the peculiar logic of so many antipress judges in the land today, Woodward and Bernstein might well have faced the probability of indeterminate jail sentences for contempt of court.

I once asked Bernstein about the likelihood of a contempt citation and he replied, "We were lucky, I guess. It could have happened." But he insisted, and none could blame him, that the power of the press in general and the Washington *Post* in particular was so great that everything would have come out "all right" anyway. Again, perhaps.

But, certainly, had President Nixon defaced, burned, or otherwise destroyed the incriminating Watergate tapes that proved he had masterminded the coverup, no one can be sure that the House Judiciary Committee would have been able to muster a majority for the articles of impeachment. Among those who believed it would have been impossible is Emmanuel Celler, devoted Democrat and Nixon foe who was the Judiciary Commitee's chairman for many years before his Congressional service ended.° So all in all, the Washington *Post*'s victory was a very fortuitous thing. Demonstrably, the power of the press rests less on righteousness sometimes than on the purest happenstance.

I have heard Soviet propagandists contend that their controlled press has a lot more power than we think. They point out that a single derogatory article in *Pravda* or *Izvestia* about a particular program is enough to kill it, that a factory worker's letter assailing a particular official frequently precedes his removal. I am sure this is true, although I suspect that both stories would be inspired. For in the case of the Soviet Union, as in all authoritarian states, we know very well that the power of the press is derived from the government and dominating party and is exercised by them for the benefit of the state.

In a democratic society in the Western sense, however, the theory is that the power of the press emanates from the people and is exercised by the press for the benefit of the people. But this is a very difficult proposition to prove.

In the case of the Washington *Post*, the people had nothing whatever to do with the Watergate expose, and Messrs. Woodward and Bernstein, supported by Messrs. Simons and Bradlee,

°In a conversation with me shortly before his death.

had everything to do with it. The people did not give any sign, except perhaps in the form of a few letters or phone calls, that they were behind the *Post*'s position until the very end, when victory was assured. On the contrary, the early mail on Watergate was anything but encouraging.

As for the case of the New York *World*, regardless of all the errors of management and other debilitating factors, what happened finally was that the people simply withheld support. They refused to buy the paper in sufficient numbers to keep it alive. And that was the end of it.

How else can people react to a newspaper in any significant way? Leaving aside demonstrations, court actions, or other propaganda devices, the people have very limited options if they are in truth the basis for the power of the press. They can either buy a newspaper or refuse to buy it, patronize its advertisers or boycott them. Comparatively few write letters to the editor, or telephone or send telegrams if they approve of something that is published. If they disapprove, the tide of communications rises but it seldom achieves the volume or the ferocity of reactions to television.

All this constitutes pretty weak proof that a mass public has within itself some mysterious quality that generates sufficient power to cause a free press to exist and flourish. The initiative would seem to be with those who face the risk of offering a newspaper to the public and taking their chances on the acceptability of what they publish, facilitated, of course, by the government's guarantee that there shall be no prior restraint on publication.

But when the people *do* react to the press in a mass movement of consequence, the effect can be sudden and drastic. For example, when the New York *World* displayed its "drastic independence" in 1925 by raising its price to three cents a copy while its chief competitors remained a penny cheaper, the paper lost almost 100,000 circulation overnight. It never recovered. In today's inflationary economy, it may be incomprehensible to a younger generation that a penny could make such a difference. But in the 1920s, when the welfare state was just a wild academic dream and people had to get along on their own without government help, a penny still meant something.

What, then, is the price of power for the press? Is it a penny, as in the case of the *World*? Or millions of dollars, which the New York *Times* and Washington *Post* spent to convince the courts of their right to publish without prior restraint? It is hard to say, because price tags on power are illusory at best. Cyrus H. K. Curtis, who made the *Saturday Evening Post* a household fixture in his time, spent many millions of dollars trying to duplicate his success in the newspaper field but failed. He found, as have so many others, that something more than money is required.

Political loyalty, too, is no guarantee that a newspaper will flourish. The New York *Herald Tribune*, the champion of liberal eastern Republicanism, failed because there simply weren't enough faithful Republicans to advertise in it and buy it. Yet, the conservatively Republican New York *Daily News* still maintains the largest circulation in the land by playing to popular taste first and glossing over its ideology except just before election day.

The concept of the individual publisher who wields great power, wisely or not, also can no longer be sustained, with few exceptions. For chain ownership and corporate management have replaced the stormy geniuses of the past and are, for the most part, the broadest repositories of the power of the press in the latter part of the 20th century.

The government, for that matter, is doing a great deal to make the position of the individual owner untenable with sharply rising estate taxes and regulations that make it difficult for heirs to continue to conduct a family-owned newspaper. Both the Federal Communications Commission and the courts also have taken positions against joint newspaper-TV ownership in the same city, forced divestiture in 16 cities, and barred any new acquisitions of broadcast properties by newspapers in the same cities. Thus, a weak paper no longer can buy into a local broadcast market.

On the positive side, the government is making possible the continued publication of more than a score of newspapers that were declared to be "failing properties" under the Newspaper Preservation Act. The law permits them to operate jointly with prosperous newspapers in the same market by merging all their major facilities except for their news and editorial departments.

It follows that neither "drastic independence" nor wealth nor righteousness nor political party regularity can ensure the power of the press. A newspaper is forever dependent on the "gut feeling" of its editors toward what it is to publish. Like Joshua, it must summon up the divine *chutzpah* to believe that a blast from journalistic trumpets will be able to level the walls of a latter-day Jericho.

There is no recourse to an oracle to tell an editor how to make a newspaper succeed. The power of the press, certainly, does not exist in a pristine stage by reason of the public will, to be turned on and off from a tap or, to revert again to Biblical lore, to gush from a stone when it is tapped by the staff of a journalistic Moses. Even chain journalism is no guarantee of triumph, moral or financial. Despite Dow Jones's success with the *Wall Street Journal*, it lost $16 million in 15 years on the *National Observer* and had to give up. And the Newhouse group, which paid a record $305 million for the Booth Newspapers, had to fold both its New York metropolitan properties, the Long Island *Press* and *Star-Journal*.[29]

To be sure, there *is* a repository of power in the press just as there is in any large and durable institution in a free country. But the quality is elusive. It manifests itself only *after* a newspaper takes a decisive position with commendable results. What we perceive as the power of the press, in consequence, is therefore based on an expectation of probable results based on past performances. And as any horse player can tell you, it is a colossal gamble to be continually betting on past performances under rapidly changing conditions.

There is quite a distance between such a power structure,

which depends on so many variables beyond journalists' control, and the imposing edifice of government authority. The press today must share with television the prime source of its power, that of newsgiver to the nation, as well as the influence inherent in the exercise of that privilege. But it cannot legislate. It cannot govern. It cannot even formulate public policy, however much it may publish on the subject.

The press cannot be made out as anything other than what it actually is—a separate institution, responsible only to itself, that was created to report on and maintain constant vigil over the other principal institutions in the United States. It is obviously very far from the equal in power of the Presidency, the Congress and the Supreme Court, as John Connally's mirage would have it. For, as a fundamental proposition, the press in this country is vulnerable when it cannot maintain a decent semblance of public support—far more vulnerable than the institutions of government.

The position is bound to trouble any thoughtful journalist. Julius Duscha, director of Washington Journalism Center, goes beyond the current unhappy reality and puts it in perspective as follows:

Of even greater concern is the lack of support one finds throughout the country for the First Amendment as it applies to the media . . . . Opinion polls show strong public support for controls over the media. Courts at all levels have increasingly looked on the media as they view any other plaintiffs or defendants before the bar. And politicians and public figures of all sorts who spend so much time courting the media for favorable attention often devote even more time in attempting to discredit the news media and cut back their constitutional rights when the news is not favorable to the politicians and other public figures.[30]

Shortly after being elected minority leader of the Senate, Senator Howard Baker of Tennessee observed, "Right now Congress doesn't trust the President, the President doesn't trust Congress, and the Court doesn't trust either one."[31] It might have been added that none of these trusted the newspapers very much, and therein lay the greatest weakness of the American press in a harsh and divisive time.

6. The Condition of the Press

During my childhood in the early years of this century, my father used to read aloud from his newspaper after dinner every evening. If my mother quietly went on with her household tasks and I slipped away from the table because I was too small to understand, he didn't seem to mind. His newspaper was his Bible.

It wasn't a great newspaper. In retrospect, I doubt that it was even representative of the better newspapers of that time. And yet, when my father brought it home, I well understood that it was a precious thing that had to be handled tenderly. Woe to me if, in trying to spell out the dialogue in the comic strips, I unwittingly messed up the paper or tore a page. It was one of the few things that angered my father when I was a child.

We were typical, I suppose, of most immigrant families of the latter 19th and early 20th centuries, to whom the newspaper was oracle and teacher, advocate and friend. To be sure, the better-educated middle and upper classes of the era generally considered themselves to be superior to their press and critics like Upton Sinclair mercilessly berated it. But such people were far removed from us. We depended on our newspaper both for news and guidance; the better people, after all, ignored us.

It didn't seem to matter to many immigrant families—certainly it didn't to ours—that the bulk of the contemporary press in America was devotedly and sometimes passionately Republican, nearly always antilabor and pointedly middle-class and white in its sympathies. Among the 2,200 dailies and 10,000 weeklies, liberal thinkers of even the mild Joseph Pulitzer variety were rare and the handful of radicals were regarded as threats to the republic.

If there were antinewspaper militants or people who mis-

trusted newspapers as intrinsic parts of the Establishment, I seldom heard of them in our small family circle. Not many union
people bothered to read the lone prolabor paper in town, and
they didn't appear to worry too much about the antilabor stance
of my father's paper except when there were strikes. Once, I
remember there was a flurry of resentment because the Hearst
Newspapers had bought the only morning newspaper in town. To
my father and his friends, the Hearst papers were anathema because they had successfully fought President Wilson in his championship of the rights of small European nations and the League
of Nations. But I never heard much bitterness over the chains.

To us, and to people like us, it was the presentation of the
news that mattered. For the newspaper was our window on the
world. In my early teens I read about the bombing of Wall Street;
the wars of the prohibition racketeers; the Teapot Dome oil scandal; the manifold marriages of Ziegfeld Follies girls; the mysterious murders of Dot King and Louise Lawson, who were among
the most glamorous of showgirls; the unfrocking of a much-mar-
ried clergyman; the financial legerdemain of Charles Ponzi, the
Boston swindler; the martyrdom of the humble fish peddler, Ni-
cola Sacco, and the shoemaker, Bartolomeo Vanzetti; the splen-
dor of J. P. Morgan's yacht; and the comings and goings of the
politically powerful at the White House. Much of this fare was
served up to us in flamboyant prose and tingling headlines that
would have abashed today's checkout-counter tabloids.

I don't think newspapers were particularly popular then, either, but probably they were a bit better off in public standing
than they are now. The difference was that we actually needed
them and we often enjoyed reading them. For the press in the
1920s still very largely resembled the historic image presented by
James Parton in 1866 at the end of the Civil War:

> There are journalists who think the time is at hand for the abolition
> of editorials, and the concentration of the whole force of journalism
> upon presenting to the public the history and picture of the day. The
> time for this has not come, and may never come; but our journalists

already know that editorials neither make nor mar a daily paper, that they do not much influence the public mind, nor change many votes, and that the power and success of a newspaper depend wholly and absolutely upon its success in getting, and its skill in exhibiting, the news.[32]

We were still living in an era in which an editor could proclaim, with engaging simplicity, that it was the duty of a newspaper to "print the news and raise hell."[33] Reading a newspaper, at that time, was considerably more than a habit. To my father, it was a downright necessity to keep himself and his family informed. This was the reason the newspaper occupied such a privileged position in our household, why we were less concerned with the paper's policies and politics than we were with the news on Page 1.

And so it is difficult for me to remember a time in my childhood, and well into my teens, when it did not give me a sense of pleasure and expectation, even excitement, to spread a newspaper on the table or on the floor, sniff the fresh ink that almost always came off on my hands, and slowly turn the pages to seek one surprise after another. This is how I began to read, and how my reading rapidly improved; how I obtained my first perception of what kind of country we lived in and what the outside world was like.

If my perceptions were flawed and my understanding imperfect, mainly because of the propaganda in the wartime American press, I did not know it. The newspaper became almost as important to me as my school work. Because it piqued my curiosity in so many ways, I discovered the wonders of our town's public library and the marvelous world of books.

It took me many years to appreciate that a single issue of a daily newspaper may present an attractive package of news, but it cannot possibly get at the truth behind the news every 24 hours. What I took for the truth in the columns of a newspaper as a child all too often turned out in later years to have been what somebody said (or guessed) was the truth. And what was presented to

me as objective reporting consisted in the main of numerous quotations of different points of view, out of which I was supposed to
decide—in my infinite wisdom—which was correct. This was the
dominant theory of how the news was presented in that ingenuous era, and it lasted for a long time.

Of one thing, however, I became firmly convinced from
childhood onward: newspapers were important because they
published the news. and in this I was not too far wrong, until
television burst upon a nation that was ill-prepared for it, changed
the patterns of our society to a stunning degree, and turned the
news business topsy-turvy.

By dwelling on the more or less idyllic relationship of a child
to a newspaper in the early part of this century, I do not mean to
make the press of that time seem any better than it was; on the
whole, with a few decent exceptions, it wasn't really very good.
My purpose is to show what an enormous change has come about
in the perception of the press in our society. For unfortunately,
the kind of press that once was considered so necessary by so
many people has now become something entirely different to suc-
ceeding generations in a changed world. No editor in full possession of his senses would argue today that it is sufficient for a
newspaper to "print the news and raise hell." And outside the
Columbia University subway station in New York City, replacing
Adolph S. Ochs's treasured slogan for the New York *Times*, "All
the News That's Fit to Print," there once was an advertisement
for the "new" New York *Times*: "It's a Lot More Than the
News."[34]

I find that American attitudes toward newspapers have
changed as dramatically as has the American concept of family
life, and perhaps the two are somehow linked in declining favor.
For one thing, the same distractions that have loosened the ties of
the family have also affected the prestige and usefulness of the
newspaper as a giver of the news. For another, in many embattled
communities in the country, obsessed by the need for protection
against street crime, it is difficult if not impossible for individual

newspaper deliveries to be made in large apartment complexes where thousands of families live.

I do not see children poring over newspapers any more; mostly, when they are not at school or at play, they sit for hours gaping slack-jawed at television without much regard for what they are watching. As for their elders, I have not heard of anybody reading aloud from a newspaper for years in anything approaching a respectful, let alone a reverent, tone. I also know of few people who regard their newspaper as a friend and ally, a good counselor in bad times. As John Oakes has observed, today's newspapers have minimal personal ties with the public. Every newspaper reporter has come across people who actually fear him (or her), who turn aside from notebook or tape recorder and plead with genuine concern, "Don't put my name in the paper."

Except during riots and other civic disturbances, that doesn't happen very often to television crews. Let a man appear on a city street with a hand-held miniature camera beside a truck with a dish antenna atop it and excited crowds will form, children and dogs will come running from all directions, and people within range of the lens will smile and wave in the hope of seeing themselves later on local or network videotape.

Crowds seldom appear any longer in front of newspaper offices, as they used to during election nights, heavyweight boxing championships, and World Series games. The only place I know of where it actually happened on election night, 1976, was in front of the offices of the Greeneville (Tenn.) *Sun* (circ. 13,000). To be sure, it didn't happen in New York City or many another metropolis across the land.

The two media—the press and television—appear in most instances to project a totally different image. The TV camera comes across as the harbinger of carnival time, which is what television means to many millions of its viewers. By contrast, the image of the newspaper is synonymous with trouble. There is more to this than the attraction of brightly colored moving pictures for the masses. Despite all the rough antiintellectual tone of the press of my childhood, it somehow managed to convey a sense of credibility to the bulk of its readers. And although it was far more fallible and less expert than today's press, it generated a greater sense of common interest. In short, the *appearance* of public service by the press of the earlier part of this century aroused greater approval than the genuine article does today. And this, perhaps, is the greatest irony of all.

Toward the end of 1976, the million or so daily purchasers of the Los Angeles *Times* must have been slightly puzzled by the opening sentence of a long article about the fate of the American press: "Are you now holding an endangered species in your hands?"[35] The piece was by David Shaw, the *Times*'s usually cheerful and often uninhibited reporter concerned with the news of the media, and it was headed:

NEWSPAPERS CHALLENGED AS NEVER BEFORE

The point of the story was that newspaper circulations were falling, that editors were trying to find new ways of appealing to readers, and that the press would have to answer the competition of television by becoming more relevant to the times. Shaw evidently believed a lot of papers wouldn't be able to make it, for his conclusion was downright chilling:

. . . what seems most likely is that the daily newspaper—or at least some daily newspapers—will survive; but—like other endangered species—they will do so only by adaptation and accommodation. The strong will become stronger—and the weak will die.

More than 1,000 of the nation's 1,756 newspapers are published by just 174 companies—monopoly operations in small-to-medium sized cities. Largely free of the economic burdens and competitive pressures of their big-city brethren, they should continue to do quite well.

In metropolitan areas, 287 newspapers already account for 63% of total circulation. Only three big cities—New York, Chicago and Philadelphia—still have three daily newspapers.* Most others have only two.

In time, say most editors and publishers, every metropolitan area—with perhaps an exception or two—will have only one large daily newspaper.

*It was common knowledge in the industry that James Hoge, upon appointment as editor of both the Chicago *Sun-Times and Chicago Daily News,* was given about three years to make the latter paper pay or else. It suspended publication early in 1978.

In each city, that newspaper will be the one that best serves the changing needs of its readers.

The uninitiated could not have been blamed for thinking, after such a mournful dirge, that the Los Angeles *Times* was either on the point of abandoning its distribution of robust dividends or going out of business entirely. But, happily, such was not the case. For the Times Mirror Company, the massive conglomerate that owns the Los Angeles *Times*, among other newspapers, led the entire industry in profits during 1976 and appeared likely to do so for 1977 as well. True, the Los Angeles *Times* did take a circulation drop of 8,000 between 1973 and 1975, a time of recession, but it gained nearly all of it back during 1976. And from 1970 to 1976, the paper actually was up by 42,700.[36] At the time Shaw wrote his piece, industry sources were reporting Times Mirror interest in taking over one or two additional leading newspapers in other large cities.

The record of the industry as a whole was even better for that particular period, showing that newspapers were more profitable than ever before in their entire history. The *Guild Reporter*, no friend of newspaper publishers, trumpeted the news to its Newspaper Guild readers (for it is always contract time somewhere in the country) with this headline:

NEWSPAPERS OUTPERFORM ALL INDUSTRY

It was true enough. For 1976, newspapers were more than 12 percent ahead of the previous year in total income and *Fortune* magazine's survey showed the press had, indeed, done better than the other industrial giants of the nation. The 18 public companies owning newspapers, including virtually all the leaders plus the major groups, had an average profit margin of 10.2 percent after taxes, while all American industry had to be satisfied with 5.4 percent. And the great chains boosted after-tax gains by about 25 percent in 1977 over 1976.

Far from being pessimistic, the statistics showed that newspapers were holding their own numerically. In 1977, there were 1,764 dailies, just one more than there were in 1946, and there were still 250 dailies with more than 50,000 circulation, an actual increase of 51 percent over 1946, which marked the end of the major period of newspaper consolidation. In 1929, there had been 2,924 dailies.

Advertising continued to be robust. Out of a national advertising total of $38 billions in 1977, newspapers had $11.1 billion, up 12 percent over 1976. TV advertising stood at $7.6 billion, with a gain of almost 13 percent over the previous year. For 1977, magazine advertising was up 21 percent to $2.1 billion and radio ads gained 11.5 percent to $2.6 billion. For 1978, the U. S. Bureau of Domestic Commerce estimated newspaper advertising revenues would exceed $12 billion.

Total newspaper employment in 1977 stood at an all-time record of 393,000, which made the industry the third largest manufacturer in terms of employment, being exceeded only by automobiles and steel.

The profitability of newspapers as a whole was all the more remarkable because newsprint, the major expense after payrolls, had more than doubled since 1970 and stood at $320 a ton in 1978. Even so, 13 large publicly held newspaper companies continued to show average net incomes of $25 million or more, with after-tax profit margins ranging from 10 percent of sales, compared with only 5.4 percent for the 500 largest industrial firms listed by *Fortune* magazine.

What, then, was the point of the Shaw story in the Los Angeles *Times*, and the seeming unanimity with which it was greeted by knowledgeable professionals? Was it the usual sanctimonious wail, so familiar in many a newsroom and adjacent plant at contract bargaining time? Or perhaps a concealed hatchet job on the competition? The advocates of conspiratorial goings-on in almost every aspect of American life would have had a hard time dredging up backing for such suspicions. For the truth was plainly written for all to see—a tremor of confidence about the future.

While it was true that the newspaper industry as a whole was enjoying the best of times, it was the very worst of times for many of the large evening newspapers in the metropolitan areas of the nation. What had happened to them was that the white flight to the suburbs had created a double hazard—a major new interest in suburban newspapers that were delivered in the afternoon plus the TV evening news programs. These suburbanites came to the city in the morning with their morning papers or picked them up on the way; as for the evening papers, their market was dwindling in the big cities under these conditions.

The 102-year-old Chicago *Daily News*—the paper of Carl Sandburg and Ben Hecht, of Edgar Ansel and Paul Scott Mowrer, of Ed Lahey and Peter Lisagor and Keyes Beech—suspended publication in 1978 with many millions of dollars in losses and a circulation that plummeted from 600,000 to 325,000 in less than 20 years. The New York *Post*, under the ownership of Rupert Murdoch, the Australian press tycoon, was reportedly losing $150,000 a month at about the same time. The ailing Washington *Star* was saved when it was purchased by Time, Inc. But the *Wall Street Journal*'s companion weekly paper, the *National Observer*, failed to survive.

The venerable John S. Knight, who had once owned the Chicago *Daily News* but sold it, summed up the position in this fashion:

> Why do great newspapers die? Well, mostly because they have lost their greatness. Secondly, evening newspapers in large markets are under heavy competition for reading time from television and suburban newspapers which emphasize local news.
>
> In recent years, the Chicago *Daily News* and many other newspapers have had a difficult time in trying to determine what they want to be. In Chicago, the *News* became half newspaper, half magazine. Its readers didn't have time to adjust to the vagaries of new editors because usually they weren't there very long.[37]

Uncertain editing and erratic readership have been continuing problems for the press for quite along time. Even when figures appear on the surface to be favorable, editors can't help worrying. Among 49 percent of editors polled by the American Society of Newspaper Editors, declining readership was named the main problem.

There is more to this than just circulation figures. Newspaper readership for more than 30 years has failed to keep pace with population growth in the United States and isn't likely to catch up in the forseeable furture. Using a base figure of 100 for the nation's population (ages 21-64) for 1946, the index of increase in population stood at 139.6 in 1976, but the index of daily newspaper circulation over the same period was only 119.7.

The weeklies have done a bit better, having maintained their numbers at a total of 7,466 in 1977 with a three million gain in circulation to 38 million from 1973 to 1977. And the fat Sunday newspapers, now at an all-time high of 665, with 52.8 million circulation, have been most stable of all.[38]

Taking the circulation slump entirely by itself, the figures do not seem to be so horrendous. What threw a scare into the dailies was a sudden drop of 2.5 million readers between 1973 and 1975 from a high of more than 63 million readers in the former year. This was a loss of about 4 percent, and recovery seemed to be lagging in 1976 with a comeback of only about 300,000 readers. In 1977, it was a bit better with a 700,000 gain to 61.7 million, but nobody was satisfied.

All of a sudden, some of the leaders in newspapering decided that perhaps the papers might benefit from better writing— scarcely an earth-shaking discovery. With a whoop of unanimity, a Readership Council was set up by the American Newspaper Publishers Association and the Newspaper Advertising Bureau. They voted to spend a million dollars a year through 1980 "to build the momentum of newspapers." Altogether, 16 professional associations rallied to the cause. To nobody's surprise the news and editorial direction of the Readership Council was entrusted to the American Society of Newspaper Editors.

The ASNE president at the time, Eugene C. Patterson, reported to his membership:

We've taken charge of the news and editorial destiny in the Readership Project's programs, not only because we ought to and want to, but because, in response to the good Mother Necessity, we had to.

We're finding, incidentally, that editors don't get no disrespect in these councils of richer brethren; on the contrary we're greeted with a welcome bordering on relief that we're taking the news/editorial reins.

Thus began the great crusade for better-written newspapers. But whether or not the Readership Project was the answer to the circulation problems of the press, editors continued to be concerned. Newspapers, after all, had suspended publication in some of the greatest cities in the land—New York, Chicago, Los Angeles, Washington, D. C., Boston, San Francisco, Detroit, Houston, and Cleveland. And others were ailing. Between 1970 and 1976, this was the position of seven major newspapers, including some of the best and most prosperous, as their circulation see-sawed: the New York *Daily News*, the national leader, was off 204,000; the *Wall Street Journal*, second largest paper in the nation, gained 192,000; the New York *Times* was off 43,000; Washington *Post*, up 30,000; Los Angeles *Times*, *up 42,700; Chicago Tribune, off 21,700; and St. Louis Post-Dispatch*, Pulitzer's paper, off 62,000 and dropping to second place behind Newhouse's St. Louis *Globe-Democrat*.[39]

Despite the concern over circulation, and the intense efforts that were being made to turn it around, the industry as a whole continued to show big profits in 1977—and that was comforting to some. Once again, in the first six months of that year, newspapers outperformed other American industries as a whole. A leading brokerage firm reported that after-tax profits of a dozen publicly held newspaper companies rose 20.4 percent in the second quarter of the year over the same period in 1976, compared with increased earnings of 11 to 12 percent for American industry in general. For the entire six-month period, the publicly held newspaper organizations showed after-tax profits of 9.3 percent, as against 8.9 percent for the same period in 1976. The reason: advertising revenues for all media are soaring at a record rate and are projected to reach $48 billion by 1980, with newspapers continuing to claim the largest share. Moreover, Americans are spending close to $4.5 billion annually to buy their papers.

The New York Times Co., one of the bellwethers of the industry, reported that net income in 1977 was up 17 percent to

$26 million on record advertising revenues. The newspaper's weekday circulation rose to 846,000, a 3 percent increase over mid-1976, and Sunday circulation was booming at 1,456,000, up 11,000 over the previous year. In May, 1977, the *Times* reported it had sold more advertising than at any other time in its 126-year history. Its second-quarter earnings of almost $7 million, or 60 cents a share, also set a record. The management credited editorial innovation for this—special sections five times a week.

Other news organizations also did well in 1977. The Washington Post Company put its net income for fiscal 1977 at $35.5 million, an increase of 45 percent over the previous year. Knight-Ridder Newspapers, Inc., earned a record $3.70 a share on a net income for 1977 of $60 million, and the Times Mirror Company, publishers of the Los Angeles *Times*, announced an operating profit increase of 58 percent for the year to $81.3 million on total revenues of more than $1 billion. The Gannett Company reported a net income in 1977 of almost $70 million, a gain of 30 percent. Other large gains for that year included those of the Dow Jones Company, publishers of the *Wall Street Journal*, with a net income of $39 million, up 30 percent, and Time Inc., with a net income of $90 million, up 33 percent. It was a banner year for most chains.

Still, nobody in the industry was taking the future for granted. There were too many uncertainties, particularly in the evening field in the big cities. In addition to the continued threat of unfavorable legislation, plus hostility from the courts, the press's critics hammered at the concentration of ownership. Ben Bagdikian wrote, for example:

> While fewer owners control more newspapers, almost all newspapers are now monopolies in their own communities. Of the 1,500 cities with daily newspapers, 97.5 percent have no local daily newspaper competition. In 1920, there were 700 United States cities with competing papers; today, there are fewer than 50. The reader has no choice even of absentee owners . . . . The chains [are] buying other chains.[41]

One of the biggest inter-chain operations was the $270 million deal through which the Newhouse chain took over the eight

Booth newspapers in Michigan plus *Parade* magazine in 1977. Other chains were also busy with major purchases in 1977 and 1978, including the $20 million purchase of the Washington *Star* by Time, Inc., subject to stockholder approval; the $125 million acquisition of the Kansas City *Star* and *Times* by Capital Cities Communications; the $60 million sale of the duPont-owned Wilmington (Del.) *News-Journal* to Gannett; and the sale of the Buffalo *Evening News* to Blue Chip Stamps Co. of California. The largest of all, subject to government and stockholder approval, was a projected $370 million merger of Gannett with Combined Communications, owners of the Cincinnati *Enquirer* and Oakland *Tribune*.

Even the most vociferous press critics were well aware that all their laments would not bring back the family newspaper. Some argued, however, that electronics would make possible new ventures in newspapering, so that a black box attached to a TV set would produce a newspaper in the home. That was scant comfort to independent publishers. One of them, John Seigenthaler, publisher of the Nashville *Tennessean*, said:

> It may be too late to question whether the movement toward chain ownership by publicly held corporations is insurmountable, as it is certainly too late to question whether monopoly ownership in a local community is good or bad. With more than 95 percent of our communities now without competing newspapers, that last issue seems, at least for the near future, a closed subject.[42]

It is not too late, however, to question whether powerful interests inimical to the preservation of a free press in the United States are likely to become involved in some of the publicly held corporations that are buying newspapers. The great industrial complexes that are in control of some of the large newspapers of France, Italy, and other democratic countries have scarcely inspired confidence and trust in the impartiality of their news reports and editorial judgment. Nor can the acquisition of the London *Observer* by Atlantic Richfield, an American oil company, be viewed with anything less than disquiet.

More than one major American industrial corporation has

toyed with the notion of taking over a newspaper or two, or even a chain. If the movement should take hold as a means of combatting what many business people feel is undue press hostility to business, quite the opposite result may be expected. For once newspaper owners accept a major financial commitment outside the media, there is a built-in conflict of interest.

7. *"Going Public" and the Public*

When a newspaper or newspaper chain "goes public" and offers its stock for sale, there is generally no outward change either in the appearance or the quality of its news report and editoral comment. But internally, there are subtle differences that take some time to develop. I remember hearing a distinguished editor, whose paper had "gone public" some months before, telling a group of friendly newspaper executives, "It's really a whole new ball game. When you go before a stockholders' meeting, you're not in any editorial conference."

Of the 169 group newspapers that are surveyed annually, 13 are dominant and their 290 daily newspapers account for about 40 percent of all daily American newspaper circulation. These were the statistics made public in 1978 by Professor Paul Jess, who compiles them annually:

Group	Mix°		1977 Activity	Daily Circulation (000's)
Knight-Ridder	34D	23S		3,560
Newhouse	29D	20S	(-1D,-1S)°	3,204
Chicago Tribune Co.	6D	4S	(-1D)	3,068
Gannett Co.	77D	45S	(+24D, +9S)	3,002
Scripps-Howard	16D	6S		1,860
Dow Jones-Ottaway	14D	6S		1,784

°D-Daily, S-Sunday. Approval of the Gannett-Combined Communications merger adds about 350,000 daily circulation to the above totals, thus making Gannett the second largest chain in terms of circulation and the largest numerically, with 79 dailies, 45 Sunday papers, the acquisition of 26 daily newspapers and nine Sundays in 1977-78.

Group	Mix		1977 Activity	Daily Circulation (000's)
Times Mirror Co.	4D	4S		1,750
Hearst Corp.	8D	7S		1,436
Cox Newspapers	19D	8S	(+1D)	1,144
N. Y. Times-Ochs Estate	11D	6S		1,029
Thomson Newspapers	58D	24S	(+1D, +1S)	1,011
Capital Cities Comm.	6D	3S	(+2D, +1S)	950
Cowles Newspapers	8D	6S	(+1D, +1S)	888
TOTALS	290D	162S	+27D, +11S	24,686

The Washington *Post* predicts an even greater concentration of press ownership. In its 1977 survey of the industry, this was the *Post*'s major finding:

Within two decades, virtually all daily newspapers in America will be owned by perhaps fewer than a dozen major communications conglomerates. Given current tax laws and economic conditions, as well as an apparent inability to challenge any media acquisitions under current anti-trust laws, the rapid concentration of press power in the hands of a few giants appears inevitable.

The public corporation is a relatively new phenomenon in the newspaper field. It evolved from the steady growth of the chains and was given a monumental push by the changes in the tax laws, which have done so much to put the family-owned newspaper out of business. When Robert and Charles Withers sold their Rochester (Minn.) *Post-Bulletin* to the Len Small chain, this was their explanation:

Not many in the next Withers generation are interested in journalism. Stiff inheritance taxes—a fear that Congress might eliminate capital gains provisions, thus permitting tax collectors to virtually wipe out the accumulated results of a couple of lifetimes of hard work.[43]

Lee Hills, chairman of the board of the Knight-Ridder Newspapers, gave this hard-headed explanation:

The tax code is biased toward and encourages merger, conglomeration, and concentration. When estate taxes became confiscatory some years ago, it accelerated the demise of almost all "family" businesses. The "skip generation" impact of the 1976 tax code, plus the equalization of the gift and estate tax rates, make it almost mandatory for prudent owners to sell out and diversify. The reformers who bemoan the loss of "small business" should examine the results of their own proposals, rather than impugn the motives of their victims.[44]

Dorothy Schiff, whose New York *Post* alone had survived all the pressures, strikes, and competitive turmoil in the New York afternoon newspaper field, made no secret of the basic reason for selling the paper to Rupert Murdoch, the Australian press tycoon. She was 72 years old and, as she told friends, her heirs would have been in no position to maintain the paper under the tougher inheritance tax laws. She sold just before they took effect.

As often as not, the owners of family newspapers initiated the negotiations for perfectly obvious reasons. They couldn't hang on, and in 1978 it was estimated that only 400 independently owned newspapers were left in the U. S.

One of the exceptions to the rule turned up in Florida, where Nelson Poynter set up an organization called Modern Media Institute, which took over the controlling interest in his newspapers, the St. Petersburg *Times* and *Independent*, after his death. While he provided for a nine-member board of trustees to run the Instituteand its academic interests, he vested the maintainence of professional control of the newspapers in a single trustee, the editor and president of the *Times*. Eugene C. Patterson, who became the trustee upon Poynter's death in 1978, explained:

> It is a very simple way to maintain professional control of the newspapers while creating the dividends that will advance the educational undertakings of the tax-exempt institute that we have established. So, that was the way he [Poynter] chose to go. Inheritance taxes, the problems of scattered stock, we all know the tremendous problems of succession in newspapers, and this is simply one town, one newspaper, one owner who chose to do it his way.[45]

But there aren't many Nelson Poynters in America. More follow the course of James G. Stahlman, the fiercely proud owner of the Nashville *Banner*, who at the age of 80 asked the Gannett Company to take over his newspaper and was satisfied when it did so. He could see no other way for the *Banner* to go.[46]

The public's role in the changing position of the press among the nation's financial and business interests has been puzzling, to say the least. Although the readers of newspapers have a greater stake than anybody else in maintaining the integrity of the press, there haven't been any public demonstrations of consequence against the proposition of chain ownership of a newspaper in a community. When an individual owner sells out these days, there usually are expressions of regret by the business people and leading advertisers,[47] but it is seldom that anybody leads a war dance against the new group ownership even though it is strange to the community.

I remember one instance in which a rugged individualist of the old school, Wally Jessup, took to the pulpits of the churches in Bremerton, Washington, a Navy Yard town, to warn against the chain that was trying to take over his paper, the Bremerton *Searchlight*. He managed to save his paper, but only for a time. Today, the *Searchlight*'s wavering beam has long been extinguished and the John P. Scripps chain's Bremerton *Sun* shines in its place. But all that happened long before any paper or group of consequence thought of "going public."

However, it is generally not the public, but editors and writers devoted to media criticism as a specialty, who continually debate the basic propositions behind the control of the press. One reason for the apparent public disinterest in new ownership is that the coming of one of the better chains into a community means the infusion of new life in an old paper. No professional of consequence argues with the easily demonstrable conclusion that a wealthy and responsible chain, with keen editorial direction, usually improves the newspaper it buys. But there also are some pretty objectionable chains that strip newspapers bare and do almost everything for the bottom line—yet even here one finds more editorial than public protests.

It is one thing to assess the importance of a chain that was dominated for so many years by John S. Knight, who won a Pulitzer Prize for his early editiorials opposing the Vietnam War and encouraged all his newspapers to pursue public service campaigns. It is quite another to contemplate the American holdings of Lord Thomson of Fleet, who proudly admitted to a visitor that the only book or newspaper he had in his office was a thick profit-and-loss ledger of all his newspaper holdings. Patting the ledger affectionately, the newspaper peer said, "These are my little cash boxes."[48]

One can respect a chain headed by Katharine Graham of the Washington *Post* group, Warren Phillips of the *Wall Street Journal*, Clayton Kirkpatrick of the Chicago *Tribune* group, Paul Miller and Allen Neuharth of Gannett, Punch Sulzberger of the New York *Times* group, and Otis Chandler of the Los Angeles *Times* group, among others. But what of a chain that fires an editor for refusing to print a rather silly attempt to make President Carter appear to condone sexual permissiveness among his staff? Or a chain that summarily dismisses a publisher after his paper printed a four-letter word on Page 1 because it touched off a slaying? As Lee Hills says, "The impact of 'chain ownership' is neither automatically good nor bad. It depends on the company."[49]

And what of the family newspapers, about which so many tears have been shed? Have they all been paragons of virtue and a boon to their communities? To be sure, everybody in newspaper work has his own list of good ones and mine includes the very best—Barry Bingham, Sr. and Jr., and their Louisville *Courier-Journal* and *Times;* the employee-owned *Milwaukee Journal* under Dick Leonard's editorship; Nelson Poynter's St. Petersburg *Times;* Joseph Pulitzer, Jr.'s St. Louis *Post-Dispatch;* and the Providence *Journal-Bulletin,* which is run by John C. A. Watkins for the family owners. But how long they will be individually run is something else again, for nearly all are, of necessity, reaching out for more broadly based operations. For many, there is no alternative. They must become chains themselves, sell out under pressure of rigorous tax laws, or go out of business.

However, not all family publishers are remembered as true

princes of journalism. During the years in which the American Newspaper Guild was being organized, under the beneficial influences of the New Deal and the Wagner Labor Act, individual owners were among the Guild's most intractable foes. If they were not as successful at union busting as Samuel I. Newhouse, the founder of one of the largest and most affluent of American newspaper chains, they were every bit as stubborn. I particularly recall one publisher in Newark, N. J., of whom it was said that he ordered a staff reduction as follows: "Everybody on this side of the room is fired, everybody on that side of the room stays." That, of course, is scarcely the image of the family newspaper as it has been handed down to us.

Another major point that independent editors make against the chains is that the "independent spirit" is sacrificed when there is a group takeover of an individually owned newspaper. To this, the chains' response is that editors in the better groups nearly always have local options in developing editorial policy and even in backing political candidates. To Eugene Patterson, for one, that isn't good enough. He puts it this way, even though he agrees that the better chains do benefit their communities:

> While quality may beget profits, the question goes on about the independent spirit. When it hurts profits, which obviously a publicly held corporation must worry about, the value of its stock is involved. Its earnings must come in. That bottom line is dreadfully important, but frequently the old independent spirit in a community will take a drop in profits because it was nobody's business but his (the independent editor) to fight a battle that needed fighting, and as time goes on, 20 years from now, if the trend continues, the bottom line must have enormous priority.

Another vigorous chain critic, Loren Ghiglione, publisher of the Southbridge (Mass.) *Evening News*, refuses to be impressed by the crusading character of the better group newspapers or the large number of Pulitzer Prizes they and their staff members have won. Like Patterson, he argues that chains put profits ahead of editorial excellence, saying,

I believe that everyone at a group newspaper is going to find it difficult not to give profitability top priority when the president and chief executive officer is saying, as [Robert] Marbut at Harte-Hanks has said, "The professional publisher has the obligation to insure that owners receive a reasonable return on the assets under the publisher's trustee-ship. He has the obligation to take the long-term view, to build the long-term franchise in the marketplace."

Ghiglione's suggestions for remedial action include changing the tax laws to favor the few remaining independents and to penalize the chains. He also wants the Federal government to set limits on the number of papers that may be owned by a group, just as the FCC limits the number of stations that may be owned by a broadcasting chain. Finally, he wants the antitrust laws applied "to slow the groups' growth."[50]

Thus, the independents are, in effect, inviting the Federal government to begin regulating the newspaper industry—the answer to many a bureaucrat's prayers. Given a continued state of adverse public opinion regarding the press, Ghiglione and other chain foes could get somewhat more government action than they expect.

The foregoing illustrates the broad range of editorial opinion today concerning the growth of the chains and the decline of the family-owned newspaper. Just about the only point of agreement on substance is that the independent newspaper is dying, at least in the daily field. Under the circumstances, there does not seem to be much use in mourning the decline of the independent spirit or wondering whether it is possible to punish the chains with heavy taxes or antitrust investigations. The point is that every chain, like any individually owned newspaper, becomes foolhardy if its managers fall victim to the belief that the power of the press can be equated with the power of government. Any newspaper risks its future if it takes an adversary position against the government and loses.

There are outstanding illustrations to support the point. Fortunately for the Washington *Post*, the Watergate gamble turned

out well. So did the gamble on the publication of the Pentagon
Papers for both the New York *Times* and the Washington *Post*.
When the Knight-Ridder Miami *Herald* went to the U. S. Supreme Court to overthrow a Florida "right of reply" law, the
gamble resulted in an 8-0 verdict for the newspaper; had it gone
the other way, all the news media would have been in the deepest trouble. As for individual newspapers, the Providence *Journal-
Bulletin* took a major risk in publishing President Nixon's income
tax returns on the basis of a leak from the Internal Revenue
Service. And among columnists, Jack Anderson has defied the
government to act against him on several occasions, notably with
his publication of secret documents showing the Nixon's administration's "tilt" toward Pakistan in the Indo-Pakistan War of 1971.

It is perfectly true, as critics contend, that such derring-do
doesn't apply to every paper, columnist, or chain in America. But
the press has the right ot be judged by its best now and then, in
common with all other American institutions, instead of being
dragged down to its lowest common denominator. Of course, any
newspaper—chain or individually owned—can coast along for
years without doing much of anything, and many do. And it is
equally true that the bottom line over the years has counted on
certain types of individual newspapers and chains alike.

But sentimental arguments aside, I am persuaded that a first-
rate chain can do as well as any individual paper in representing
its community—provided it retains a system of editorial control
that is independent of the business office. Some say that this will
not be possible much longer—that the press itself will stifle its
own freedom. Others contend that the business office—the
dreaded counting house—already has taken over in most major
newspaper organizations, as it has in television.

I am not at all sure that this is so. For one thing, I heard the
same things being said by eminent nonjournalists—and quite a
few low-paid journalists, too—when I broke into the business
more than fifty years ago. For another, any sophisticated business
manager knows that a paper is finished when it loses its reputation

for editorial integrity, just as any sophisticated advertiser knows that it doesn't pay to try to dictate editorial policy for papers that are large enough to defend themselves. Where business has out-weighed editorial considerations, it is often at the bottom level of American journalism—not usually at the top, so far at least.

Whether or not this principle will remain valid constitutes the public's gamble in accepting the growth of some of the largest communications conglomerates in history. On this, like it or not, we have now staked the future of the free press in the United States. For if independent editorial control cannot be maintained where it counts most, then it doesn't really matter if the system is based on conglomerate ownership, newspaper chain ownership, or the individual proprietor. Once editorial policy becomes the property of the counting house, the free press in the United States will be doomed to extinction. And Federal antitrust action, if taken, will only tend to confirm it.

8. *The Mission of the Press*

With all the contending forces that are struggling for primacy over the American press, it is no wonder that its mission in today's society is a mass of contradictions.

Like all American institutions, it depends on the government to protect its freedoms. Yet, it is the only institution that regards the maintenance of tension with government as a necessity.

Its reporters are assigned to daily contact with the most im-portant personages, officials and organizations in the land, not to be impartial recorders of fact, but quite frequently to be adver-saries.

It is accountable to no outside authority under the First Amendment, except for the laws that apply in general to all. Still, it demands accountability from everybody else.

While it shares in the common responsibility of all Americans to uphold national security, it reserves to itself the right to publish sensitive or even secret information whenever it deems such action to be necessary.

It is perceived by its readers to be certifying the truth of all the news it publishes, but even the newest reporter soon learns that news and truth are not necessarily synonymous.

Its columns are open to any legitimate advertiser, but consumers ofter ask it to attack those same advertisers.

It is an engine that is fueled by public exposure, but its own inner workings are seldom held up to public view even in this day of the publicly held news corporation.

It is also a business that cannot on occasion avoid exposing the ills of other businesses; a profession that anybody may enter merely by proclaiming himself to be a journalist; an employer of labor and a party to union contracts, but it is often critical of labor unions.

At best, a considerable section of the public has therefore looked upon its press as a necessary annoyance. At worst, it has been denounced as the tool of infernal meddlers, a disgrace to all proper socety, and a menace of sorts to the survival of the republic. At one time or another, it has managed to offend just about every powerful group in the land, including its own advertisers. So its public relations, since the glory days of World War II, have descended to a level well below freezing.

These are the disorderly circumstances that lead totalitarian societies to call the free press an absurdity. No wonder dictators take over the newspapers upon assuming power! Since the main elements of the broadcast media are already under government control everywhere except in the United States, they are less of a problem. All of which makes the mission of the press in the United States, as the largest and most powerful of the remaining open societies on earth, a matter of crucial importance for all peoples.

There is no pat definition of the mission of the press in America. Journalists themselves often disagree violently over what it should and should not do, which is only to be expected. In a pursuit that is at once so competitive and so aggressive, so filled with rancor and criticism, it is understandable that journalists must go their separate ways even if they are likely to fall into greater error by so doing. Walter Lippmann once observed: "The theory of a free press is that the truth will emerge from free reporting and free discussion, not that it will be presented perfectly and instantly in any one account."[51]

That, however, is only a part of the story. When the first Joseph Pulitzer exhorted his heirs never to be satisfied with merely covering the news, he sounded another of the dominant themes of the American press. It has been variously phrased over more than two centuries, nearly always in the high moralistic terms that have also characterized much of American governmental policy at home and particularly abroad. When Andrew Hamilton called upon a New York jury to free John Peter Zenger on a charge of libel against the colonial government, he invoked the "Cause of Liberty—the Liberty both of exposing and opposing arbitrary Power by speaking and writing Truth."[52] And the revolutionary press, in the words of Arthur Meier Schlesinger, Sr., "influenced events both by reporting and abetting local patriot transactions and by broadcasting kindred proceedings in other places."[53] Horace Greeley, in founding the New York *Tribune* in 1841, dedicated it to reform: "Anti-Slavery, Anti-War, Anti-Rum, Anti-Tobacco, Anti-Seduction, Anti-Grogshops, Brothels and Gambling Houses."[54]

The most uncompromising of abolitionists, William Lloyd Garrison, began his *Liberator* with flaming editorial defiance: "I will be harsh as truth, and as uncompromising as justice. On this subject I do not wish to think, or speak, or write with moderation . . . . I am in earnest—I will not equivocate—I will not excuse—I will not retract a single inch—AND I WILL BE HEARD."[55]

Not even the excesses of the brawling partisan press of the early part of the 19th century stifled the American journalist's passionate interest in uplift, crusading, and reform. In the latter part of that century, the voice of Pulitzer was heard declaiming against injustice and vowing "drastic independence" in the conduct of his newspapers. And there was a barbaric yawp from Chicago: "Comfort the afflicted and afflict the comfortable!"

Even Adolph S. Ochs, in pledging "to give the news impartially without fear or favor" when he acquired the New York *Times* in 1896, felt obliged to add that his paper would be "for no more government than is absolutely necessary to protect society, maintain individual vested rights, and assure the free exercise of a sound conscience."[56]

In the best of American journalists, there has always been a touch of the prophet, which is odd in those who profess to be simple news-givers to the nation. There are editors who argue that advocacy does not befit the journalist, but the hard truth is that the great journalists—and many of the lesser ones—have always been advocates. Nor have they been ashamed to attack their fellow-journalists for falling into error or failing to perform their duty.

Ralph McGill, the illustrious liberal who became both the voice and the conscience of the South in the battle over civil rights, pleaded with his fellow editors to permit the publication of ideas they detested. And when some refused after the 1954 school desegregation decision of the United States Supreme Court, he wrote: "I must enter a *mea culpa* plea for my own profession of journalism and that of local television and radio. Some of the failures of our regional press and other media to offer truthful, honest leadership have been tragic and contemptible in spirit and in the encouragement of extremists to violate the law."[57]

It remained for Edward R. Murrow, in his major speech to his associates in broadcast journalism, to phrase this warning of Armageddon:

During the daily peak viewing periods, television in the main insulates us from the realities of the world in which we live. If this state of

affairs continues, we may alter an advertising slogan to read: LOOK
NOW, PAY LATER. For surely we shall pay for using this most powerful instrument of communications to insulate the citizenry from the hard
and demanding realities which must be faced if we are to survive.[58]

Perhaps the most universal and widely accepted principle of
action for American journalists was enunciated by Elmer Davis
and broadcast at the height of the McCarthy era of witch-hunting
for Communists in government:

The first and great commandment is, Don't let them scare you. For
the men who are trying to do that to us are scared themselves. They are
afraid that what they think will not stand critical examination; they are
afraid that the principles on which this Republic was founded and has
been conducted are wrong. They will tell you that there is a hazard in
the freedom of the mind, and of course there is, as in any freedom. In
trying to think right you run the risk of thinking wrong. But there is no
hazard at all, no uncertainty, in letting somebody else tell you what to
think; that is sheer damnation.[59]

One would suppose that such noble sentiments would endear
the journalist to the American public, but, as has already been
shown, this is unfortunately not the case. The mistrust of the press
in the infant republic, which led Alexander Hamilton to fight the
insertion of a free press guarantee in the Bill of Rights, has persisted in different form to current times.

It was even present in colonial America. The 17-year-old Ben
Franklin, then a printer's apprentice, fled from Boston "because I
had already made myself a little obnoxious to the governing party
and . . . it was likely I might, if I stayed, soon to bring myself into
scrapes."[69] He was in many a scrape later with his publications
and eventually he made his mark not as a journalist, but as a
statesman.

Since Franklin's time, not may famous Americans outside the
profession have celebrated their beginnings as journalists with a
mission. We have had no Winston Churchills, no Georges Cle-
menceaus, no Theodore Herzls and, perhaps fortunately, no Karl
Marxes. The only journalist who ever made his home at the White
House was the ex-editor of the Marion (Ohio) *Star*, Warren Ga-

maliel Harding, who became one of the worst of our Presidents. The most renowned practicing journalist in the U. S. Senate in the last generation was the ex-city editor of the Grand Rapids (Michigan) *Press*, Arthur Vandenberg, who was originally appointed to the post and not elected until after he had established a political reputation.

It is understandable, given the lack of public respect for the journalist's mission and the absence of charismatic public leadership, that the American people more often than not are impressed by charges that the press is both wicked and authoritarian. This has been a staple of reformers since the era of Upton Sinclair, in his *The Brass Check*, early in the century.[61]

What is far more difficult for the public to understand is the evolution af adversary journalism in its modern guise, for its acceptance requires a certain amount of trust and faith in the intent of a crusading newspaper. And this, quite frequently, the public is unwilling to give until it has been demonstrated beyond all reasonable doubt that the newspaper—or other news organization— is right. If the mission of the journalist as advocate arouses mistrust, the concept of the journalist as adversary often becomes doubly suspect.

It is true that there always have been both advocates and adversaries in American journalism, but today's swing toward an adversary position by a number of leading newspapers is quite different from anything the press has done previously in American history. While it was based originally on the press's mistrust of government, it has broadened into a general suspicion of many another power center. And it has penetrated numerous medium- and smaller-sized newspapers, a few of the more vigorous weeklies, the news magazines, the bolder elements in both radio and television journalism, and even the wire services on occasion.

Every editor and correspondent has a different idea of the historical perspective that brought about such a dramatic shift in the mission of the press. It is not a simple matter, therefore, to trace the evolution of this concept by citing public statements or actions. Nor can any precise date be put on the emergence of the journalist in the image of Messrs. Woodward and Bernstein, with an overlay of Ben Bradlee.

This much is reasonably certain: until journalists willingly accepted the term "adversary journalism," it had existed mainly in the American legal system. In the clash between prosecution and defense, or plaintiff and defendant, the theory holds that the truth eventually will be perceived by judge and jury, working together or separately. Sometimes, the legal adversary system doesn't work very well, as was shown when four persons convicted of first degree murder were freed through the efforts of Gene Miller, a Miami *Herald* reporter. But that is another story.

Nobody is quite sure when this legal concept moved into journalism and was embraced by much of the press's leadership, both liberal and conservative, as a proper description of its posture toward many of our major power centers, headed by the government. A legal scholar, Benno C. Schmidt, Jr., suspects the shift came during the 1960s and he is probably right.[62]

The old theory of adversary journalism (only it wasn't called that) was based in the main on political alignment. That is to say, if the mayor or governor or President was a Democrat and the publisher of the paper was a Republican, there could usually be very little agreement between them. This attitude came to full flower and withered during Franklin D. Roosevelt's four Presidential campaigns, which he won although he had fully 80 percent of the press against him.

The more vindictive publishers tried every trick of which they were capable to undermine public faith in FDR. William Randolph Hearst, Sr., ordered his editors never to permit the use of the term, "New Deal," in his papers and had it changed to "Raw Deal," even in the news columns. Papers like the archconservative New York *Sun* ridiculed Social Security by publishing pictures of citizens with dog tags around their necks, stamped with a Social Security number.

This was the journalism of political partisanship, practiced with a vengeance, but it didn't work. FDR always had the upper hand because he invariably used the power of his high office to dominate the headlines on Page 1, leaving the publishers with their little-read editorial pages, and he also was the acknowledged master of radio oratory. But so far as is known, neither he nor his foes considered that they were practicing adversary journalism.

Neither did the fiercely aggressive President Truman, who also had more than his share of battles with the press and seldom came off second best. The picture of the victorious Truman, holding aloft the Chicago *Tribune*'s headline that proclaimed his defeat in the 1948 Presidential election, is one of the emblems of the kind of journalism that was used against him.

If the futility of old-fashioned political opposition to a popular President began to dawn on even the most die-hard among conservative publishers in the 1950s, the bankruptcy of so-called "objective" reporting of McCarthyism also gave editors something to think about. For each of Senator McCarthy's unsubstantiated charges was published in flaring headlines by a large section of the press that seemed anxious to believe that there were, indeed, hundreds of concealed Communists in government. The papers that dared to oppose McCarthy were so few in number that their voices were almost smothered. It was not until Edward R. Murrow's revealing "See It Now" broadcast on March 9, 1954, that the whole nation heard the voice of reason:

> We proclaim ourselves, as indeed we are, the defenders of freedom—what's left of it—but we cannot defend freedom abroad by deserting it at home. The actions of the junior senator from Wisconsin have caused alarm and dismay among our allies abroad and given considerable comfort to our enemies. And whose fault is that? Not really his; he didn't create this situation of fear, he merely exploited it and rather successfully. Cassius was right. "The fault, dear Brutus, is not in our stars but in ourselves."[63]

It is hard to convey the disillusionment that so many editors of varying political persuasions felt in the aftermath of the storm over McCarthyism. They had seen FDR elected four times over the opposition of 80 percent of the press. To make matters worse, they—the editors—now realized that they had let themselves be victimized by a charlatan who played on their weakness for the journalism of "fact," whether there was any truth in the facts or not.

There were mighty vows for reform at conventions of editors. In an effort to convince a skeptical public that the press never again would abet the rise of a McCarthy, there was a hesitant turning to the practice of interpretive reporting and analysis by papers that had never before permitted much of it to be done by their own staffs. Checks were run on provocative statements made by speakers of national renown. But for Adlai E. Stevenson, it remained "a one party press in a two party country."[64]

Everything seemed to return to normal during the Eisenhower Presidency. The country was at peace. Times were better. No President since FDR had been more popular, more acclaimed, more trusted. The smiling face of "Ike"—wherever he appeared—seemed to give everybody reassurance in the rightness of the American way.

And then, completely without warning, everything went awry when the Russians shot down Francis Gary Powers's U-2 spy plane on May 1, 1960. The government of the United States was publicly humiliated when it first denied the overflight, then was forced to admit it had lied. Worse still, after first denying Presidential responsibility, President Eisenhower—the sainted "Ike"—admitted that he was responsible. As a result, the Summit meeting with the Russians in Paris blew up—and so did Eisenhower's temper.

Under the sharp questioning of Senator William J. Fulbright, the chairman of the Senate Foreign Relations Committee, the President flared, "Look Senator, this is modern-day espionage. In the old days I could send you out or send a spy out and if he was caught, disavow him. But what do you do when you strap an American-made plane to his back, Senator?"[65]

If the incident had a traumatic international effect, it was no less of a shock for the American press, which had to face up to the bitter truth that it had been deceived by the President of the United States. And this was no ordinary President, but the victorious Allied commander of World War II. If "Ike" could not be trusted, who could? The citizenry, always practical in such matters, appeared to be somewhat more philosophical about the incident. After all, many people reasoned, wasn't it a part of the government's duty to spy on the Russians as they spied on us? And wasn't it necessary to take risks such as President Eisenhower accepted in authorizing the U-2 overflights?

But most editors, regardless of their political philosophy, didn't see it that way. It was very hard for them to accept the dictum of the ancient radical journalist, I. F. Stone: "Every government is run by liars and nothing they say should be believed."[66] There was still an illusory feeling in many a newsroom throughout the land that the word of the government of the United States ought to be respected.

In the changeover to the Kennedy administration, the brillance of a modern Camelot dispersed the gloom for one brief, shining moment. But very soon, rumors of an imminent invasion of Cuba by anti-Castro forces with American support swept through Washington. Nor did the new President's assurance against a Cuban involvement by American armed forces set the rumors at rest.

Arthur Meier Schlesinger, Jr., a Presidential adviser, acted at the President's request to kill a story called "Our Men in Miami," which had been submitted by Gilbert Harrison of the New Republic—a "devastating account of CIA activities among the (Cuban) refugees," Schlesinger called it. Not long afterward, President Kennedy himself persuaded the New York Times not to publish a detailed account by Tad Szulc of the imminent invasion. The version that did reach print was so thoroughly laundered that not even the CIA could have taken offense.

It was a stupid blunder, both for the President and the New York Times, as the abysmal failure of the Bay of Pigs invasion demonstrated. In the appalling aftermath, the President—after initially lecturing the press on the need for self-regulation—told a *Times* editor, "If you had printed more about the operation, you would have saved us from a colossal mistake." And Schlesinger, while calling the *Times*'s act "patriotic," added," I have wondered whether, if the press had behaved irresponsibly, it would not have spared the country a disaster." The *Times* itself thundered:

> A democracy . . . our democracy . . . cannot be lied to. This is one of the factors that make it more precious, more delicate, more difficult, and yet essentially stronger than any other form of government in the world . . . Not only is it unethical to deceive one's own public as part of a system of deceiving an adversary government; it is also foolish . . . . "[67]

One would have thought, after successive strategic failures at deceiving the press and the people by a Republican and a Democratic administration, that the government would choose the path of rectitude for at least a short time. But such was not the case, as developments in Vietnam demonstrated. Kennedy led the nation into the treacherous morass of secret warfare in Vietnam apparently without thinking of the consequences. And the press, after being outraged by the deception over the Bay of Pigs, let him do it. As late as the summer of 1963, there were only a handful of correspondents for American news organizations in Saigon. A year later, after Lyndon Baines Johnson had become President following Kennedy's assassination, there were still only about a dozen correspondents. Although most of them gave valiant warning of disaster if the United States escalated the war, they were not listened to—even by their home offices—until it was too late.[68]

Out of the Vietnam debacle came the basic outline of the theory of adversary journalism in its modern guise. It has frequently been assumed, principally by writers who know little or nothing about journalism, that this was primarily a liberal position. But quite the contrary is true. The harsh and skeptical attitude toward the government and other major power groupings in the land was assumed by Vietnamese hawks and doves alike, for they realized that they had been used like parrots to repeat government propaganda to the public.

Furthermore, it is very difficult to assume, as so many nonjournalists have, that this was an ideological move led by disappointed and chagrined liberals. Once the Tet offensive had shown the basic weakness of the American military position and forced President Johnson to fold up his plans to run for reelection, publications as conservative as the *Wall Street Journal* and the Chicago *Tribune* gave up the notion that this war could be "won." And the most voracious hawk of all, *Time* magazine, became the most insistent critic of the government's Vietnam policy.

There was no other way for the press to go. Its integrity had been undermined by successive administrations, without regard to political allegiances or obligations. In consequence, the old notion of political journalism as a standard for supporting or attacking the government was as dead as Arthur Brisbane. And what of the leaders of journalism who had gone along willingly, even patriotically, with dubious governmet positions only to find that the government had studiously, deliberately, even strenuously, misinformed them? It made sense to most of them that the press should try to regain a decent amount of standing with the public by separating itself from the government and adopting a critical position henceforth.

It was at this juncture that Neil Sheehan, the Pentagon correspondent of the New York *Times* and perhaps the bitterest opponent of the Vietnam War among all the correspondents, delivered the Pentagon Papers to his newspaper. There never was any serious debate at the *Times* about whether or not to publish these secret documents on how we sank into the Vietnamese quagmire. The only question was one of method. As the *Times* told its readers editorially:

A fundamental responsibility of the press in this democracy is to publish information that helps the people of the United States to understand the processes of their own government, especially when those

processes have been clouded over in a hazy veil of public dissimulation
and even deception.

As a newspaper that takes seriously its obligation and its responsibilities to the public, we believe that, once this material fell into our hands,
it was not only in the interests of the American people to publish it but,
even more emphatically, it would have been an abnegation of responsibility and a renunciation of our obligations under the First Amendment
not to have published it.[69]

Althought the Nixon administration had taken the *Times* and
the Washington *Post* to the U. S. Supreme Court in a vain effort to
halt publication, there really wasn't a partisan issue in the case
and the press itself divined none. When the 1972 Pulitzer Prize
Jury in Public Service met under the chairmanship of Stuart Aw-
brey, editor and publisher of the Hutchinson (Kansas) *News* and
scarcely a flaming liberal, the verdict of the five editors went
unanimously for the *Times*. A prize for the *Times*, the jurors said,
"can reaffirm to the American people that the press continues its
devotion to their right to know, a basic bulwark in our democratic
society."[70]

In the later debate within the Advisory Board on the Pulitzer
Prizes, the issue of whether to recognize the *Times* for its publication of the secret documents troubled a good many editors. But
finally, it was no liberal but one of the staunchest of conservatives
who made the decisive argument. Vermont Royster, then the editor of the *Wall Street Journal*, said, "Many things about the Pentagon Papers trouble me. But I'm sure of one thing. If I had them,
I would have published them."[71] And on that basis, the *Times* was
awarded the Pulitzer Prize gold medal for public service for 1972
over the stated opposition of the Trustees of Columbia University.[72]

Thus was the most distinctive professional support given to
the dawning concept of adversary journalism. It seemed to be a
virtual signal to the American press to go forth and do likewise.
And less than two months after the announcement of the Pulitzer
Prize for the Pentagon Papers, this is exactly what the Washington *Post* began to do with the "third rate burglary" at the Watergate complex. One cannot look into Ben Bradlee's mind and de-

duce that the *Times*'s exclusive on the Pentagon Papers goaded
him into gambling that his two young reporters would get somewhere with the Watergate expose. But certainly, it didn't do anything to dissuade him. He had been among those who voted for
the *Times*'s prize.

True, once both the press and broadcast media were drawn
into the Watergate inquiry by the Washington *Post*'s initial disclosures, there was a revival of partisanship. The more conservative
Republican papers did try initially to defend Nixon, but very soon
realized how hopeless it was. By the time of the House Judiciary
Committee hearings, Nixon had lost every defender of consequence among the press. The last nail in his political coffin was
hammered home by the Chicago *Tribune* in an editorial, written
in part by the editor, Clayton Kirkpatrick, demanding his resignation.

In this manner, the press set its course toward a continuation
of adversary journalism. And the broadcast media served as a
gigantic national amplifier for every disclosure, large and small,
whether it affected the government or lesser power centers.
Some, including knowledgeable insiders, argued that it was a temporary phenomemom brought about by the vulnerability of the
Nixon administration and the necessity for a different kind of
newspaper journalism to combat the influence of television journalism. But at best, that was a half truth and not a very good one
at that.

Daniel Patrick Moynihan, later to become a U. S. Senator
from New York, even theorized that media hostility toward government could be ascribed in large part to the recruitment of
"more and more persons from middle- and upper-class backgrounds" who were university-trained to elitist, anti-Establish-
ment attitudes.[73] This was just about the silliest argument of all,
for it presupposed that every green kid from Harvard or Columbia could walk into a newsroom and do just about as he pleased—
that editors and publishers had abdicated all responsibility to
some semi-beautiful young people.

Max Frankel, in the New York *Times*, gave the proper answer when he argued that adversary journalism came to pass because of "the conduct of government itself" and went on:

You must begin by noting not the power for occasional deception in the White House, but the habit of regular deception in our politics and administration . . . It is the damnable tendency toward manipulation that forces us so often into the posture of apparent adversaries.[74]

Frankel might well have added that the press, out of self interest, whether enlightened or not, also had to act to defend it own credibility with the public at a time when there was rising public skepticism over the intentions of government, regardless of what party was in power. Indeed, after the Carter administration took office, the more liberal newspapers were the ones that appeared at first to be the most active among his adversaries. Was this irresponsible journalism—taking an opposing position merely for the sake of cultivating the image of an adversary? To quote Helen Thomas, the chief White House correspondent for United Press International and an impartial reporter by nature and professional commitment: "White House news is carefully managed and sanitized. Carter has as many secret appointments as his predecessors. We still go into his office two or three times a day like the thundering herd, but only when someone in the heirarchy has decided there should be coverage."[75]

At the end of the President's first year in office, after 22 televised news conferences in the nation's capital, she had not changed her mind. She wrote that White House Press Secretary Jody Powell, "likes to manage the news and undoubtedly would do more of it if he could." She also reported that he favored the TV networks and had warned the President he could not expect "fair treatment" from the newspapers.

La plus change . . .

This, then, is the age of the aggressive journalist. What it comes down to is that a major area of the press is committed for the indefinite future to a position of challenge and conflict—the essence of adversary journalism. We now have, and shall continue to have, journalists who are both advocates and adversaries, who will inevitably strive to look behind the news while trying to present it as it happens. What effect this will have on the shaping of the news can scarcely be forecast, but it is troublesome to contemplate. Almost certainly, it will broaden the mission of the journalist far beyond the old concept of event-oriented news. A lot of things are therefore likely to be brought to public attention that will continue to inconvenience, and perhaps embarrass, one or another of our major power centers, including the government.

The events of a single year, 1977, will serve to illustrate the position with dramatic impact. During that year, these were among the newspapers that actively campaigned against abuses in government with the following results:

The Houston *Post*'s judicial investigation helped bring about the removal of an associate justice of the Texas Supreme Court. The Boston *Globe* successfully attacked a series of abuses in public office. The Philadelphia *Inquirer* uncovered both illegal and brutal practices in the Philadelphia Police Department. The continuing inquiry into South Korean efforts to bribe Congressmen was stimulated by exclusive revelations in the Washington *Post*.

In Florida, the Fort Myers *News-Press* disclosed how federal funds for needy farm workers had been misused. In Kentucky,the Louisville *Times* exposed financial mismanagement in a county school system. In Georgia, the Columbus *Ledger* brought to light voting irregularities in Phenix City, Ala., just across the state border. In Wisconsin, the LaCrosse *Tribune* and Racine *Journal-Times* jointly revealed legislative abuse of the state's tax-financed telephone system.

The Lufkin (Texas) *News*, winner of a Pulitzer Prize public service gold medal in 1976, went on in the following year to fight both the state attorney general's office and the Texas Welfare Department to disclose the neglect of patients in some of the state's nursing homes. In Montana and West Virginia, newspapers were active in obtaining new state laws to knock down secrecy in government.[76]

It is difficult to say how far the press is likely to push the adversary concept, but certainly it shows little sign of moderating its position. The strength of the developing opposition inside and outside government will, of course, have something to do with the outcome. But what will count more than anything else will be the determination of the press to continue to exercise its obligations under the First Amendment, as well as its rights.

This is more than a crisis of confidence in the press. It is, basically, a crisis of performance. For the press over the long run is going to be judged, as it always has been in this country, by what it is able to accomplish in public service.

THREE

THE PRESS AT BAY

1. "Why Can't You Be Like the British?"

MOST OF the arguments of the judges, lawyers, and government administrators who seek to restrain and discipline the Amrican press are based on their admiration for the British system of justice.[1]

"Look at the British!" goes the refrain. "The British press is so gentlemanly, so concerned with doing the right thing. It doesn't print anything it isn't supposed to, and Britain is still a great democracy. Why can't our journalists be gentlemen, too?"

It all seems so logical, so sensible, an object all sublime, until you ask the members of the British press what *they* think. And they don't agree, for the most part, with the notion that the British system meets the requirements of the free press in a manner superior to that of the United States. In fact, with the exception of a few newsroom barristers and similar types, British journalists would be very happy to work under American conditions.

The reason for the polarity of view is quite easily explained. Since the British have no written Constitution with a free press guarantee contained in a Bill of Rights, the courts have the power to strike their own balance between the rights of the free press, on the one hand, and the assurance of fair trial, on the other. It is only natural that the judges have chosen to limit publication or broadcast of proceedings before them to the barest minimum on

133

the somewhat questionable grounds, to an American journalist, that almost anything the news media may do would prejudice the public for or against a defendant. The people's right to know finishes a poor second behind the awesome power of this judicial oligarchy.

Only Parliament could change the unequal balance in Britain between the courts and the press. But Parliament, always strongly influenced by the British concept of law and its legal-minded M. P.'s, shows no inclination to do so, particularly when a Labor government is in power. In consequence, the British judiciary's power to find a journalist in contempt of court and put him in jail is so great and so ruthless in its application as to be frightening.

Charles Wintour, a British editor, writes: "Within the past 30 years, editors have been sent to gaol and heavily fined for contempt offences." He cited in particular the case of Silvester Bolam, editor of the London *Daily Mirror*, after the paper accused a murder suspect of being a "human vampire" in a particularly shocking case. Lord Chief Justice Goddard four days later called the editor and his paper a "disgrace to British journalism," jailed the editor for three months, fined the paper £10,000 ($28,000 at that time) and costs, threatened the proprietors with dire punishment if the offense was repeated. The fact that the suspect was convicted did not change the court's mind. In another case involving a newspaper called *The People*,which had published an editorial about an alleged "vice king" entitled, "Arrest This Beast," it turned out that the arrest already had been made; as a result, the publisher, the editor, the reporter, and even the printers all were convicted of contempt and punished.[2]

To keep editors out of trouble, an institution known as the "Night Lawyer" has come into being in the newsrooms of most of London's nationally circulated newspapers. It is this lawyer's business to stay in the newsroom at night, read all doubtful material that could bring editors into conflict with the courts and advise them on what, if anything, they may publish without suffering unpleasant consequences.

Rivaling the British journalists' justifiable fears of judicial contempt power is the strength and harshness of British libel law, which is far more pervasive in its effect than American libel procedures and devastating in both its cost and punitive potential. Here, too, the "Night Lawyer" is expected to intervene whenever necessary to stave off libel suits by altering dubious copy or killing it altogether. Understandably, editors go against legal advice in Britain at their peril.

Professor Albert G. Pickerell of the University of California, Berkeley, writes:

> Over a year's time costs of the Night Lawyer systems are substantial, but proprietors operate on the theory that if once a year the barrister prevents even the threat of a libel suit the expense has been justified. Libel actions are costly to defend, jury awards are unpredictable and often seem erratic. Also, as an additional hazard, a newspaper losing a libel action would almost certainly be assessed all costs—both his and the plaintiff's—and these can be enormous.[3]

In addition to civil suits for libel, the British press has been confronted with the threat of a revival of actions for criminal libel, a part of the law that has been unused for years. And this goes far beyond the inconvenience of paying heavy damages plus costs if found guilty; it could mean a stiff prison term as well. To quote Anthony Lewis of the New York *Times*, who has won two Pulitzer Prizes for his coverage of the administration of justice in the United States, on British law: "To American eyes [Britain] seems a libel-happy country. Hardly a week passes without some public figure suing over an alleged defamation that would pass without notice in the United States."

In the United States, to be sure, there are libel lawyers of repute who are often consulted by journalists over the use of sensitive material. But the lawyers do not sit in newsrooms, as a rule; nor do they, for that matter, dare to encroach upon the editor's prerogative to decide what shall be printed or broadcast and what shall be omitted. The melancholy truth is that the British press, so weakened by economic adversity and the hostility of three studies by Royal Commissions, has become subordinate to both the courts and whatever governments may be in power. It is fair game for almost anybody who wants to sue, from Prime Minister to charwoman.

There is good reason for the Congress of the United States, as well as the American bench and bar, to be casting longing glances at the defensive posture of the British press. For the British place great store by restrictions on publication in such statutes as the Criminal Justice Act of 1967, the Children's and Young Persons' Act of 1933, and the laws governing matrimonials (suits for separation, divorce, etc.). But the particular law in which the Congress of the United States would be interested is the law on contempt of Parliament, which contains all-pervasive restrictions against the press. This is even tougher than the contempt of court statute, for it makes the press liable for every act or omission which "obstructs or impedes any member or officer of either House" in the discharge of their official duties, or which has a "tendency, directly or indirectly" to produce such results.

A journalist may also be found in contempt of Parliament for "diminishing respect for the House," for circulating false reports of debates, and for premature publication of committee procedures or evidence before a committee. One wonders how such laws would have affected the publication in the United States of such accounts as the relationship of a dancer (professionally known as the "Argentine firecracker") to the Hon. Wilbur D. Mills of Arkansas, or the relationship of Miss Elizabeth Ray to the Hon. Wayne L. Hays of Ohio.

Those accused of violating Parliamentary privilege in Britain are worse off, in some ways, than the targets of both contempt charges and libel actions. For a journalist brought up on such an accusation has almost no judicial recourse. He has no right to be represented by counsel. He can't even cross-examine the witnesses who appear against him. And, under the law, his demeanor is taken into account in determining his guilt or innocence— which is quite a challenge for even a law-abiding British M. P.

Beyond that, the British press is up against the stiffest and most unyielding kind of government secrecy, applied with all the arrogance of which the upper-class British civil servant is capable. Those who administer the British Official Secrets Acts would never dream of permitting their press to publish disclosures about the failures of British intelligence, clandestine actions of various kinds, or some of the other sensitive material about weaponry and troop dispositions that regularly appear in the American news media. I have heard it said that Richard Nixon, under British law, could have gotten away with his insistence that national security was involved in the Watergate coverup. But that, naturally, can only be conjecture.

Broadly interpreted, the Official Secrets Acts make it an offense for anybody holding an office to give unauthorized news of anything to any person. A government publication states the position as follows:

The Official Secrets Acts make unlawful the unauthorised communication of information about matters which must remain secret in the interests of the safety of the State. They also make unlawful the unauthorised communication of information obtained by any person owing to his position as holder of an office under the Crown, or as a contractor or employee of a contractor of the Crown, as well as the unlawful receipts of such information.

The British government makes the law operative with the formal dispatch of a D (for Defense) Notice to the British news media, asking that nothing be disseminated on a certain sensitive matter. Although compliance with a D Notice is not mandatory, the warning is usually respected. When it is violated, and it has been in rare cases, the offending news organization seldom has any defenders in high places. And the Official Secrets Acts, like the contempt actions and libel laws, are strongly enforced.[4]

Now and then this suffocating policy of secrecy and press regulation produces a backlash even among well-disciplined Britons. A few years ago, the Fulton Committee on the British Civil Service wrote:

The public interest would be better served if there were a greater amount of openness; the increasingly wide range of problems handled by government and their far-reaching effects upon the community as a whole demand the widest possible consultation. There are still too many occasions when information is unnecessarily withheld.[5]

To which Harold M. Evans, editor of the London Sunday *Times*, added with heartfelt emphasis: "Nothing so perpetuates and aggrandizes error as secrecy. It is a lesson of a thousand furtive exercises of a monopoly of power. It is a lesson once learned always remembered—until the next crisis."[6]

Those who are painfully familiar with the limitations on British journalism have often said that editing a British newspaper is like walking through a minefield blindfolded. If British journalists tolerate their lot in gentlemanly fashion, with only a few exceptions, it is primarily because they can do very little to try to change it.

It would be difficult, if not impossible, to fasten the entire British system of restraints on the American press, although I am sure that many will continue to advocate it. In the first place, the American press is in a much stronger position to resist than its British counterpart, being much larger and wealthier and far more diversified in its interests. In the second, even if some features of the British system should come into use here (and it would require virtual repeal of the First Amendment to do it), I doubt that enforcement would be possible. The controls that can be administered in a relatively small country like Britain would require an army of administrators plus billions of dollars in tax revenues to impose on a press that was determined to resist in a country as large as the United States.

It just wouldn't work. And the government that tried it might find itself in the midst of a Constitutional crisis, for respect for the quality of justice in the United States sometimes rivals the press for low standing in the public view. Certainly, there is a considerable difference in character between the type of people who administer justice in Britain and some of those who function in the same manner in the United States.

That, basically, is the reason courts merit public trust in the United Kingdom and have the support of public opinion in applying strictures against the press. For since the Act of Settlement of 1701, not a single judge in England and Scotland has been dismissed from the bench. Not one in almost 300 years! In fact, the only judge anywhere in the United Kingdom to have been removed from the bench since 1701 was Sir Jonah Barrington (1760-1834), a judge in the Admiralty Court in Ireland. He was separated from his post in 1830 by vote of both Houses of Parliament after being found guilty of pinching funds paid into his court for his own purposes. So in the whole of the United Kingdom, not a single judge has been removed from the bench in almost 150 years.

The last time an attempt was made against a judge in the United Kingdom was in 1867, the target being Sir Fitzroy Kelly. And in 1843, charges were heard in the House of Commons that James Scarlett, 1st Baron Abinger, had been "partial, unconstitutional, and oppressive." But in both cases impeachment efforts failed. Thus, for more than 100 years, no judge in the United Kingdom has suffered impeachment.[7]

It is understandable that such an excellent judicial record could scarcely be expected from the much larger judicial establishment in the United States, where judges are often the product of politics and the question of judicial fitness is sometimes brushed aside. While I have no desire to be offensive, and am well aware of the honesty and probity of most American judges, it must be pointed out that we have suffered numerous judicial scandals in recent years at county, state, and federal levels. And too many judges have been obliged to resign under pressure or have been removed.

It would take considerable time and effort to arrive at a statistical estimate of judicial failure at the Federal level and in the 50 states. But a sufficient indication of what has been going on in this country does happen to be available in the records of the Pulitzer Prizes, which, while far from a complete registry of the deeds and misdeeds of the judiciary, do cover some of the highlights over the past six decades.

The following awards are listed:

A public service prize for the Riverside (California) *Press-Enterprise* in 1968 "for its expose of corruption in the courts in connection with the handling of the property and estates of an Indian tribe in California and its successful efforts to punish the culprits."

S. Burton Heath of the New York *World-Telegram*, a reporting prize in 1940, "for his expose of the frauds perpetrated by Federal Judge Martin T. Manton, who resigned and later was tried and imprisoned."

John T. Rogers of the St. Louis *Post-Dispatch*, a reporting prize in 1927, for "the inquiry leading to the impeachment of Judge George W. English of the U. S. Court for the Eastern District of Illinois."

Other prizes have been given to newspapers and individual journalists for blocking questionble judicial appointments. These include an award to William J. Eaton of the Chicago *Daily News* in 1970 "for his disclosures about the background of Judge Clement F. Haynesworth, Jr., in connection with his nomination for the U. S. Supreme Court." In 1966, the Boston *Globe* won a public service prize "for its campaign to prevent the confirmation of Francis X. Morrissey as a Federal District Judge in Massachusetts." And in 1935, the Sacramento *Bee*, in California, won another public service prize "for its campaign against political machine influence in the appointment of two Federal judges in Nevada."

In a case involving the highest court in the land, William Lambert, a Pulitzer Prize winner, disclosed in *Life* magazine in 1969 that Associate Justice Abe Fortas had accepted but later returned a $20,000 check from the family foundation of Louis E. Wolfson, an industrialist who was later imprisoned for stock manipulation. While Justice Fortas denied that he had ever intervened in the Wolfson case or that he had intended to do so, he resigned from the Supreme Court after serving for four years.

I do not mean to infer that the press, by itself, is capable of overseeing the courts. Other cases involving judges in one way or another have been uncovered by the Congress, the various state legislatures, and by the judicial establishment itself. At lower levels, in the immediate past, a New York judge was scathingly criticized for his conduct on the bench by that State's courts. Also, two judges retired in Florida under threat of impeachment and the chief judge resigned.

The record, incomplete though it is as cited here, can scarcely go very far toward inducing the press in this country to accept a strong-arm judiciary, as is the case in Britain. It is a rare editor or publisher who would willingly accept the kind of controls that have so seriously weakened the combative spirit of the British press.

A few of the more cynical members of the American bar, with whom I have discussed the position privately, have argued that the record of the British bench may not be as good as it appears to be and that the American judiciary therefore should not be judged by what amounts to an invidious comparison. They advance the somewhat surprising premise that if the British jurists were subjected to the same uncompromising press surveillance that American judges must undergo, the British system, too, might emerge as something less than perfect.

This is a touching, if somewhat backhanded, affirmation of faith in the probity of the American press. But the American bench and bar really can't have it both ways. If they want the British system of press regulation, they must also accept the kind of spoon-fed press that goes with it. It is worth noting that Henry Fairlie, a British journalist resident in the United States, has written that the American insistence on the "right to know" is "the most ludicrous of claims for the press to make"—that "there is no 'right to know' anything."[9] It is quite a comedown from the great

John Delane, the editor of *The Times*, of London, who stirred up
a storm in the 19th century by breaking the Peel cabinet's secret
decision to repeal the Corn Laws, and who overthrew the Aber-
deen cabinet by disclosing the pitiable plight of the British army
during the Crimean War.[10] That, however, is the measure of the
decline of British journalism and the courts must share in the
responsibility for it.

The American press already has agreed, mistakenly I believe,
to limit its coverage of criminal proceedings in accordance with
various press-bar guidelines that have been drawn up voluntarily
in numerous states. This has not been sufficient to please the
American Bar Association, some members of which are in a mood
to demand nothing short of unconditional surrender from the
press. Nor does it seem to have improved the standing of the
press in the public's estimation.

At the time of the storm over judicial "gag" rulings against
the American press, it was no hard-line editor, but one of the
most distinguished of American jurists, the 88-year-old Harold R.
Medina, who wrote that there always have been "people who
liked the British system of using the contempt powers of the
courts to reduce press coverage of criminal trials to a scanty minimum."

It was Judge Medina's opinion, later affirmed by the United
States Supreme Court and discussed elsewhere in this volume,
that such "gag" orders were unconstitutional. He also argued it
was an infringement on First Amendment rights "to clamp a lid
on every source of information so that there would be no news."

This was the burden of his advice to the press:

Why the public has not made vigorous and sustained protests
against these omnibus gag orders is a mystery to me. Probably one of the
reasons is that the average citizen thinks these orders facilitate the enforcement of criminal laws.

But the truth is directly to the contrary. They may merely lighten
the burdens of a busy judge or serve as a cover-up to conceal corruption. The First Amendment is the most important of our precious free-

doms. It serves to let in the light so necessary to the proper functioning of our democracy.

And we must remember that unless every single one of us tries to understand and to fight for these First Amendment freedoms they will become eroded and lose their strength . . . .

As I never did like censorship of any kind, I have a little unsolicited advice to the news media:

First, I would stand squarely on the First Amendment itself. I used to think guidelines might be helpful. Now, I believe them to be a snare and a delusion. And the same is true of legislation. Nor do I like any part of the latest American Bar Association proposal . . .

Second, I would make no compromises and no concessions of any kind.

Third, I say fight like tigers every inch of the way.[11]

Judge Medina's advice, as might be expected, was widely published and sagely approved in numerous editorials, mostly unread by the public. But the press as a whole paid little heed to his warning.

The legal process of slicing up the First Amendment in bite-sized pieces, like so much salami, continues apace both through voluntary agreements and court decisions that restrict the flow of information to the news media. Worse still, the twin threats of restrictive legislation and punitive antitrust actions have by no means been dissipated.

What the British press is today, bullied and brow-beaten by both the British government and its courts, the American press need not become tomorrow. But it had best look to its defenses before it is too late.

2. The Uses of National Security

While I was at the Pentagon one summer during the Korean War, an official of consequence wanted to show me something that had just come over the wire service printers. He led me to a double-locked door with the forbidding legend, "SECRET—NO ADMITTANCE," behind which I could hear the machines pounding

away. "Why hide the news tickers?" I asked, thoroughly aston-
ished. My escort open the door with an apologetic air. "I don't
really know. I guess it was the only place they could find to put
them."

Whether that was true or not, the placement of the wire
service machines was symbolic in one sense. For the military
mind, with few exceptions, cannot seem to separate the function
of gathering the news from that of gathering intelligence. No
matter how often it is pointed out that news is for public dissemination and intelligence often involves the tightest secrecy, military people deeply believe that reporters should be their allies in
the defense of the nation. And sometimes it is almost impossible
to disabuse them.

I remember that the students at the Air War College, following a lecture I gave there on the American press some years ago,
fairly bombarded me with questions about the role of the American newspaper in helping to uphold the security of the nation.
Finally, a bemedaled colonel of Marines stood up and demanded:
"Why *shouldn't* we issue false information and have the press
print it to fool the enemy, just the way they do with us? The
Russian papers all help their government and their armed forces.
Why can't the American papers be more helpful to us?"

I suggested that the essence of the conflict between the
United States and the Soviet Union was precisely the difference
between the freedoms we are guaranteed by our Constitution and
those that are denied to the Soviet peoples—that our press is free
to criticize our government and the Soviet press is not. The rationale was received in cold silence.

Insensitivity to the distinction between news and propaganda
is not peculiar to the fighting men in the American armed forces.
Soon after becoming the Secretary of Defense in the Kennedy
administration, Robert Strange McNamara was deeply concerned
about published reports of American military weakness in various
newspapers. He demanded, "Why should we tell Russia that the
Zeus [antimissile] developments may not be satisfactory? What

we ought to be saying is that we have the most perfect anti-ICBM system that the human mind will ever devise."[12]

The propaganda virus sometimes infects even professional journalists of long standing when they go into government service. Arthur Sylvester, for many years the Washington correspondent of the Newark *Evening News*, became McNamara's Assistant Secretary of Defense for Public Affairs and thoroughly startled his erstwhile colleagues after the Cuban missile crisis of 1962 by ing, "I think the inherent right of the government to lie to save itself when faced with nuclear disaster is basic." It didn't help much when he later elaborated on this policy as follows: "The government does not have a right to lie to the people but it does have a right in facing an enemy to disseminate information that is not accurate and is intended to mislead the enemy."[13]

All this was of a piece with General William Tecumseh Sherman's response to a Civil War correspondent who said he had come to get the truth about the conflict: "We don't want the truth told about things here—that's what we *don't* want! Truth, eh? No, sir! We don't want the enemy better informed than he is!"[14]

The full flower of that policy, as it developed under the Johnson and Nixon administrations, was the Vietnam War and Watergate. It is behind the movement to clamp the American press in the vise of an Official Secrets Act.

The agitation for some form of restraint upon the American press to buttress naitonal security has intensified with the advancement of the atomic age. Until the atomic bomb was dropped on Hiroshima on August 6, 1945, such pressures had been confined in the main to wartime censorship efforts. But with the passage of the Atomic Energy Act of 1946, national security became an overwhelming consideration for the government in time of peace as well as war. President Truman wrote:

One event occurred in 1945 of such magnitude that it was to revolutionize our relations with the world and usher in a new era for humanity, the fruits and goals and problems of which we cannot even now fully grasp. It was the atomic bomb. With it came the secret of how to harness nuclear energy. I now had a responsibility without precedent in history. The decisions I had to make and the policies I would recommend to Congress on the use and control of atomic energy could well influence the future course of civilization.[15]

Truman accordingly closely followed the drafting of the Atomic Energy Act and saw to it that provisions for secrecy, satisfactory to the government and the military, were written into it. While the news media are not specifically mentioned, there is no doubt that they are covered by drastic provisions for punishment up to and including the death penalty upon conviction of unauthorized disclosure of "restricted data." The definition of "restricted data," moreover, is so broad that it includes the manufacture and utilization of atomic power and fissionable material as well as atomic weapons for war. Under the terms of the act, only material cleared for publication by the government may be used by the news media.[16]

The psychological effect of the act, in many ways, proved to be almost as important as the legal prohibitions against unauthorized disclosures. Among the civilian leadership at the highest levels in the executive and legislative branches, the zeal to protect national security became, in some instances, virtually an obsession. Those who had served in the armed forces in one way or another, including every President from Truman on, were particularly affected. The phrase, "need to know," became more important than "right to know." And any message from Rio, Accra, Singapore, or New Delhi that was marked "eyes only" was treated by American officials as if it had been a contribution to the Holy Writ.

All this might have been more convincing as an article of faith if there had been a corresponding reaction within the armed forces. But from the Pentagon to the most isolated Army post, Air Force base, or Navy installation, it was business as usual. Beginning with the B-36 controversy in the late 1940s, the pressures of interservice rivalry created the usual number of leaks of classified information that were intended to influence Congressional sentiment, public opinion, or both. There were publicity flaps over the presence of Soviet submarines off the American Atlantic coast at budget-making time with such regularity that it became a very poor joke. And the junkets of Congressmen and prominent citizens to so-called sensitive military installations developed to such scandalous proportions that CBS finally did a documentary about it, "The Selling of the Pentagon."

I do not mean to infer that concern over national security is ill-placed or that top-secret messages consist in the main of warnings to guard the total amount of coffee beans purchased by the armed forces as a state secret.[17] Anybody who has served in the Pentagon for any length of time knows that there is a mass of properly classified data that should not be—and generally is not—made public in order to safeguard national security. I can testify that, in my own occasional service as a Pentagon consultant over an eight-year period, the military was well able to safeguard those secrets it could not afford to disclose.

That, however, is not the main issue in the coverage of national defense and the national interest. For when military appropriations of upward of $100 billion a year are at stake, the uses of national security too often become blurred in the tremendous heat of interservice rivalry and industrial competition for military contracts. And that is the heart of the matter.

Every reporter in the Pentagon knows of officers who have risked their careers by leaking classified documents in order to benefit their own branch of the service or injure rival branches, usually both. It is nonsense to say that there should be laws to stop this kind of thing. There already are laws in abundance, and they are continually violated in military matters.

Ah, yes, there are always wrathful investigations after every leak, and outraged civilian administrators promise that heads will roll. It doesn't often happen, however. I recall seeing a much decorated officer at an out-of-the-way military center in a foreign land and being told that he had leaked a certain document to the press, accepted reassignment out of Washington—and a promotion for his pains.

It is into this no man's land of distorted values, double-dealing, and deceit that the press must venture if it is to cover the story of national defense and satisfy the national interest. No other independent agency is equipped to do it on a day-to-day basis. And almost at once that involves the troublesome, and immensely difficult, subject of dealing with the publication of classified information, leaked or not.

There are several ways of approaching this issue. The most direct and drastic would be the promulgation of an Official Secrets Act to halt all dissemination of classified information for any reason whatever. This is the course that President Carter is reputed to have favored before he began campaigning for the White House. To the uninitiated, it would seem that a properly enforced and administered Official Secrets Act would take care of the problem.

However, it may be argued that if the current laws against disclosure can't be enforced effectively, why would a new one be treated with any more reverence? And if journalists choose to go to jail rather than reveal their sources to some country judge, is it illogical to suppose that they would take the same course if they believed it necessary to violate an Official Secrets Act?

Such a spectacle of all-out resistance by American journalists would make a mockery of all the grandiloquent claims that are made for American respect for human rights. And if I know anything at all about the character of the American journalist, I am convinced that this would be the ultimate end of the passage of an Official Secrets Act.

Franklin D. Roosevelt, the most consummate politician to occupy the White House in this century, knew exactly what he was doing when he rejected proposals for a censorship law for America in World War II—the only major combatant nation to take such action. While there was field censorship, of course, as there had been in World War I, the press and radio otherwise were put entirely on their honor and willingly worked with the Office of Censorship in a policy of voluntary compliance.

Under these seemingly shaky circumstances, the greatest of wartime secrets—the making of the atomic bomb—was kept from the media until President Truman told of the destruction of Hiroshima.[18] The feat was made possible primarily because government, people, and press were more united than they have been since in a common purpose.

The unity began crumbling in the Korean War, which opened with General Douglas MacArthur's refusal to institute even field censorship. But once his rash advance to the Yalu drew the Chinese army into the fray, and press criticism mounted, MacArthur clapped all correspondents under a stringent censorship that was relaxed only with his removal from the high command.[19] It just didn't work, despite wartime conditions. And in Vietnam, the situation became so chaotic that effective censorship, even in the field, never was possible.

To suggest that an Official Secrets Act in peacetime would meet any different fate is to defy all precedent.

There is an alternative that seems better because it relies more on self-discipline in the Rooseveltian tradition and less on the force of law, but it, too, has a catch. Former Secretary of State Dean Rusk, now a professor at the School of Law at the University of Georgia, delineates this position as follows:

I am not in favor of a general Official Secrets Act which would impose upon private citizens a responsibility for retaining government secrets. I am a radical in support of free speech and free press for reasons set forth long ago by people like John Milton, John Stuart Mill, Thomas Jefferson, and many others.

In my view it is the duty of the reporter to try to get the story. There are times when it is the duty of a public official to keep his mouth shut. The resulting tension is necessary and wholesome in a free society, and we should not try to remove that tension by law. codes of ethics, or agreements between adversary parties.

I do expect representatives of the news media to obey the law. The First Amendment provides a constitutional guarantee to say and write what one wishes. It is not a license to trespass, bribe, steal property or knowingly receive stolen property, or to commit any of the other common crimes in the name of getting the news. I am not prepared to say that no one is above the law except reporters.[20]

Rusk's view is representative of a cautiously liberal tradition. It approximates the quotation attributed to Walt Whitman that *Newsday*, the Long Island newspaper, carried at its masthead for many years but dropped with its dawning conservatism: "Be liberal, be liberal, be not too damn liberal." In one sense, Rusk goes beyond the majority legal position of attempting to maneuver the press into an inhibiting thicket of laws and voluntary agreements. In another, he places the press in what appears to be an indefensible moral position of committing or abetting crimes to get at the news.

But where are the crimes that the press has committed? The United States Supreme Court, in the case of the purloined Pentagon Papers, ruled that the government had failed to prove its charges that national security would be irreparably harmed by the continued publication of the documents. When Jack Anderson published classified State Department papers showing an American "tilt" toward Pakistan during the Indo-Pakistan War of 1971, the government failed to react to his implicit challenge and didn't even move to prosecute. When Jack White published President Nixon's income tax documents in the Providence *Journal-Bulletin*, an Internal Revenue Service official was disciplined for allegedly being implicated, but nothing was done to either White or his paper.

To quote Federal Judge Murray L. Gurfein of the Southern District of New York, in denying the government's plea for a preliminary injunction in the Pentagon Papers case:

A cantankerous press, an obstinate press, an ubiquitous press, must be suffered by those in authority in order to preserve the even greater values of freedom of expression and the right of the people to know. These are troubled times. There is no greater safety valve for discontent and cynicism about the affairs of government than freedom of expression in any form.[21]

It is a grievous misrepresentation of the press's position to imply, as some do who should know better, that it acts out of a desire to create shock and sensation in matters affecting national security, or that it wants to sell a few more papers. There are a lot easier, less expensive, and less risky ways to boost circulation. Nor are responsible reporters ever authorized to ransack government files with reckless and mischievous intent or to expose a covert operation just for the hell of it.

Journalists have only their ability and their integrity to sustain them. Take away either one, and they are bound to be totally discredited.

Only the yahoos on the far right reacted angrily to Seymour Hersh's well-documented disclosure of the My Lai massacre, which led to the conviction of Lieutenant William L. Calley. To the nation at large, the exposure of this shameful outrage by American troops was both proper and necessary. And when Hersh later revealed the secret bombing of Cambodia, certainly an illegal and improper act by the Nixon administration, nobody advocated punishing him (except possibly some of the more fanatical military people). It was an instance in which a reporter and his newspaper, the New York *Times*, collaborated to inform the public of the underhanded actions of its government. The same was true of the disclosures of American involvement in the overthrow of the Allende government in Chile.

At no time in recent history was the issue to print or not to print illustrated more dramatically than in the campaign of the CIA to prevent the press from publishing the story of the agency's effort to raise a sunken Soviet submarine from the floor of the Pacific Ocean. Although parts of the story already had leaked in Washington, the CIA invoked national security and for 39 days in 1975 persuaded the elite press of the country not to use the story.

Even more shocking, when *Rolling Stone* magazine tried to get
the record of the agency's security efforts under the Freedom of
Information Act, the government fought in court to keep secret
the details of its secrecy campaign. That, too, was labeled national
security but it became the "Glomar Explorer" coverup.

It turned out to be more of a tragicomedy, once the papers
were given up, in which William E. Colby and others of the CIA
twisted arms and breathed imprecations at the New York *Times*,
Los Angeles *Times*, Washington *Post*, Washington *Star*, *Time*,
Newsweek and all three networks. It was quite a lineup.

Moreover, most of them proved to be pushovers for the CIA
in this particular instance. The New York *Times*, for example,
went on record in a letter to Colby, offering to withhold the story
if others did. The Los Angeles *Times* hinted at its sources, but
agreed to keep the secret. So did the Washington *Post*, writing,
"It is all agreed with you that it is not anything we would like to
get into."

The moral, as expressed by Charles B. Seib of the Washington *Post*, was that the press "at least in its upper reaches is easy to
con." Easy, except for Jack Anderson, who broke the story over
the Mutual Broadcasting System in a radio newscast with this
explanation: "I don't think the government has a right to cover up
a boondoggle. I have withheld other stories at the behest of the
CIA but this was simply a cover-up of a $350-million failure—
$350 million literally went down into the ocean."

Under the rules of the news business, once the story was
broken, all others were released from their pledge of secrecy and
the CIA's oceanic misadventure was made public by the press
and broadcast media. The nation emerged undamaged from the
experience; as usual, the CIA's plea of national security was exposed as a fraud that covered up only its own ineptitude.[22]

It is clear, both from this experience and the two Cuban
crises in the Kennedy administration, that the news media do
heed government requests not to use sensitive information. The
trouble is that, in most instances, the voluntary coverups backfire

and discredit those who participate in them when the public at last is let in on the secret.

It follows that the Rusk formula, which would place the press on its honor not to breach national security, is bound to create more controversy instead of lessening it. There are a number of reasons for this, the most important being that there is no agreement on what constitutes national security.

The law may be what the Supreme Court says it is, but national security, alas, is quite often not what the government says it is. For this unhappy conclusion, Richard Nixon must remain Exhibit A.

It does not follow—indeed, it cannot follow—that the press is the sworn enemy of government, that adversary journalism obliges a reporter to suspect every official act. This, as Norman Isaacs has written, is a "gross disservice to journalism." "We need to be *reporting*, not lining up news sources as automatic enemies," he says.[23]

That is the way it was—before the riots in the inner cities, the despair over Vietnam, the disillusionment over Watergate. After all, it was the enthusiasm of the press that helped sell a skeptical public on the concept of a United Nations organization, and many since have blamed the press for overselling. Secretary of State George Marshall, too, gave generous credit to the press for helping put over the Marshall Plan for the restoration of Western Europe after World War II. And James Reston disclosed that he had known for a year that U-2 spy planes were overflying the Soviet Union, yet the New York *Times* did not publish the story until Francis Gary Powers's plane was shot down over the Urals.[24] Reston wrote:

The old tradition of the American press was that anything a government hides, except during open and declared war, was wrong, probably wicked, and therefore should be exposed; but a press demanding unlimited freedom for this principle today could in many cases risk the nation's security. Yet the problem cannot be solved simply by saying that the operations of the intelligence services of the government are none of the public's business.[25]

This is the perplexing part of the situation for the press. For despite all the evidence of the frailty of government in handling sensitive situations, many an editor cringes a little at the notion that he, and he alone, must make the decision whether to disclose news of a sensitive nature that has fallen into his hands. If he is right, he will gain no particular advantage. Spiro Agnew to the contrary, Pulitzer Prize juries generally are not sympathetic to borderline disclosures affecting the national interest and most awards in such cases are granted only after strenuous debate. And if the disclosure turns out to be either wrong or based on poor judgment, then irreparable harm may be done to the originating news organization. Roy Howard's erroneous United Press bulletin that touched off the "false armistice" of 1918 toward the end of World War I will never be entirely forgotten. Nor will Ed Kennedy's premature bulletin signaling the end of World War II in Europe ever be recognized as a glorious feat by the Associated Press.

Contrary to prevalent public impressions, there *is* a severe form of punishment for journalists and news organizations that do violence to professional standards in dealing with national security or other matters of importance. For when they lose the trust and respect of their colleagues, both advertisers and the reading public become aware of the change in short order. The damage can be great. William Randolph Hearst, Sr., was embarrassed by his World War I association with a German agent named Bolo Pasha. And the Chicago *Tribune* even today remains sensitive over criticism that it disclosed the breaking of the Japanese code in World War II. Unless there are special circumstances to justify their conduct, disaccredited war correspondents are seldom hailed as martyrs to the free press. And even so spectacular a crusader as Jack Anderson was obliged to make a public apology to Senator Thomas Eagleton of Missouri for wrongfully accusing him of convictions for drunken driving.[26]

The press is not omnipotent. It does not claim to be. The First Amendment, for that matter, does not require it to be and the courts still leave room for error in the United States in their judgment of what is libelous and what is not. This, however, cannot and must not serve as an excuse for the irresponsible use of sensitive material affecting national security in the news media.

Too often, it is assumed that journalists do act both capriciously and irresponsibly. Bob Considine, the columnist, once told the story of an irritable general who complained that a young reporter was creating a lot of trouble in his command by publishing stories criticizing a new fighter aircraft that was undergoing supposedly secret tests. "What am I going to do with a guy like that?" the general asked in despair. Bob murmured, "General, why don't you shoot him?"

Much that the journalist does depends on point of view. What seems arbitrary and unreasonable to the military can, on occasion, appear to the journalist to be the highest concept of professional duty. Which does not mean that every reporter goes out on a story with a collapsible halo in his back pocket, to be taken out and exhibited with a flourish to convince the public of his angelic intentions. There are, unfortunately, lousy reporters in the news business just as there are quacks in the medical profession, shysters in the law, and heartless frauds among the clergy. In journalism, the competition for the relatively few editorial openings each year is so great that the hacks usually don't last very long. Professional responsibility is more than just a phrase to be mouthed with unctuous mien at editors' conferences.

If the press's critics could assume that its integrity is at least equal to their own, that might be the beginning of reason in dealing with the problems of news in sensitive areas that could affect national security. It does no good whatever to consider that almost anything the press does these days resembles a Grade B movie scenario of the 1920s. Reporters don't come bounding joyously into the city room with a satchelful of classified documents yelling, "Scoop!" And editors don't rush to feed them into the nearest Video Display Terminal for immediate publication.

The reality is considerably more circumspect. What usually happens in responsible news organizations that pick up a sensitive piece of defense information is that the highest executives take over, demand additional background, call in lawyers if necessary and then ask for the comments of responsible government officials. The more sensitive the story, the longer it takes to arrive at a decision to use or withhold. Sometimes, as in the case of the U-2 or the CIA salvage operation, publication is deferred for a long time; on other occasions, as in the instance of the Bay of Pigs, important elements of a story may be left out. Now and then, as in President-elect Eisenhower's secret journey to Korea to try to end that war, the government releases the story when the mission is completed. But it is not good judgment to rush to use a story of major importance without checking and rechecking sources.

At the height of the excitement over the Watergate expose, the impatient Woodward and Bernstein sometimes were in despair when, at the last moment, they were told by their managing editor, Howard Simons, to hold up or kill a story if they had their doubts. "I don't care if it's a word, a phrase, a sentence, a paragraph, a whole story or an entire series of stories," he said. "When in doubt, leave out."[27]

I applied this familiar professional principle in the late 1950s when I was asked by the Air Force to recommend some way of resolving a bitter dispute between the press and the missile command at Cape Canaveral, Fla. After the Russians put Sputnik in orbit in 1957, the press had built up every subsequent American missile shot as an earth-shaking event. But when one fizzled, the reaction was appalling. What the Air Force wanted to do was to exclude all reporters and bar all publicity, which was manifestly impossible; any missile shot, good or bad, could be seen and heard for miles around. Instead, I suggested a moratorium on advance publicity and a guarantee that the news media would be given the unrestricted right to use film, still pictures, and news reports from the moment a missile was fired. The system worked well, and without strain, particularly after the Americans began piling success on success in shooting for the moon. Eventually, the press and broadcast media also agreed not to monitor unscheduled secret test firings—a program that continues to this day.[28]

Thus, the broad outlines already exist for a program of voluntary cooperation between the news media and the government in the handling of sensitive information bearing on national security. What it really amounts to is an extension of the successful voluntary program that lasted throughout World War II under the direction of Byron Price, who was on leave from the Associated Press. I don't believe it is necessary to have another Price office because there aren't that many calls for consultation by the news media. The existing machinery at the White House and in the Pentagon is quite sufficient to handle reportorial inquiries, as long as there is some assurance of responsiveness on the part of the government. Merely to say, "Don't print or broadcast," and imply that violation of these instructions is tantamount to treason will not get very far with the press. Editors, for their part, should be willing to defer a decision on using sensitive information at least until the government presents its argument for delay or a complete halt on dissemination.

None of this has to be set down in codes, plans, or affirmations of professional conduct. To formalize such an understanding is to raise suspicions in the media that the ultimate intent is some form of censorship. Worse still, the public is likely to suspect, possibly with reason, that formal cooperation between press and government—particularly in peacetime—means that neither can be believed in military matters.

This may seem like little more than an extension of the status quo, and perhaps it is. The generals and admirals certainly are not going to like it, but then most of them are worse at accepting criticism than even the press, which is pretty low on the scale of human tolerance. As Winston Churchill once said of democracy, it's a terrible way of running things—except for all those other systems that are worse.

Two wartime laws for press regulation, the Espionage Act of 1917 and the Trading with the Enemy Act, still remain in effect but neither has been invoked in recent years. John Foster Dulles, while Secretary of State, mentioned the latter statute in 1957 during an argument with Arthur Hays Sulzberger, then the publisher of the New York *Times*. The paper had protested Dulles's limitation on the number of correspondents to be admitted to mainland China, something that didn't happen until 14 years later. Sulzberger even went so far as to accuse Dulles of abridging freedom of the press. To which Dulles replied with this rather unique interpretation of the First Amendment:

> You suggest that our policy with respect to Americans going to China "abridges the freedom of the press." The Constitutional "freedom of the press" relates to the publication and not to the gathering of news . . . . United States foreign policy inevitably involves the acceptance of certain restraints upon the American people.[29]

Dulles, a formidable legal authority, never pushed the point because the *Times* dropped the argument. But his view of the First Amendment has been revived from time to time and it could come before the Supreme Court some day, tortuous though it may be in its attempt to separate the gathering of the news from the process of dissemination. This is by no means the only effort that has been made to twist the law of the press to suit the convenience of the government. It goes a long way toward explaining the reluctance of journalists in general to formalize and codify their procedures.

The professional arrangements to which the press so often consents are not without their own hazard, and this is likely to make the most capable and experienced reporters look foolish when their own approved methods are used against them. The State Department is especially adept at this, as has been demonstrated by every Secretary of State since the time of John Foster Dulles; the art of not telling the truth without being caught in an outright lie is one of the staples of foreign policy.

I do not mean to write, or even insinuate, that our Foreign Service depends for its effectiveness on slippery practices up to and including dishonesty in its relations wih the press. This is more likely to apply to other agencies of the government such as the CIA, which is somewhat more committed to following the practices of General William Tecumseh Sherman. In the State Department, the routine procedures of journalism have simply been turned to the advantage of the government, usually with the unintended cooperation of that peculiar breed of journalist known as the diplomatic correspondent.[30]

The institution that is often used to produce these results is the backgrounder, under which the news source is guaranteed a certain amount of anonymity in return for permission to use whatever information develops in the interview or news conference. While the practice goes back many years in the history of the chanceries of Europe, particularly the Quai d'Orsay, it did not come to the United States until World War II.

Ernest K. Lindley, a correspondent for *Newsweek*, is generally credited with originating it in the U. S. Unable to persuade officials in sensitive positions to speak for publication, he worked them around to talking to him "on background." And thus was reborn in the United States an ignoble tribe of anonymous informants, including such shadowy characters as the informed source, the official circle, the senior official, the government spokesman, the diplomatic source, the usually well-informed source, the trustworthy source, and the source who is close to all the other sources. When the journalist wearied of plagiarizing the less remarkable ideas of these paragons, he could—and did—fall back on their cousins in the backgrounding retinue—those familiar with the situation, friends of the administration, critics of the administration, people who know the government's view, visitors from, travelers to, experts in the field, leading authorities, well-qualified persons and close associates. Finally, there was always that eminent figure, *sans peur et sans reproche*, the impartial observer, who could on occasion turn out to be the reporter himself.

Could the operatives in the State Department's offices on Foggy Bottom be blamed for adopting this less than illustrious platoon of dummy sources as their own and using them on every occasion that warranted it? I for one never have thought of blaming officialdom. This was—and remains—something that journalists have done to themselves because of the intense pressure most of them feel to produce a story every day.

This wasn't precisely what President Wilson had in mind when he initiated the Presidential news conference; nor did it accord, for that matter, with his oft-enunciated principle of open covenants openly arrived at (which he never practiced). It turned out to be a game at which any number could play, although the end result sometimes turned out to be public confusion.

The line between giving information for background, which is intended for use, and talking off the record, which supposedly is to be kept in confidence, often becomes so vague that almost anything may happen.

As early as 1948, in an incident of which I have personal knowledge, Secretary of State Marshall called the three American wire service reporters to an off-the-record briefing in Paris at which he disclosed his plans for a NATO alliance. His apparent purpose was to seal up the Associated Press, United Press, and International News Service until the right moment. However, the UP man, H. R. Shackford, already had heard about the NATO proposal from French sources and broke the story. His punishment was a public announcement barring him from State Department briefings, which didn't last very long.

Secretary of State Dulles, who fancied himself a manupulator of the press, also got into trouble with backgrounders. In 1953, he told a few Washington correspondents at a background dinner that he was thinking of a Korean peace plan that would include cessationof hostilities near the 38th Parallel and a UN Trusteeship for Taiwan. When the correspondents dutifully sent up the trial balloon, ascribed to an unnamed high official, the outraged journalists who hadn't attended the dinner promptly revealed Dulles as the source, upon which he ungracefully denied the whole business.

In 1958, Dulles again created a flap over a backgrounder. As Secretary of State, he announced in Newport, R. I., that the United States wasn't sure whether to defend the Nationalist-held islands of Quemoy and Matsu against the Chinese Communists. Then, invoking the background rule, he turned himself into a "high official" who warned that the United States was prepared to fight for the islands if necessary. When the reporters again acted as obliging dummies for this diplomatic ventriloquist, his predecessor, Dean Acheson, revealed that Dulles was the "high official."

In an effort to avoid such embarrassment, Secretary of State Rusk in the Kennedy administration invented what he called "deep background," by which he intended to discuss sensitive foreign policy matters with selected reporters on condition that they used the session only as a learning experience. The "trusties" played along with him and "deep background" worked very well until others began using the same device with different ground rules.

What finally happened was that President Carter's cover was blown early in his administration when he gathered reporters around him, in carefully selected groups, to talk to them on "deep background" about his views of such problems as the Middle East, the Soviet Union, tax reform, and welfare. The White House press office had explained that Carter wanted to give the reporters an insight into his "impressions" and "thought processes." The result was a sudden fusillade of stories, ascribed to no source whatever, which purported to give the President's views. Some began with the old dodge, "It was learned that . . . . " while other grounded themselves on reportorial belief. The *Wall Street Journal*, however, announced:

"The President's views on tax revision, as well as other subjects, were given to a group of reporters yesterday under ground rules that barred identification of the source." It was one kind of hidden persuasion that didn't work.

Norman C. Miller, chief of the *Wall Street Journal*'s Washington bureau, explained, "I think you ought to cut it [identification of source] as close as possible without breaking any ground rules. I personally don't have any trouble with backgrounders by officials of government in relatively small give-and-take sessions where there's a true opportunity for exploration of the official viewpoint and it can be tested."

Others weren't so sure. Seymour Topping, managing editor of the New York *Times*, informed the White House in high displeasure that his paper wanted the "deep background" briefings discontinued and explained, "The New York *Times* objects to background briefings in which news is made available for publication on a nonattributable basis . . . . We feel our readers are entitled to as much information as we can give them about sources, particularly in reporting government news." Howard Simons, managing editor of the Washington *Post*, didn't go quite that far although he also disapproved. But, he added, "We couldn't have done Watergate without the use of unnamed sources."[31]

The point should not be disregarded. The objection is not to the protection of sources, which is a journalistic obligation, and remains the basis for nearly all investigative reporting. What is wrong about the way sources are concealed in much reporting about foreign affairs, and some other categories of news, is that it puts reporters in a false position. They become a part of an elaborate government masquerade, the end result of which is to try to persuade press, people, and government that all is well in Washington, D. C. For a few drinks, a plate of meat and potatoes or a junket on a government aircraft, both they and their news organizations risk the leveling of charges that they have—temporarily at least—become a part of the government apparatus. And in the hands of a clever government official working on any kind of nonattributable basis, this is exactly what happens.

Nobody in recent history was better at manipulating the press for his own ends, and incidentally the support of American foreign policy, than Henry Kissinger in both the Nixon and Ford administrations. During his Middle East "shuttle diplomacy," his briefings of reporters on his plane as a "senior official" became an intrinsic part of his style of operations. Through this device, he was able to float trial balloons and otherwise test the willingness of Egyptians and Israelis to agree on some kind of temporary pullback from the 1967 front lines.

Now and then, he would take liberties with the truth in briefings that otherwise were devoted to fairly solid information. Once, he told reporters before leaving the United States that he was bound for Damascus to receive a list of Israeli prisoners of war which he wanted to give to Israeli negotiators as a sign of Syrian good will. However, when the Kissinger reportorial entourage was airborne after having dispatched the story, a reporter who had stayed behind learned that Kissinger had been given the list by the Syrian ambassador before taking off.

Sometimes, too, the optimism with which government officials try to clothe almost everything they do falls flat. For example, during the "shuttle diplomacy" operation, Kissinger told reporters before leaving Cairo that he was making progress on a Sinai disengagement—a good story for them at the time. While aloft on the way to Israel, however, he conceded he had been overly optimistic but it was too late for the reporters to do much about the story that day.[32]

William Beecher, correspondent for the Boston *Globe*, was one of the relatively few reporters who were critical of Kissinger's methods while assigned to cover him. The "senior official," the reporter wrote, is to his accompanying press corps "informative, witty, charming, illusive, misleading, cunning, liked, distrusted, abused, and protected . . . . He has raised the practice of manipulating the press to an art form of diplomacy."

And what of the other reporters who formed Kissinger's journalistic palace guard? Beecher wrote that while they are sometimes frustrated "at the duplicity of the official's approach," he added bluntly, "They stop short of going so far as to risk a divorce . . . . It means too much to them personally and professionally."[33]

Finally, the identity of the "senior official" became so obvious that some of the most protective of the correspondents gave up. CBS News identified the "senior official" as someone who was stout and wore glasses. Gannett News Service explained that the "senior official" often referred to Kissinger himself. The New York *Times* chose to drop the use of "senior official" entirely and attributed Kissinger's information by saying that reporters on his plane were told about certain developments without identifying the source. The Associated Press was the principal news organization that stuck unvaryingly to the "senior official" identification. Beecher wrote in the Boston *Globe* on one occasion: "On the ground at 9:30 P. M., the senior U. S. official was last seen entering a long black limousine with Nancy Kissinger."[34]

Kissinger was so adept at handling his captive audience of reporters while aloft that he seldom got into trouble. But on the ground, even he suffered a comeuppance when he went too far. During the Indo-Pakistan War of 1971, while he was White House adviser on national security affairs, he threatened India during a background briefing. Next day, Senator Barry Goldwater was so angry that he inserted the entire background briefing in the Congressional Record and identified Kissinger as the source. It didn't bother the ebullient diplomat. Soon, on "deep background," he was warning the Soviet Union to restrain India or else. And this caused the Washington *Post* to blow his cover, but he didn't mind. It wasn't long before he became Secretary of State.

The reporters covering Kissinger offered this defense as given by Kenneth J. Freed, then the State Department correspondent of the Associated Press:

Recognizing the advantage Kissinger has in the charade, most reporters who cover the Secretary continue playing the game because it has its uses from a news point of view . . . . To get an insight into what is really going on or to understand the trend of events, reporters covering Kissinger need as candid an explanation as they can get from as high an official as possible. Talking under background rules also gives reporters an opportunity to question the secretary with minimal inhibitions.[35]

It also gave Kissinger an opportunity to have minimal inhibitions about the quality of the news content in his answers. The journalists' rules suited him beautifully. He knew those rules and used them better than the reporters did.

In a judgment on the Kissinger legacy, Leslie H. Gelb wrote in the New York *Times*:

Kissinger exceeded all of his predecessors in imparting information and providing explanations of policy to these institutions [the press and Congress]. He told them more and misled them more. His briefing of newsmen on the Paris cease-fire accords was a model of extensiveness and lucidity, but he said no secret agreements or understandings had been reached—and Nixon, it was later revealed, had made a number of secret commitments to Hanoi about postwar aid and the withdrawal of American civilian advisers, and to Saigon about the resumption of American bombing of North Vietnam in the event of violations.
His 1975 testimony before Congress on the Sinai disengagement agreement between Israel and Egypt was a marvelous exposition of the intricacies of American diplomacy in the Middle East, but he played games here, too. Several months earlier, when it had seemed there would be no pact at all, Kissinger had agreed with the Israelis not to blame anyone for the breakdown of his latest round of shuttle diplomacy. No sooner did he get on his aircraft to return home than he started blaming the Israelis. His public position was that neither was at fault; privately, he told another tale—the one he believed.[36]

It was a lot simpler for the reporters when Kissinger left office and the Carter administration chose Andrew Young as the ambassador to the United Nations and self-described "point man" for foreign policy. On his first trip to Africa as a diplomat, the

forthright Young brushed off reporters' attempts to explain the
rationale behind the concepts of on-the-record, off-the-record,
simple background, and deep background. "What's the difference?" Young asked.

Next thing that happened, his comments on Britain, Sweden,
Russia, and the Borough of Queens in New York City as havens of
racism were on the TV evening news and spread across the front
pages of the nation. He rejected the speeches the State Department had cleared for him and spoke off the cuff—"winging it," in
his words. For a long time he didn't seem to be sure what reporters considered to be news and what was not—and it didn't worry
him in the least. He was as uninhibited as Kissinger was controlled and, of course, he made a better story.[37] He wasn't trying
to con anybody, which might have been fine for the self-respect
of the diplomatic correspondents, but it didn't do much for
American foreign policy.

At the time of the Soviet dissident trials, Young embarrassed
the President by charging, in an interview with the French Social-
ist daily, LeMatin, that there were "hundreds, perhaps thousands" of political prisoners in the U.S. Carter rebuked him and
he apologized but the press still didn't get very high marks from
the public for its treatment of the ambassador. As Jesse L. Jackson
said on an earlier occasion, "It's time the truth Andy Young
speaks gets the primary attention."[38]

One of the most troublesome aspects of the continued debate
over national security is the posture of mutual suspicion that is
maintained by the press and the government's principal investigative agencies. We now know that the CIA has had numerous
operations in the past in which it hired American and foreign
journalists overseas and permitted some of its agents to pose as
foreign correspondents. We also have learned that the FBI in the
past monitored literally hundreds of newspapers that were critical of its activities. While both agencies proclaim their return to
virtue and swear by all that is holy that they have halted such

pernicious practices, they have made the news media very uneasy. Suspicion, once raised, is not easily overcome.

The most definitive investigation of the CIA's operations involving the press was conducted by the New York *Times* toward
the end of 1977. The inquiry established that the CIA had had
between 30 and 100 American journalists on its payroll abroad at
various times and used others without pay as "assets," whether
they knew it or not. It was also shown that the CIA had owned or
subsidized more than 50 news organizations, and the propaganda
and lies they disseminated sometimes were picked up and published as the truth at home. Moreover, the investigation disclosed,
a dozen or more CIA operatives were enabled to use the creden-
tials of American news organizations as "cover" for their intelligence work.

An investigation by Carl Bernstein in *Rolling Stone* magazine
placed the total number of journalists who cooperated with the
CIA at around 400, probably because he lumped together those
who were paid, those who worked for nothing, and those who let
themselves be used without knowing it. Joseph Alsop, the most
prominent journalist identified by Bernstein as a cooperator, admitted it and said, "Yes, if you have a chance to help your country, it is your job to do so. I've never taken orders. I've never
done anything I haven't believed in."

Stanley Karnow, a foreign correspondent, wrote that while
he had refused a CIA offer of employment, he and others had
considered it a matter of routine to exchange information with
the CIA. As he put it: ". . . Information is the best leverage for
acquiring more information, and he who keeps his lip buttoned is
not going to learn much."*

All this wound up in a series of hearings by a House subcommittee, during which William E. Colby, former head of the CIA,
conceded that propaganda planted by the agency abroad had

_____

*I respectfully dissent. In many years of newspaper work and research for books, I
frequently interviewed CIA people but never found it necessary to trade information. I do
not recall that I was beaten by the "Traders" on anything of importance.

been fed back to domestic news organizations and treated as genuine. It was even given a name by CIA operatives: "domestic blowback." And while Colby tried to minimize the damage, he did admit, "That is a problem." He added that the CIA sometimes had issued warnings to the American news media not to touch certain stories.

As a result of these disclosures, the CIA pledged that it would halt its clandestine relationships with the personnel of American news organizations and and not seek new ones of its own accord, that it would not deal with nonjournalist employees of an American news organization unless the organization itself approved, and that it would not normally let its operatives pose as news correspondents. It had an important reservation, however, which was that the director of the CIA could make exceptions. Also, the CIA specified that it would accept any information offered by correspondents, full-time or part-time. As for correspondents of foreign news organizations, the CIA restrictions did not apply.

All in all, the position between the CIA and the press remained quite strained. The public, for its part, had good cause to be concerned over the relationships between the intelligence community, where the rule is "need to know," and the news business, where the rule is "the right to know." The two continued to remain at odds.

In the field, however, business continued with a few cautionary moves by both sides. There has always been, and there continues to be, a perfectly legitimate intermingling between real correspondents and "spooks," as CIA people are known. They discuss information (if they trust each other), check it, sometimes issue new information, and in some cases exchange it. It is a part of the news business to seek information wherever it may be found and th CIA, after all, remains a first-rate government source.

The rule for correspondents is, "Let the buyer beware." Or, as I have phrased it to many generations of aspiring foreign correspondents, "Everybody is trying to sell you something, including the CIA, but you don't have to buy. And what you buy you must examine carefully before you use it." Just because a CIA operative offers some information and denies something else means little to an experienced correspondent, who knows that anything fed to him in such a manner must be made subject to the most careful check.

The only trouble is that the public does not appreciate the fine points of this kind of reporting. In consequence, the effect of the disclosures of CIA interference with the news media can only be to undermine further the amount of credence the public can place in news dispatches, particularly those sent from overseas without a clear statement of sources. However loudly editors may proclaim that the public has a right to be assured that correspondents for American news organizations are not also working for unseen paymasters who influence their work, and that the correspondents themselves have a right not to be suspected as spies, the record makes it very hard for a critical section of the public to believe in any guarantee of the sanctity of the news.

The surveillance of newspapers by the FBI is even more serious. It came to light when the Charleston (W. Va.) *Gazette* obtained documents under the Freedom of Information Act that showed the FBI had conducted criminal checks of its owners and editors after the newspaper had criticized the activities of J. Edgar Hoover while he was the agency's director. From photocopies of the *Gazette*'s FBI file, it was also deduced that the agency had monitored many other newspapers and even sought to discipline news organizations that questioned its inquiries.

Two of the newspapers directly involved, the Louisville *Courier-Journal* and *Times*, learned that the FBI had kept a running file on critical items published about its activities and investigated the papers' owners, policies, and personnel. Barry Bingham Jr., editor and publisher of the papers, commented: "I'd like to think that era is over and, if it is, I am relieved. But it has worried me for a long time that so much official investigation of citizens and the press has gone on . . . I fear it will take a long time for these attitudes to be washed out of the system."

The inquiries into the press, the Senate's report made clear, were a part of the government's intelligence campaign that caused its investigative agencies, including both FBI and CIA, to index the names of more than 300,000 Americans, keep files on 1,000 organizations, open nearly 250,000 pieces of first-class mail, list 26,000 citizens for detention in a national emergency, and subject others to secret harassment. It was not something of which every American could be proud.

The Senate report said: "The free flow of information, vital to a responsible and credible press, has been threatened as a result of the CIA's use of the world media for cover and for clandestine information-gathering." That judgment also could have been applied to the FBI's disciplinary campaign against the American press.

The principal weapon the news media were able to use to defend themselves against such unwarranted government actions was the Federal Freedom of Information Act. Like all the "Sunshine Laws" and "Open Meetings" laws that had been approved at both Federal and state levels, it was an imperfect instrument, but it did become possible, within limits, for the press to discover what the government was doing.

In the first ten years of its existence, the use of the FoI Act provided information on the CIA's experiments with drugs to control the human mind, attempts to assassinate foreign leaders, the training of local police as burglars, and the suppressed details about the espionage convictions of Julius and Ethel Rosenberg as atomic spies.

In 1976, the act's 10th year, about 150,000 requests for information were made by various organizations and persons to government agencies. Of these, 25,000 were denied in whole or in part, and 3,700 appeals were decided with about 400 finally yielding information. Some agencies placed exorbitant fees on their research services, notably one case in which the General

Services Administration wanted $2,000 for copies of contracts with a single real estate company. But for the most part, fees were nominal. The service, however, was slow.[39]

In most conflicts over fact and policy in the field of national security, the public is far more likely to believe the government than the press. The government, after all, is more potent as a molder of public opinion. Its resources are infinitely greater than those of the press. And, as every President has realized since the advent of the television era, it is possible to blunt the opposition of the press by appealing directly to the public through the broadcast media.

Many in this country are still so bemused by the trauma of the Vietnam War era and Watergate that they do not realize how defensive a large section of the press has become in dealing with news affecting national security.

But editors who read their mail and ponder over the vagaries of public opinion are well aware that they do little to make themselves popular by giving heavy play to news that discredits or otherwise tends to injure national defense. Even if the papers are right, they often do not get public credit for their efforts. It is both illogical and wrong-headed, but it is abysmally true that a considerable section of the public still believes it unpatriotic to criticize the armed forces.

In this area, as a result, the government has recovered at least a part of its credibility to date and the press has not. Even the revelations of CIA misconduct, timely and justified though they were, did not arouse the public to cheers of approval.

Historically, the press has nearly always operated at a disadvantage in making an aggressive examination of the government's requirements and performance in the field of national security. After the St. Louis *Post-Dispatch* forced a revival of the Senate's inquiry into the Teapot Dome naval oil reserve scandal in the 1920s, it took almost four years before a former Harding cabinet official, ex-Secretary of the Interior Albert B. Fall, was sent to jail.

It was more than two years after the Wasington *Post* began dig-ging into Watergate that President Nixon's pretense of acting for reasons of national security was shown to be a mindless fraud and his resignation followed.

It may well be, as critics on the conservative side have main-tained, that some of the press has been overzealous in trying to uncover wrongdoing in the twin fields of military power and for-eign policy. But can any responsible person seriously contend that American actions in South Vietnam, Chile, the Dominican Repub-lic, Zaire, and Cuba should not have been held up to the most searching scrutiny? Is it possible that anybody of consequence would want to keep secret the CIA's long surveillance of thou-sands of American citizens or its somewhat crazy venture into mind control?[40]

On the basis of a considerable career as a reporter, plus a sketchy experience as a part-time government servant, I would conclude that over the long haul the government has used the press to a much greater extent than the press has abused the government. For when the government speaks, it is with the voice of ultimate authority. But the press, in making its disclo-sures, frequently is obliged to conceal its source with the use of a gobbledygook language that reporters themselves often do not comprehend. And it does have to rely on leaks from government sources for much of its primary information.

The passage of restrictive or punitive legislation, assuming such action was possible, would not change these circumstances. In a government establishment of 2.8 million office holders and employees on the Federal level alone, there is bound to be dis-agreement and dissent over controversial policies. When the Pres-ident and his chief deputies give the command, "Forward!" not everybody automatically falls into line. This is, fortunately, not an authoritarian state and the dissenters invariably find a way to make their sentiments known, covertly if not openly. To that end, the press is their conduit. How else is the public to be informed of the disadvantages of a developing policy within the government, or the flaws in policy that already has been adopted? It is a rare administrator who throws himself on his knees before Congress, the people, or the press and confesses that what he has done was not worth doing. The bureaucrat is trained to admit no wrong.

I once knew a distinguished ambassador who was displeased with the formulation of a new State Department policy that affected the government to which he was posted. His protests, he knew, were being routinely brushed aside. What he did, therefore, was to disclose to a few trusted correspondents the full texts of his top secret arguments to the State Department with the result that his protests landed on Page 1 of some of the leading newspapers of the land and were amplified and commented upon in the evening news programs. The policy to which he objectd was modified and eventually dropped.

There was an even more spectacular demonstration of dissent within the Carter administration when the President enunciated his policy of opposing Federal payment for abortions, which seriously affected poor women. Some two dozen of his own appointees met for two hours with Presidential Assistant Midge Costanza in protest. They had the support of a Cabinet officer, Patricia Harris, Secretary of Housing and Urban Development. Not unremarkably, this outburst came to the attention of the news media and was widely and favorable commented upon.[41] Under what kind of law in a democratic society could something like this have been suppressed?

Those who would sanitize the American press and turn it into little more than a house organ for government and huge private interests can have little comprehension of the benefits of openness in a democratic society. All they can see are the drawbacks, of which there are many. But let the press be weakened as an investigative agency and the "watchdog" function over the actions of government will devolve almost entirely on Congress—a Congress that is notoriously responsive to the need for maintain-

ing local military establishments, bringing home big defense contracts, and dipping into the pork barrel on every occasion to
benefit local interests.

To raise the question in such a situation is to answer it. There
is a demonstrable need for an agency independent of government
to maintain constant vigil over government, particularly in the
field of national security. For better or worse, all we have is the
press.

3. Trial by Congress

Congress and the press have had a rather peculiar relationship in much of American history. It may not be actuated by hate,
except in the cases of those in Congress who were turned out of
office when the press began poking about in their affairs. But it
certainly isn't love, either. The position approximates that of the
enigmatic characters in the Jean-Paul Sartre play, *No Exit*, who
must find some way to get along with each other because they are
all stuck in the same place through eternity.

The members of the House and Senate, being the duly
elected representatives of the people, are well aware that the
press is going to cover them closely whether they are at home or
in Washington, D. C. Some adjust to the ordeal of constant scrutiny of all public (and some private) acts with grace and cheerful-
ness. Others bitterly resent the intrusions of the press. But all
fully realize that their political lives depend in large part on how
well they can communicate through the press with the electorate
back home and their luck, or lack of it, in presenting a favorable
image on television.

Congress, therefore, tolerates the press and the broadcast
media beacuse of what they can do *for* its members and at the
same time broods over what is done *to* them. Over two centuries,
this ambivalent feeling has resulted in Congressional investigations of both reporters and editors, citations for contempt against

them, jail terms for a few, expulsion from the House and Senate press galleries for a lot more. It also accounts for the latent hostility against the news media that sometimes is painfully in evidence, particularly in any legislation having to do with broadcasting.

The case of Daniel Schorr illustrates the position in all its ramifications. Dan Schorr was a respected investigative reporter for CBS News in Washington, one of the few effective ones in broadcast journalism. He was a graduate of the College of the City of New York, a reporter, editor, and foreign correspondent for newspapers and wire services from his 18th year, and had served CBS with distinction for 23 years. For his foreign correspondence, he won an Overseas Press Club prize; for his coverage of Watergate, an Emmy award.

Here was no irresponsible tyro, no wild-eyed zealot, but a substantial member of the Washington press corps. And yet, when he reached the age of 60 in 1976, a time in life when most people muffle their impulses under the drab cloak of discretion, something happened to Dan Schorr. He had been covering the House's Select Committee on Intelligence, headed by Otis Pike, a New York Democrat, and was appalled by what he had learned of the misdeeds of the CIA. Once the committee's report was drafted, he and other reporters were able to determine in advance what some of its conclusions would be. On the basis of calculated leaks, CIA report stories began appearing in the press and, among other places, on CBS Evening News.

Soon, Schorr obtained a copy of the report before it was made public and determined that the full text should be published. He gave the document to the *Village Voice*, a New York weekly, which put it out and at once created an uproar. Long afterward, Schorr said miserably, "If I had know then what I know now, I would have had the report duplicated and thrown all the copies from the CBS Building on 52d Street, New York."

The House was outraged, and the news media were thrown on the defensive. CBS News decided to fire Schorr, but agreed at the same time to give him severance pay and let him draw two more years' salary in addition. It occurred to both parties that, if the news got out before the House finished its investigation, the case might be prejudiced. Accordingly, they agreed on a "cover-up" statement (Schorr's terminology), in which he was merely "relieved of all reporting duties." CBS then paid Joseph Califano, later to become the Secretary of Health, Education, and Welfare in the Carter administration, a total of $150,000 to defend Schorr before the House.

Rep. Charles W. Whalen, Jr., an Ohio Republican with an excellent record on free press legislation, wrote: "Mr. Schorr's transmittal of the 'leaked' report to the *Village Voice* presents the House with a rare opportunity to wreak vengeance against what many members view as their mortal enemy—the press."

The House moved resolutely toward a confrontation with the news media on the issue. On February 19, the House found that the "alleged action of the said Daniel Schorr may be in contempt . . . of this House." It thereupon directed the Committee on Standards of Official Conduct, the Ethics Committee, to conduct an investigation for which $150,000 was appropriated five weeks later.

Rep. Thomas P. (Tip) O'Neill, the House Majority Leader, tried to derail the inquiry resolution before its passage by moving to refer it to the Rules Committee. But he was beaten by a whopping margin of 219-172. The House showed, by its vote, that it wanted to make an example of Schorr, at least at that particular time. Schorr wrote:

> My problem, friends in the press advised, was that I had made the press establishment feel threatened by breaching several of its cardinal rules. I had made my own decision about publishing the Pike report, causing many editors to worry about the precedent for staff discipline. Though meeting all my employer's needs, I had disposed of a document that raised questions of property rights. (I had assumed it was the public's property.) I had involved television in an argument with Congress when Congress was looking balefully at the broadcast industry anyway. And I had flaunted the idea of press disclosure when the disclosure was

retreating before a secrecy backlash, and the press was fretting about public hostility to the news media.

There was a lot of huffing and puffing by the House Ethics Committee and its chairman, John J. Flynt, Jr., a Georgia Democrat, who seemed to have taken personal umbrage at Schorr's refusal to name the source from which he had obtained the report. The FBI and the committee's own investigators tried for six months to crack the big secret but, in the end, had nothing to show for their $150,000 mission.

Throughout, the Republican leadership of the House which might have been expected to try to capitalize on the incident, adopted the role of interested bystander. The Minority Leader, John J. Rhodes of Arizona, once suggested mildly that if Schorr persisted in his refusal to disclose his source, "So be it, that is his privilege as a newsman."

Flynt wouldn't give up. Eventually, on September 15, this contrived minidrama ended in a confrontation. Schorr was summoned before the House committee as a witness and ordered to reveal his source. The implicit threat, if he again refused, was severe punishment in the form of a citation for contempt of Congress, a fine, and probably a stiff jail sentence.

Schorr doggedly stood his ground. He cited the First Amendment and argued with eloquence against what he considered to be a Congressional invasion of the rights of a journalist. "To betray a source would be to betray myself, my career, and my life," he said. "I cannot do it. To say I refuse to do it is not saying it right. I cannot do it."

Chairman Flynt warned Schorr nine times that he faced a fine and imprisonment for his stubborn attitude. But the reporter refused nine times, saying "My rights to withhold my sources are protected by the First Amendment, which is absolutely essential to the free press of this country." He argued, too, that he had violated no House rule because he obtained the report before the House voted to keep it secret on January 29.

Toward the end of the hearing, help came from an unexpected source. A member of the committee, Thad Cochran, a Mississippi Republican, told him, "I support you 100 percent in your refusal to name your source."

So did seven other members of the twelve-member committee. Chairman Flynt was beaten. Schorr escaped the harrowing experience of facing the entire House of Representatives, which would have been the next step if that committee had turned against him. But his career suffered a marked change of direction, for his rather comfortable discharge took effect once he had been cleared and he left CBS. At first, he took to the road as a college lecturer, taught for awhile at the University of California, and then published a book about his experiences, "Clearing the Air."

Anthony Lewis made a fitting comment after it was all over: "Judges and legislators are coming to understand how strongly the press feels about this issue."[42] But the incident didn't cause the House to adopt a more elevated and less jaundiced view of the mission of the journalist. Part of this may have been due to the mixed press notices that Congress usually receives. These were somewhat worse than usual at that juncture because of the Congressional sex scandals, the outcry against alleged Korean bribery of some of the less honorable members, and dilatory action on considerable pending legislation. But mostly, the attitude of Congress was exactly what it had been for some years, and a substantial part of the Congressional membership reflected to a large extent the public's disenchanted view of the press.

It wasn't long after the Schorr investigation that the entire Washington press corps began feeling the heat of Congressional disapproval. Rep. David R. Obey, a Wisconsin Democrat and the chairman of the House Committee on Administrative Review, publicly attacked reportorial perquisites in the capital. These included 181 free parking spaces reserved for the press, free telephone calls totaling $23,000 a year, and more than a million dollars a year in public funds to maintain the House and Senate Press

Galleries with a staff of 24 government employees whose sole
duty it is to help reporters. Remarked Obey,

> Reporters raise hell with the Congress, and chew us out about free
> parking places. They don't talk about the fact that they have free park-
> ing spaces too.
> What disturbs me most when I think about the national press is that
> I see the same developing pattern. . .that I see within the Congress
> itself. . . . We are both susceptible to the same temptation to overdram-
> atize, to overreach for stories and headlines and, I am sorry to say, to
> pander to popular prejudices. . . . It is disturbing to me to see that
> same. . . cheap shot, one-a-day style, growing in the national press.

Obey and Wisconsin's Senator Gaylord Nelson had sponsored a bill, which Congress passed, that called for the financial
disclosure by its membership of all outside income. Now the Congressman suggested that he might sponsor legislation requiring all
journalists covering Congress to make the same disclosures. He
explained:

> When a reporter comes in to talk to me, he knows where I stand,
> because I have disclosed everything. I'd like to know everything about
> him, too, so I can know what special baggage he brings with
> him. . . . Doesn't the public have a right to know if a science writer has
> large holdings in drug company stocks?

Obey didn't carry out his threat, however. He conceded that
such a law affecting the press might be unconstitutional. However, his criticism of journalistic hypocrisy touched a sensitive
area. While it is the policy of numerous leading news organizations to pay for reporters' travel and tickets, there is still an aston-
ishing amount of free-loading in the news business. The free services that journalists receive from Congress and other branches of
the Federal government also exist, to a greater or lesser extent, in
most state legislatures and city governments and even at the
United Nations headquarters in New York.

As James M. Perrry wrote in the last days of the *National
Observer*, "We may be more vulnerable than we think. But no,
we shouldn't be required by the Congress to disclose our outside
income. We really are different, even if we don't always deserve

our constitutional protection. But I think Obey should introduce
the bill anyway, just to provoke debate. We really are riding too
high."[43] It may be worth some reflection that the *National Observer* suspended publication two days later, although death was
due to journalistic anemia and not at all to anything the government did or did not do. Just how high the press may be riding
depends entirely on the angle of observation.

There are some who say, "Why all the fuss? You can't expect
Congress to like being bad-mouthed by the press. And anyway, it
used to be a lot worse in the good old days." That is perfectly
true. Beginning with William Duane, editor of the *Aurora*, who
was jailed for 30 days in 1800 for contempt of Congress, journalists from time to time have learned to their dismay that Congress,
when displeased, can play very rough. The House in 1846 ex-
pelled the New York *Tribune*'s correspondents because of "abusive" reports about an Ohio Congressman. Correspondents for
the Washington *Times* were removed from the press galleries that
same year for alleging corruption in the settlement of the Oregon
boundary dispute. And in 1857, a reporter for the New York
Times, James Simonton, was held in contempt when he refused to
reveal to a House committee the source of his allegations that
several Congressmen had taken bribes. "I cannot," he said, "without a violation of confidence, than which I would rather suffer
anything." After 19 days in custody, he was released with the
approval of the House, which by that time became convinced he
would never disclose his source. Moreover, three Congressmen
resigned in connection with the charges—which did more than
anything else to vindicate him.

The outcome of two other congressional investigations of the
press are also important. One was a Senate committee's inquiry in
1915 into the New York *Times*'s own financing following a series
of editorials that attacked a bill to purchase German shipping that
had been interned after the beginning of World War I. Charles

Ransom Miller, the *Times*'s editor in chief, concluded his testimony as follows:

Inquisitorial proceedings of this kind would have a very marked tendency to reduce the press of the United States to the level of the press that crawls on its belly every day to the foreign office or to the government officials and ministers to know what it may say or shall say—to receive its orders.

The second instance was a Senate investigation of Communist influence in the news media during the 1950s while McCarthyism still was a factor in almost everything that happened in Washington. It began with the admission of a CBS correspondent that he had had Communist affiliations, but it soon centered on the New York *Times* in 1955 and 1956. The moving spirit of the inquiry was Senator James O. Eastland of Mississippi, whose Senate Internal Security Subcommittee subpoenaed more than a score of *Times* employees. After two *Times* copyreaders had been fired and an assistant editor had resigned under pressure after pleading the Fifth Amendment before the Eastland Committee, the *Times* defiantly editorialized:

We cannot speak unequivocally for the long future. But we can have faith. And our faith is strong that long after Senator Eastland and his present subcommittee are forgotten, long after segregation has lost its final battle in the South, long after all that was known as McCarthyism is a dim, unwelcome memory, long after the last Congressional committee has learned that it cannot tamper successfully with a free press, the New York *Times* will still be speaking for the men who make it [the *Times*], and only for the men who make it, and speaking, without fear or favor, the truth as it sees it.[44]

This is not to say that Congress habitually slams the door in the face of the free press. Quite to the contrary. Some of the most progressive legislation in support of the press in this century orginated as a result of the many hearings and investigations conducted by the Moss Subcommittee on Government Information in the House. Such forward-looking legislation as the Freedom of Information Act and the various "Sunshine" laws, designed to produce more open meetings and open records, could not have come to pass without a great deal of effort in both houses of Congress. With few exceptions, however, the press did not seem particularly grateful for the assistance. Private individuals and agencies have used the Freedom of Information Act to a greater extent than the press. As for the "Sunshine" legislation, there has been a good deal of newsroom grumbling that the laws were too complicated, too ineffective, or both. The net result has been— and continues to be—a somewhat less than trustful relationship between Congress and the press.

It is one of the signs of the times in Congress that Morris K. Udall, the Arizona Democrat who sponsored the Newspaper Preservation Act, was the first to call for a Congressional study of the growing concentration of newspaper ownership.

The Newspaper Preservation Act benefited failing newspapers in 23 cities by permitting them to merge their operations (except for the editorial department) with those of prosperous newspapers in the same city. That earned Udall the gratitude, temporarily at least, of many publishers.

However, his new bill was aimed in the direction of antitrust action against the chains and his friendly press evaporated very quickly. Eugene Patterson, who was the president of the American Society of Newspaper Editors, asked, "Is not a chain operation. . .going to be inviting. . .Justice Department scrutiny?[45]

There was a lot of conjecture over the Arizonan's motives. Probably, he was disturbed over the growth of chain operations in his own state. In any event, he said in an address before the National Press Club:

I dread the day all newspapers look and read alike, when there will be less difference in daily newspapers than between the Big Mac and the Whopper—and less flavor.

I seriously worry about the absence of local publishers and editors with real roots in the community. A leader whose concern goes beyond advertising lineage and newsprint costs. . . .

I recognize that talk of regulation of newspapers is an area of special caution because of the First Amendment and the incompatibility of government control and the free press. but the business of publishing is also the business of selling advertising, which no one has contended is exempt from antitrust laws. For it is true that one can drive out competition and do great damage to consumers with a newspaper cartel even as with an oil cartel. . . .

Today, what the titans of the chains want is profits—not power— just money. I fear that the quest for profits and higher dividends for their growing list of stockholders will transcend their responsibility to maintain an independent and dedicated influence in the community.[46]

What Udall proposed specifically was a commission that would examine the press and other basic industries, such as steel and automobiles, over a three-year period, with special interest in various criteria such as efficiency, innovation, social impact, price, and profit. Those that did not perform well, he suggested, would be given "remedies. . .tailored to specific conditions."

The silence of the House's Democratic leadership after he introduced his measure was deafening. And not many members even wanted to comment on it, for it was not something to cheer about. Very few seemed ready to take on the chains, with their considerable influence in the broadcast industry, not to mention the remainder of the news media in the nation. Some pointed out privately that three Royal Commissions that had investigated the decline of the British press had done nothing to take it out of its economic tailspin. Others saw it merely as a device to encourage greater attacks on the press.

Regardless of the ingrown prejudice with which many in Congress viewed the press, it became evident soon after Udall made his proposal that it would not get very far. Indeed, being the supple politician that he is, he changed course and introduced another newspaper bill in the House, the Independent Local Newspaper Act, which was intended to save the local newspaper from the chains. It proposed to amend the Internal Revenue code by allowing the establishment of trust accounts to pay off publishers' estate taxes. For the family papers that already had been absorbed by chains, it was no help at all; for the rest, it provided a mere glimmering of hope. The movement was too far advanced to be reversed.

Udall's original proposal remained the subject of intense discussion among his colleagues and in the press. In the Senate, Senator Edward M. Kennedy indicated strong interest, as well. The chains reacted for the most part with sophisticated reserve, with Lee Hills observing for the Knight-Ridder chain:

> Mr. Udall assumes that bigness *per se* is bad in newspaper publishing companies. We don't accept that assumption. Our size and resources help us assure quality. There are more than 170 companies which own one or two newspapers. Knight-Ridder, the largest in terms of circulation, has less than 6 percent of total U. S. daily circulation. While there are many excellent locally owned newspapers, most of the best are owned by companies which own two or more newspapers. Knight-Ridder's reputation for improving newspapers is well known. . . . However, we readily concede that many newspapers, whether independent or group-owned, do not have the same commitment to excellence.[47]

Elsewhere, the reactions to the monopoly inquiry ranged from "very dangerous," Eugene Patterson's comment, to the Topeka *State Journal*'s complaint that Udall showed "a vast dearth of common sense" and faith in the free press. *Editor & Publisher*, the trade magazine, limited itself to a few lines: "If Rep. Udall could pass a law returning all newspapers now owned by groups private and public to their orignial owners, in 25 years the concentration of ownership would be the same as it is today unless confiscatory taxes on individual owners and their heirs are changed." And Claude Witze, a veteran journalist, summed it all up: "The trend toward central ownership of some daily U. S. newspapers is none of the Federal government's business. Why doesn't somebody say so?"[48]

The trouble is that most of these comments miss the central point, which is that the nature of the news business has changed. What we have in this country no longer resembles the simple corporate setup of the early 20th century, in which news was disseminated by newspapers that—except for rare cases—were affiliated with no other commercial interest. Some of the modern chains and all the conglomerates deal in news, books, televisison, paper mills, magazines, and a diverse category of other products. In a few, news is a mere byproduct; in others, a showcase attraction to pull in customers for other offerings. The time has not yet come when oil and steel and automobile companies are ready to own newspapers as they do abroad, but it could happen here at almost any time. There is nothing to stop them.

So it would be a mistake, I think, to dismiss Udall's challenge out of hand. Both the immensely profitable nature of the news business as it is organized today, and the diverse operations of the proprietary interests, make newspapers potential targets for political action. The adverse nature of public opinion toward the press does nothing to improve the situation and it is even worse toward television, which is far more vulnerable to government action. From attacks on television violence in 1976, critics became even more voluble in 1977 and 1978 on the general subject of excessive sex on the tube.

But the three great broadcasting chains continued to increase their profits despite that. Even though CBS Inc., was no longer the broadcast leader in ratings of popularity, it set records in net sales, income, and earnings per share in 1977. The company's net income was $182,008,000, an 11 percent increase over the previous year, on net sales of $2,776,000,000, a 24 percent jump over 1976. That was equivalent to $6.50 a share for the year, up from $5.75. It was noteworthy that CBS Inc., besides being in the news and entertainment business, also owned a book company, a number of magazines, a car rental company, some musical instrument companies, 67 retail stores, and a toy company.

RCA, the parent company of the NBC broadcasting chain, also set records. Its $247 million earnings for 1977 represented a 39 percent gain over 1976 on sales of $5.92 billion, up 10 percent over the previous year. That set pre-tax profits at a new high, with earnings of $3.23 a share, up from $2.30 in 1976. As in the case of CBS Inc., RCA was in a lot of businesses other than news and entertainment, among them book publishing, frozen foods, a car rental company, and electronic products.

ABC, Inc., which again led in the popularity ratings for 1977, estimated its earnings for the year at $6 a share, up from $4.05 a share in the previous year, on a net income of $71,747,000. Like its giant rivals, ABC Inc., was branching out in numerous directions from news and entertainment—theaters, books, magazines, records, and the National Insurance Law Service.[49]

The largest of the conglomerates in print journalism was Time Inc., with its $90-million 1977 net income. While its magazines accounted for 35 percent of its income, it also owned newspapers, a book company, a film company, a forest products company, companies that make interior wall products and bedroom furniture, and some TV stations.

By contrast, such large chains as Knight-Ridder, the Chicago Tribune group, and Gannett remained predominantly daily newspaper operations, although each has some TV interests as well. The Times-Mirror Company was more diversified, operating book companies, magazines, television stations, newsprint mills, and directory printing in addition to its newspapers.

The two individual newspapers with the most prestige in the nation, the New York *Times* and Washington *Post*, also were expanding into other fields, including books, television, and magazines. The *Post*, in addition, benefited from the growth of *Newsweek*, an affiliate, and the prime challenger to *Time*.

In forecasting some form of government inquiry into the entire field, taking the conglomerates and the news operations together without differentiation, Kevin Phillips wrote: "The question. . . is whether the self-interest of vested establishments and the indignation of the general populace are reaching a level of mutual reinforcement. If so, and I for one think so, the form taken by any legal, economic, and political corrective measures will be all-important for American democracy."[50]

But with Congress deeply divided on numerous issues that were of more immediate importance to the nation, the prospect for action on Udall's antitrust measure remained dim, and Phillips continued to be a lonely prophet.

For the future, I don't see how an organization that operates primarily in the news field will have much to fear, for it can properly base itself on the First Amendment. But the position of the conglomerates may not be as strong, particularly if some commercial interest like an oil company enters the news field.

Anthony Lewis has observed that the press was meant to be "outside the established order" by the framers of the Constitution."[51] That is eminently true even today. But if the news business in part or whole is swallowed up within the established order and jumbled together with all manner of commercial interests, there is legitimate concern over whether it can continue to justify its special protection under the Constitution.

Organizations that deal primarily in news are different. No sensible person denies them the right to earn a reasonable profit on their investment, for if there is no financial security for the press it cannot maintain its independence. It also would be difficult to deny singly owned newspapers the right to broaden their financial base and acquire other news properties in a nation with the stringent inheritance tax laws we now have. Thus, the principle of the newspaper chain, which goes back to Benjamin Franklin in American history, can scarcely be negated at this late date.

If critics are to press their argument that being big is bad, the question then is, "At what point does the size of a newspaper chain become objectionable? And how can it be proved that its operations are less desirable than those of a smaller chain or those of an individual newspaper?" It would seem very difficult to uphold the premise that there should be one rule for large news organizations and another for smaller ones.

There are, clearly, limits beyond which government regulatory commissions cannot go. The Federal Communications Commision, for example, would have quite a First Amendment fight on its hands if it tried to extend its jurisdiction to monitoring the news. The same is true of the Securities and Exchange Commission, which has jurisdiction over the stock offerings of publicly held newspapers, newspapers groups, and other media corporations, but could scarcely expect to develop that right to affect the content of the news or editorial opinion. It would run counter to public policy in the United States, as it exists at this particular time.

But public policy can take rather violent swings under the stress of adverse public opinion. Thus, Admiral Stansfield Turner, director of the CIA in the Carter administration, recognized that somebody in government might "blow the whistle" and inform the news media if the CIA ever again tried to conduct secret drug experiments on American citizens. It was quite a switch from the usual official denunciation of "leaks" to the press and a somewhat different image of what could be expected in these times from a patriotic American. It was also a response to the low public tolerance of governmental error.

The press can expect a similar reaction from the public—and perhaps the government—if its ownership is further absorbed into the general industrial and financial pattern of the nation. The eternal outsider was meant to stay outside, to remain aloof from the Establishment, not to be escorted to the head of the table.

Nobody was very happy about the duPont ownership of the Wilmington (Del.) News-Journal, including the duPonts themselves. In 1978 the papers were sold to the Gannett chain for $60 million. There was scattered participation of industry in other newspapers, notably a railroad company in Florida and copper interests in Montana.[52] This kind of ownership should be abandoned, not encouraged, if the press is to regain even a part of its standing with the American public.

One of the most sensitive aspects of American journalism has been the treatment of conflicts of interest in the handling of the news. In politics, those with an overt interest in the fortunes of a particular party or candidate have been disqualified from reporting the news or handling it. In business and finance, the relatively few journalists who betrayed their trust by writing about securities in which they had an interest were promptly removed upon discovery.

The same rule applies to an even greater extent in media ownership. No question of propriety was raised when the *Wall Street Journal* investigated charges of corruption among such corporate giants as Lockheed and United Brands, and the *New York Times* dissected the affairs of Gulf and Western. But could a news organization with heavy commitments outside journalism undertake such activities? To many, they simply would not be credible.

Britain currently is experiencing some of the dubious results of industrial expansion into journalism. What is happening in Fleet Street is far from reassuring. Lord Beaverbrooks's London *Daily Express*, for example, has fallen into the hands of a businessman, Victor Matthews, whose first instructions to his staff were to believe in Britain and publish good news.[53] Evidently, he thought he had taken over a house organ, not a newspaper. The irascible Beaverbook would have howled in displeasure, but Matthews was not conscious of error. After all, that was the way he ran the Cunard Lines and the Ritz in London.

The American press, fortunately, is in a much stronger position and need not depend on business and industry to bail it out. But the trend toward an expanded conglomerate press, nevertheless, is disquieting, and Udall's proposal constitutes a yellow light, a cautionary sign. It is not yet the threat that some take it to be, or a portent of government regulation through antitrust action, because it doesn't seem to have all that much support. But somewhere down the road, it may appear in different guise as a red light, a full stop, against the growth of an industrially minded conglomerate ownership. News is too important to be left to those who have an essential conflict of interest with its fair, full, and honest presentation.

The struggle against long-pending restrictive legislation in Congress is of more immediate consequence than the Udall study project. The Reporters Committee for Freedom of the Press has warned that these proposals, as originally drafted, amounted to "an Official Secrets Act which would give the government wide-ranging new criminal powers to severely restrict the First Amendment rights of the press to report—and the public to receive—the news."[54]

The warning is well founded. What remains unsettling about the situation is that, so far, few journalists have taken part in the fight and the public has shown an appalling lack of interest in the proceedings.

As an entirely technical matter, the problem originated with the long pending redrafting of the Federal Criminal Code, which is a worthy and necessary project. President Nixon sent it to Congress early in 1973 with distinguished bipartisam sponsorship, and it became known as S-1 (Senate Bill No. 1). Nothing happened for almost a month. Then, Senator Edmund S. Muskie of Maine completed a study of the 100,000-word document and publicly denounced it as an "attempt to stifle the flow of official information to the public." Senator Birch Bayh of Indiana, one of the bill's sponsors, angrily withdrew and tried to amend it, saying, "I believe that if S-1 were enacted in the form approved by the Subcommittee [on Criminal Laws and Procedures of the Senate Judiciary Committee], the state of our criminal law and the protection of our civil liberties would, without exaggeration, recede a full century."

Senator Alan Cranston of California set about at once to "defang" S-1 with this explanation: "We seek to protect legitimate national defense and foreign policy secrets without threatening to throw into jail conscientious Federal employees who blow the whistle on wrongdoing in government and investigative reporters who report it."[55]

The three liberal Democrats, with some support from like-minded colleagues and an activist section of the press, waged an unremitting fight on S-1 for three years, and it finally died in committee in December 1976, without ever reaching the Senate floor. Then, what was heralded as a new bill, the Criminal Code

Reform Act, was introduced in 1977 under the sponsorship of Senator Edward M. Kennedy of Massachusetts, a liberal Democrat, and, until his death that year, Senator John L. McClellan of Arkansas, a conservative Democrat. It had the approval of Attorney General Griffin Bell.

The new bill, S-1437, also 100,000 words in length, soon was dubbed "Son of S-1."[56] That is close to what it turned out to be, even though some of its most poisonous provisions were knocked out before it was passed by the Senate, 72-15, on Jan. 30, 1978, and sent to the House. There the American Society of Newspaper Editors and other media representatives finally decided to make a stand following the urgent warnings of the ASNE's Committee on Freedom of Information.

Anthony Day, editorial page editor of the Los Angeles *Times* and chairman of the ASNE FoI Committee, wrote that S-1437 had "fatal flaws" that posed "a grave threat to the press":

> I think that for the press to be complacent is a serious mistake. The bill's sections on the press (as indeed does the bill as a whole) tilts the law against the citizen and its press spokesmen in favor of the government.
>
> It is my personal view that the press should not be misled by the bill's supporters' claim that it "merely codifies existing court decisions." Some of these court decisions. . .infringe press liberty. To put the stamp of Congress upon them strengthens them and gives the courts and the government a new base from which to proceed further toward curbing the press in the name of justice.

The following were the provisions of the Senate-approved bill that aroused the most concern before the House, particularly at a time when some members of Congress were under investigation for accepting bribes from the South Korean government:

CRIMINAL CONTEMPT (Sec. 1331). This would make it a crime for a reporter to protect his confidential news sources.

HINDERING LAW ENFORCEMENT (Sec. 1311). This would make it a crime for a reporter to hide or refuse to give up notes or film out-takes (unused film) of interviews with news sources suspected of being involved in a crime.

In a floor debate, Senator Kennedy argued that this section would not necessarily be used against a reporter unless the notes were actually under subpoena. But obviously, he could not give a guarantee of what an individual judge would do in a specific case.

CRITICIZING A WITNESS (Sec. 1324). This would make it a crime to publish a news article or editorial that "improperly criticizes" a witness at a trial or Congressional hearing, if the criticism causes "economic loss or injury" to the person's business or profession.

REFUSAL TO PRODUCE CONFIDENTIAL INFORMATION (Sec. 1333). This would make it a crime for a reporter to *initially* refuse to obey an order calling for confidential news sources if the order is upheld on appeal, even if the reporter thereafter freely volunteers such information.

LEAKING "PRIVATE" INFORMATION TO PRESS (Sec. 1525). This would make it a crime for a past or present government employee to inform the press of government crime or other news, based on information submitted to the government in "private," as defined by any law, regulation, rule, or order. (However, if a government employee leaks information to law enforcement officials, he will not be prosecuted. He takes a risk only if he talks to the press!)

SEALING CRIMINAL RECORDS (Sec. 3807). This would permit Federal courts to seal permanently public arrest, indictment, and conviction records of first offenders under 21 who have been convicted of posessing heroin or other drugs, and have been placed on probation.

"These proposals," Day concluded, "would impinge directly on the ability of the press to gather news from confidential sources that often enable the press to expose corruption. . . . Beneath the bland and often turgid legal language of the bill. . .can be discerned the thrust of the legislation and it is ominous for the press."

Among the bill's provisions that were stricken before the House took final action were measures to make it a crime to publish a "stolen" government document or report, to criticize government officials "improperly," to retain possession of a government document intended for publicaton, and to publish a government report (i. e., the Pentagon Papers) without permission. Also dropped was a provision that would have made it a crime to publish a news article or editorial in violation of a court-approved gag order, even if the order was later declared invalid.

The Reporters Committee for Freedom of the Press took this position:

> We believe, in general, that the principles of the First Amendment never authorize any agency of the Federal or State governments to issue a prior restraint on the publication of news unless—as the New York *Times* and Washington *Post* argued in the Pentagon Papers case—the government can prove "clear and present danger to the national security of the United States."
>
> Following this principle, it is our position, with reference to this bill, that it can never be a Federal crime for a news person or news organization, acting in good faith under the First Amendment, to publish news in violation of a court order—except for the "clear and present danger" situation.

The evidence is clear that Congress is being pushed steadily in the direction of some form of press regulation, regardless of the outcome of the fight over S-1437. When two such dissimilar and differently motivated administrations as those of Presidents Nixon and Carter basically agree on a philosophy of dealing with the press, as exemplified by the original versions of S-1 and S-1437, then the press must take warning.[57]

The position cannot be viewed with equanimity. It can scarcely be an accident that the Democratic and Republican leadership of Congress, with few exceptions, joined in backing S-1 when it came to the Senate during the Watergate scandal.

To be sure, S-1 died unmourned. But it is also unfortunately true that the process of defanging, to use Alan Cranston's colorful term, took three years and succeeded only after a tremendous effort and a nationwide educational campaign by the press. It might well have been enacted if the Watergate scandal had not broken wide open.

What is one to think when much of S-1's punitive philosophy was incorporated in the original version of S-1437, the work of two of the most useful and distinguished Democratic Senators? How can one interpret the dismaying reality that the goals of the "Son of S-1" seemed in some respects to coincide with the views attributed to President Carter some years before his election to the nation's highest office?

It is all very well to say that the President's views are now modified, that S-1437 has been cleansed of some of its worst features, and that the government really does not intend to try to put the press on a leash. In an election year—the mid-term Congressional elections or the quadrennial Presidential elections— most office-seekers vow their fealty to the ideals of the free press and swear by all the other freedoms guaranteed in the First Amendment.

But the public and the press must judge by actions, not fine words, and the actions to date—to put it mildly—have been most disturbing. The Schorr investigation, the criticism of the press's prerogatives, the Udall antitrust proposals, the revised Criminal Code Reform Act—all these are of a piece. The purpose, regardless of whether it is attained or not, is to put the press on the defensive, to try to force newspapers through one means or another to tone down their bent toward investigation of government misdeeds, to muffle their adversary relationship under the cotton wadding supplied by Congress.

To anybody given to reflection over the lessons of the past, there is something symbolic in the fact that S-1 was formulated in the Justice Department while it was directed by the ever abrasive John Mitchell. No journalist can forget that it was he who led the attack on the Washington *Post* when it first began unraveling the tangled skeins of the Watergate plot. But in the end, the newspaper he threatened turned out to be the public benefactor and it was *he* who was convicted and sent to prison.

That in itself should give Congress reason for careful thought before it moves toward an Official Secrets Act, now or in the future. As Salvador de Madariaga pointed out many years ago, those who ignore history are condemned to relive it.

4. The Judgment of the Courts

The press has so few well-wishers outside its own ranks that it indulges in an orgy of self-congratulation whenever it wins a significant court case. This is as illusory a demonstration of security as resting the fate of a marriage on a waterbed, which is likely to leak.

When the Supreme Court struck down the government's attempt to suppress publication of the Pentagon Papers and permitted the New York *Times* and Washington *Post* to resume their disclosures, the former called it a "ringing victory." But the Solicitor General of the United States, Erwin N. Griswold, remarked, "Maybe the newspapers will show a little restraint in the future."[58] This caused John S. Knight, always the realist, to warn, "The press. . .may not be giving sufficient thought to the possibility that actually a precedent has been set for further or future restraints on the right to publish."[59]

In the light of subsequent events, Knight proved to be more nearly correct than the New York *Times*'s optimistic editorialist. For when the judicial offensive to curb the press was halted in one direction, it changed course and set off on another tack. Nor is it likely to cease in the foreseeable future.

"Any system of prior restraints of expression comes to this court bearing a heavy presumption against its constitutional validity," the Supreme Court held in its majority decision in the Pentagon Papers case. That system has an honorable history going back three centuries to the English common law, as interpreted by Blackstone's *Commentaries*:

The liberty of the press is indeed essential to the nature of a free state; but this consists in laying no previous restraint upon publications, and not in freedom from censure for criminal matter when published. Every freeman has an undoubted right to lay what sentiments he pleases before the public; to forbid this, is to destroy the freedom of the press; but if he publishes what is improper, mischievous or illegal, he must take the consequences of his own temerity.[60]

This is the philosophy that led to the adoption of the First Amendment to the United States Constitution. For 140 years thereafter, not even an attempt was made to challenge the right of publication without prior restraint. Then, in 1931, a landmark Supreme Court decision was handed down in Near v. Minnesota. Chief Justice Charles Evans Hughes wrote in the majority opinion:

The fact that the liberty of the press may be abused by miscreant purveyors of scandal does not make any the less necessary the immunity of the press from previous restraint in dealing with official misconduct. Subsequent punishment for such abuses as may exist is the appropriate remedy. . . .[61]

Justice Hughes held that the press's immunity could be limited only in exceptional cases. But, as Professor Thomas I. Emerson pointed out subsequently, the high court left in "considerable confusion" the question of what exceptions could be made in the general refusal to apply prior restraints. He wrote:

He [the Chief Justice] gave as examples certain obstructions to the conduct of war, obscenity, and incitement to violence. But the reasons for making these exceptions are unclear—some of them do not even involve expression—and the whole matter remains obscure.[62]

This is the circumstance of which the courts took advantage in their efforts to balance the Constitutional guarantees of free press and fair trial. To be sure, the excesses of general court and crime coverage by the sensational press gave judges ample provocation for action, but it was a long time before they did anything, despite some of the legal circuses that were made out of notorious murder trials.

After one of the worst judicial exhibitions of the century—the murder trial of Bruno Richard Hauptmann in 1935—the protest of the American Bar Association took the form of Canon 35, a professional rule prohibiting picture-taking during trial proceedings. That, however, did very little to halt the carnival in which supine judges, sensational journalists, and publicity-seeking lawyers shared the blame for the shame of the courts.

The event that shocked the conscience of the nation, the murder of President Kennedy in Dallas on November 22, 1963, also touched off the public's reaction against the news media. For after 50 million witnesses on television watched the murder of Lee Harvey Oswald, who had been arrested for the slaying and brought before the cameras, the Warren Commission blamed both the news media and the police for the breakdown in law enforcement.

Soon the Supreme Court began to take firm action to restore the rights of those under arrest and others who faced trial. The murder conviction of Danny Escobedo, a Chicago laborer, was set aside in 1964 because he had not been permitted to consult a lawyer before making an alleged confession. In the following year, the fraud conviction of Billie Sol Estes, a Texas financier, was reversed because his trial in a Texas state court, despite Canon 35, had been televised live over his objection.[63] In 1966, Ernesto A. Miranda, an Arizona truck driver, also won a reversal of a rape conviction because he had not been informed of his right to counsel, or that statements he made would be used against him.

The high court struck its strongest blow, and the one that most severely affected the news media, in the reversal of the murder conviction of Dr. Samuel Sheppard of Cleveland in 1966. It held that "virulent publicity" had made a fair trial impossible. "Trials are not like elections," Justice Tom C. Clark wrote in the majority decision. "Due process requires that the accused receive a trial by an impartial jury free from outside influence."[64]

It was soon after the Sheppard decision that judges began to clamp down on press coverage for fear of having verdicts in their courts set aside. Defense lawyers, in cases in which their clients were found guilty amid excessive news coverage, often attacked the press in filing their appeals. It was a heavy price for the news media to pay for the excesses of the past.

But the courts, once they stirred from their lethargy, continued to apply pressure against both print and broadcast journalists to a point that sometimes was unreasonable and self-defeating. Some editors charged that the prevailing doctrine against prior restraint on publication had been virtually abandoned.

The climax of this legal offensive came in 1975 when Judge Hugh Stuart of Lincoln County, Nebraska, issued an order that limited the state's news media in their coverage of a mass murder in Sutherland, Neb. Although a farm laborer was convicted of the killings early in 1976, Nebraska news organizations and others carried the case to the Supreme Court. Thus, the issue was joined in Nebraska Press Association v. Stuart. Once again, on June 30, 1976, the high court by a 9-0 decision reaffirmed its position on prior restraint against publication and struck down the "gag" order. And once again, a loophole was left when Chief Justice Burger wrote: "However difficult it may be, we need not rule out the possibility of showing the kind of threat to fair trial rights that would possess the requisite degree of certainty to justify restraint.[65]

In consequence, there were mixed opinions about the effect of the Nebraska decision. Professor Benno C. Schmidt, Jr., of the Columbia Law School, warned, "Although the Nebraska case deals only with prior restraints, it will certainly influence other aspects of the fair trial–free press problem. . . . A more extreme reaction on gathering news may also be stimulated by the decision."[66]

Floyd Abrams, a distinguished New York lawyer who was active in a number of First Amendment cases, expressed the belief that the Nebraska case made it "all but impossible" for such sweeping "gag" orders to be entered in the future. He conceded, however, that courts retained the power to seal off sources of information by restraining court personnel, witnesses, lawyers, and others. These latter restraints, which were not direct restraints of the press itself, drew the fire of the Reporters Committee for Freedom of the Press. In testimony before the Senate Judiciary Committee, the committee's representatives also listed such directives as "gag" orders. "We are facing a plague of gag orders issued by both Federal and State judges barring the press from publishing court news," the committee's statement said. It was made clear that the main thrust of the complaint was against "censoring public proceedings, public records and public fugures involved in civil and criminal cases."

Jack C. Landau of the Newhouse Newspapers, who had presented the committee's views, later explained:

We. . .believe that gag orders orders which directly restrain publication are virtually outlawed.

There is a semantic problem. We include in gag orders orders issued by judges sealing court records, authorizing secret court proceedings and stopping defendants, witnesses, attorneys and others from commenting to the press.

What has happened is that the judges, now prohibited from stopping newspaper presses from publishing, are simply cutting off information at its source.[67]

The committee doucumented a total of 50 judicial restraints directed against the press in the nine years before the Nebraska decision, 38 of them between 1974 and 1976. Within a year after the Nebraska case, it counted at least 17 judicial restraints on information about court cases that were pending in federal and state courts—and more followed.

Among those who protested was Arthur Ochs Sulzberger, publisher of the New York *Times*, who told a judicial conference:

I think we can see the clear and present danger of a lack of judicial restraint. . . . When the rights of free press and fair trial conflict, the remedy is not for the one to seek to triumph over the other, but to find an accommodation; not for the courts to trample on the First Amendment by barring publication, but to protect the rights of the accused by changes of venue, or sequestering of juries, or instructions from the bench or—if absolutely necessary—by ordering a new trial.[68]

Still, the indirect "gags"—the closing of sources of information—persisted in many parts of the nation. In the District of

Columbia, a judge sealed a formal complaint in a baby-selling case and thereby blocked the efforts of the news media to report on it. The Supreme Judicial Court of Massachusetts barred the Cape Cod *Times* from coverage of a bank's complaint against the State Banking Commission and approved the sealing of docket entries in the case. The sealing process also was resorted to by a Virginia judge to frustrate the Richmond *News Leader*'s coverage of charges against a corporation involved in fatalities attributed to the chemical Kepone.

A coroner's report was sealed by a North Carolina judge to keep the Raleigh *News & Observer* from publishing it in connection with the killing of a fugitive. An Ohio judge sealed pretrial proceedings in a murder case to prevent publication by the Akron *Beacon Journal*.

The Rockford Gazette in Illinois was ordered by a judge not to publish editorials critical of the local court system. And in Kentucky, a judge sealed a formal complaint in a sewage contamination case to forestall publication of details by the Louisville *Courier-Journal*.

But the case that finally set the alarm bells ringing was the Supreme Court's 5–3 decision in 1978, in the Stanford *Daily* case, that gave police the right to search any newsroom or the premises of any other innocent organization or person for evidence of a crime, merely by obtaining a search warrant. Here at length was the basis for the dread "midnight knock on the door."

Now there were not many editors who refused to face up to a tough situation. William F. Thomas of the Los Angeles *Times* called the decision "incredible, terrible." Maxwell McCrohon of the Chicago *Tribune* exclaimed, "Outrageous." Joseph Pulitzer Jr. of the St. Louis *Post-Dispatch* saw the press's "watchdog" role as "gravely jeopardized." John Hughes of the *Christian Science Monitor* believed the ruling made possible the "gravest abuse."

Such concern was justified. In the first 195 years of the Republic, there had been no searches of news offices by police bearing search warrants. But from 1970 to 1978, there had been a dozen, three of them within a year before the Stanford *Daily* decision.[69]

It was clear enough to all concerned that the investigative function of the press had been weakened. Worse still, this was a case that affected the rights of every citizen under the Fourth Amendment, not only the press, against "unreasonable searches and seizures." Even in Congress, where remedial legislation was proposed, the impression grew that the Supreme Court had gone too far—that subpoenas and hearings rather than search warrants were preferable before the premises of innocent people could be searched.

Of course the press was accused of overreacting. But this time it took a particularly obtuse editor to conclude that the judicial rampage could be ignored.[70] At length, in a few places, some journalists were sufficiently aroused to take protective measures. In Pennsylvania, for example, about 80 editors, broadcasters, and heads of professional journalism organizations formed the First Amendment Coalition to fight all judicial restraints, including gag orders, closed hearings, and secret sessions.

John V. R. Bull, one of the founders of the coalition who acted with the support of his newspaper, the Philadelphia *Inquirer*, wrote before the Stanford decision:

> It seems to me that our society—our unique experiment in self-government—is today facing a crisis of epic proportions. It is a crisis—brought on by understandable longings for privacy—that threatens to eat away at the very foundations of our open society. It is a crisis that has intensified in recent years, aided and abetted by the judicial system, and implemented with glee by all sorts of public and semipublic officials.

Edward Miller, executive editor of the Allentown (Pa.) *Call-Chronicle*, said of the position of courts and the press in Pennsylvania, "Open warfare is going on in many counties."

The Los Angeles *Times* editorially attacked "judicial tyranny in the courts" and charged them with "claiming the power of wide censorship over the American people, a censorship that strikes at the heart of democratic government."

Philip Kerby, the Los Angeles *Times*'s Pulitzer Prize-winning editorial writer, added this estimate of judicial irresponsibility: "Judges, like other human beings, find power delightful, and I have no doubt they would find absolute power absolutely delightful. But our system of government was intended to prevent any public official from experiencing the reality of that seductive pleasure."

Now and then, a favorable court decision would give heart to those who quite sincerely believed that the danger of eroding First Amendment rights was exaggerated. Such a ruling came from Chief Judge Irving R. Kaufman of the U. S. Court of Appeals for the 2nd Circuit, who held that journalists cannot be forced to disclose either the opinions or the thoughts they held when they were preparing a news story.

The decision, reached by a 2-1 vote of the three-judge appeals court, was in a libel suit by Anthony B. Herbert, a former Army officer, who contended he had been defamed in a 1973 CBS "60 Minutes" program that threw doubt on his charges that officers had covered up American troop atrocities during the Vietnam War. A lower court had ruled that Barry Lando, a CBS producer, would have to tell what he was thinking about when he prepared the program. Judge Kaufman wrote,

> Faced with the possibility of such an inquisition, reporters and journalists would be reluctant to express their doubts. Indeed, they would be chilled in the very process of thought. The tendency would be to follow the safe course of avoiding contention and controversy—the antithesis of values fostered by the First Amendment.
> We cannot permit inquiry into Lando's thoughts, opinions and conclusions. . . . [71]

While the Supreme Court considered the Herbert case, it came down on the side of the press when it ruled unanimously that newspapers cannot be criminally punished for publishing truthful information about secret government proceedings. The case involved the Norfolk Virginian Pilot, which was fined $500 in 1975 by a state court for publishing an accurate story that a local juvenile court judge was being investigated for disciplinary action. The Virginia Supreme Court upheld the conviction and the state law under which it had been obtained but the high court upset both the ruling and the law, declaring that judges' reputations could not be protected at the expense of free speech and a free press.

However, most judicial decisions at various levels were more severe in the First Amendment cases, provoking this comment from Judge Harold R. Medina of the U.S. Court of Appeals of the 2nd circuit:

> The muzzling of the press is the remedy which is all too readily available and which requires the least effort by a busy judge. . . . We all know the tieup between the political bosses and the selection of judges. . . . Does it require extended argument to demonstrate that these [judicial] gag orders, this muzzling of the press, may be used as a cover-up to prevent the detection of lax criminal enforcement or downright corruption?

The most scathing comment of all came from Reg Murphy, publisher of the San Francisco *Examiner*. When informed that the appeals court, on grounds of prejudicial publicity, had upset the conviction of a man who had kidnaped him while he was editor of the Atlanta *Constitution*, Murphy said, "I presume the judges would like the trial held on Guam or in the Bavarian Alps before a jury which speaks no English and knows no American customs."[72] The second trial, held in Key West, Fla., resulted once again in the defendant's conviction.

If the press had hoped for an outburst of public indignation over the apparent excesses of the judges who applied restraints against court coverage, it was disappointed. Indeed, the most sweeping prohibition to date was approved by the New York State Court of Appeals, the most prestigious high court in the land next to the Supreme Court itself. By a 4-2 vote, it barred the press from all pretrial hearings concerned with the admissibility of evidence unless the press could prove there was an "over-whelming public interest" in continued coverage.

The case involved the suppression of a transcript of a pretrial hearing. The hearing was for two alleged slayers of a Rochester, N. Y., policeman and it was held to determine whether evidence against them had been obtained illegally. The Gannett Company, publishers of the Rochester *Democrat & Chronicle* and the Rochester *Times-Union*, secured a ruling from the Appellate Division of the State Supreme Court that the trial judge had erred in refusing to permit coverage of the proceedings. The ruling also granted the papers access to the sealed records. Meanwhile, the two defendants had pleaded guilty to lesser charges.

Despite the guilty plea, the State's highest court, ruled on the case because the issue involved was of "concrete significance." The majority not only upheld the trial judge but broadened its decision to include all pretrial hearings in the State in these terms:

> To allow public disclosure of potentially tainted evidence, which the trial court has the constitutional obligation to exclude, is to involve the court itself in an illegality.
>
> This potential taint of its own process can neither be condoned nor countenanced. To avoid becoming a link in the chain of prejudicial disclosures, trial courts have the power to exclude the public from pretrial suppression hearings.
>
> At the point where press commentary in those hearings would threaten the impaneling of a constitutionally impartial jury in the county of venue, pretrial evidentiary hearings in this State are presumptively to be closed to the public.

The appeals judges then proceeded to place the burden for justifying coverage on the press itself and charged it with the responsibility for producing evidence of an "overwhelming public interest" in keeping the courts open. Judge Lawrence H. Cooke protested in his dissent:

> To allow closure on the mere showing that press commentary would "threaten" the impaneling of an impartial jury affords almost no protection to First Amendment rights, for the simple reason that in cases of notoriety it will always be possible to show some risk of prejudice. Of greater concern [is that] the burden of proof has been turned around. . . . This presumes that the press should be excluded and discourages the use of alternatives to closing the courtroom.

Within a short time in 1978, the Supreme Court itself sanctioned the validity of limiting news coverage in criminal trials. What the high court did was to reject press pleas against "gags" on coverage of criminal trials in Ohio and South Carolina. Thus, the lower courts were given the strongest kind of encouragement to continue to limit what the press could hear and report on in criminal trials.

In the South Carolina case, involving charges of conspiracy to defraud the United States against a state senator and two other persons, a Federal judge ordered all participants not to make prejudicial statements outside the court. A similar order was issued by an Ohio judge in the case of a defendant who had held 13 people hostage in a Cleveland office for nine hours.

The high court also refused to interfere with a Pennsylvania judge who closed pretrial proceedings in the second murder trial of the ex-president of the United Mine Workers, W. A. Boyle, and ordered all the records impounded. It merely sent the case back to the lower courts, which in effect gave the "gag order" judges the authority to do as they pleased.°

There was no doubt that the high court took a very dim view of the activities of the press, something that created a stir among the members of the Washington press corps. Jack C. Landau, director of the Reporters Committee for Freedom of the Press, protested that the Supreme Court had created "a chaotic situation where nobody really knows with any certainty what the law is." And the New York *Times*, commenting on the equally damaging position of the New York State Court of Appeals, said that the court had "undermined" what it called "a basic assumption about American justice—that it is public business and should be conducted in the open."

The widening breach in the application of the First Amendment, however, continued to leave the public unmoved. As a

---

°Boyle was again convicted of first degree murder on Feb. 18, 1978 at Media, Pa., in the 1969 assassination of his union rival, Joseph Yablonski.

result, the courts were further encouraged to invoke the ever-powerful contempt citation against individual reporters and editors in an effort to uncover the sources of articles displeasing to the bench. And this was the ultimate disgrace to any free society, for journalists went to jail rather than to submit to a violation of their rights. Had they complied with the demands of the bench, they would have destroyed their own credibility and rendered further investigative reporting impossible. And the courts, of course, were well aware of it.

Until the 1970s, there had been comparatively few punitive contempt citations against journalists. One of the earliest of modern cases involved Martin Mooney, a reporter for the New York *American*, who served a 30-day sentence for contempt of court in 1935 rather than disclose his sources in a gambling inquiry. Another widely publicized contempt sentence was given to Marie Torre, a columnist for the New York *Herald Tribune*, who refused to reveal her source in a controversy over the singer, Judy Garland, and went to jail for 10 days in 1957. There were a few cases involving journalists of less prominence, but the press on the whole wasn't particularly aroused.

In 1972, however, the Supreme Court took a decisive step with a landmark ruling on the issue of contempt as it affected the press. By a 5-4 vote, the high court decided in Branzburg v. Hayes that journalists could not claim the protection of the First Amendment if they refused to disclose confidential sources and confidential information to grand juries on demand. It was a sledge-hammer blow against confidentiality for journalists.

Those involved in the case were Paul M. Branzburg, then a reporter for the Louisville *Courier-Journal*, who had refused to tell the source of his information in a series about illegal drugs; Earl Caldwell, a New York *Times* reporter who balked at disclosing his source of information about the Black Panther Party; and Paul Pappas, a newsman for WTEV-TV, New Bedford, Mass., whose contempt citation also was based on secrecy regarding his Black Panther sources.

It was the position of the reporters, on appeal from their convictions in separate cases, that the government should not expect to use them as agents by applying pressure through the courts; to do so, they argued, would deprive the public of independent sources of disclosure and contravened the purposes of the First Amendment. But Justice Byron White, writing the majority opinion with the support of four justices whom President Nixon had appointed, declared: "The Constitution does not, as it never has, exempt the newsman from performing the citizen's normal duty of appearing and furnishing information relevant to a grand jury's task."

Justice Potter Stewart, in a minority opinion in which Justices William J. Brennan and Thurgood Marshall concurred, warned that the high court's decision was in effect an invitation to government "to undermine the historic independence of the press by attempting to annex the journalistic profession as an investigative arm of the government."

The dissent continued:

The full flow of information to the public protected by the free press guarantee would be severely curtailed if no protection whatever were afforded to the process by which news is assembled and disseminated. . . . Without freedom to acquire information, the right to publish would be impermissibly compromised.[73]

Despite the noble rhetoric of the minority, the damage had been done. The press now was thrown almost entirely on its own resources, which meant in the main its influences within its community, to protect its reporters. Just about the only judicial comfort it could find in the high court's decision was a suggestion by Justice Lewis Powell, who sided with the majority, that a grand jury should show "a legitimate need for law enforcement" before proceeding against a reporter or editor.

The net result was that more reporters were punished for contempt. Peter Bridge of the Newark (N. J.) *Evening News* went to jail for defying a grand jury's demand for his sources in a criminal case. Larry Dickinson and Gibbs Adams, two reporters for the Baton Rouge (La.) *Morning Advocate* and *States Times*, were convicted of criminal contempt and fined because they had defied a court order and published information obtained in open court proceedings; even though the order was subsequently held to be invalid, an appeals court ruled that the reporters should have obeyed the court order for as long as it was in effect.[74]

It was inevitable that some of these cases would be carried to the Supreme Court as news organizations sought relief from the oppressive features of Branzburg v. Hayes. And in 1976, two such cases did come before the high court. One involved William Farr, who had served 46 days in jail for contempt of court for refusing to reveal the source of an article he had written about the Charles Manson murder trial in the Los Angeles *Herald Examiner*. He was finally freed by Justice William O. Douglas of the U. S. Supreme Court but was involved in litigation for years thereafter. He is now on the Los Angeles *Times*. The other case involved four members of the staff of the Fresno *Bee* in California, who had refused to disclose the source of grand jury testimony the paper had published in connection with a bribery trial.

When the Supreme Court refused to hear the appeals of either Farr or the Fresno Four, it was apparent that Branzburg v. Hayes was to be the standard for some time to come by which the courts judged the conduct of journalists. Since Farr already had served in excess of the five days of his original sentence, the lower courts did nothing to revive the criminal case. But the Fresno Four went to jail for 15 days—Managing Editor George Gruner, Ombudsman James H. Bort, Jr., and Reporters William Patterson and Joe Resoto. Finally California Superior Court Judge Hollis Best released them because he was convinced they would never give in. The evidence, he said, showed there was "an articulated moral principle in the news media" against the disclosure of sources.

The Supreme Court, however, continued to rule against newsmen by refusing to hear such cases. Late in 1977, it turned aside a plea by James E. Shelledy of the Lewiston (Idaho) *Trib-*

une, who had been given a 30-day contempt sentence for refusing to disclose to a judge his source in a drug enforcement case. What Shelledy had done was to quote an unnamed source in criticism of the actions of a law enforcement officer, who had promptly sued for libel. The judge wanted the unnamed source, pointing out that the agent had a right to know who his accuser was. But Shelledy said he would rather go to jail than violate the journalists' unwritten code. While he was spared from prison for a time by technicalities, his case was not viewed with equanimity by some of his colleagues in Idaho. They did not think his position was very strong,[75] primarily because of the unnamed source in a libel case.

Worst of all, a New Jersey judge jailed New York *Times* reporter M. A. Farber and heavily fined his newspaper for refusing to yield confidential files in a murder case on July 24, 1978. Both rejected the court order and appealed. Farber's inquiries had helped bring Dr. Mario Jascalevich to trial in Hackensack, N.J., on a charge of killing five hospital patients with curare. It was further evidence that journalists would endure prison rather than deliver up their sources, and the good faith of their profession, to bench and bar.

It was not too long ago that journalists were telling each other that the libel laws of this country had virtually been suspended. This was, of course, journalistic hyperbole, one of the accursed weaknesses of the profession. For with rapid change in the character of the Supreme Court through death and retirement, libel once again became a weapon to be used against the press.

Now, the high court's relentless progression toward a tight set of libel laws indicates that the news media had better beware. One distinguished legal authority, Alan U. Schwartz, has gone so far as to warn of "the destruction of the press's necessary role as a critic of the judiciary." He has called the current era "a time of dark caution for the press, and therefore for the country."[76]

The liberalization of American libel law, which lulled journalists into a false sense of security, occurred in the latter days of the Warren Court. The key decision was the adoption of the New York *Times* Rule in 1964, when the Supreme Court under Chief Justice Earl Warren agreed that the First Amendment provided a defense for the press against libeling a public official.

The decision came on an appeal by the New York *Times* from an Alabama jury verdict that granted $500,000 damages for libel to L. B. Sullivan, commissioner of public affairs for Montgomery. Commissioner Sullivan argued that he had been injured by what he called unretracted falsehoods in an advertisement in the *Times*, sponsored by a civil rights group.

The high court ruled against Sullivan. It held that the press may criticize public officials and even commit errors of fact as long as it is not guilty of malice, which was defined as "to knowingly lie or recklessly disregard the truth." The majority decision said:

> The Constitutional guarantees require, we think, a Federal rule that prohibits a public official from recovering damages for a defamatory falsehood relating to his official conduct unless he proves that the statement was made with "actual malice"—this is, with knowledge that it was false or with reckless disregard of whether it was false or not.[77]

For the next seven years, the press fairly reveled in a whole series of favorable Supreme Court decisions on libel cases. Nothing quite as heartening as this had happened in a long time. So, as usual, the aura of self-congratulation at meetings of editors and publishers was almost suffocating in its effusiveness.

What happened in brief was that the high court extended the New York *Times* Rule about public officials to an even broader category called "public figures." This finally included "a private individual [involved] in an event of public or general concern." One could scarcely blame a happy editor for exclaiming, "We're libel-proof. Nobody can sue us now and hope to collect."

There is no optimist, alas, who is more foolhardy than the newsroom optimist—and more subject to self-delusion. In too many instances, editors misread a temporary advantage they had gained in the courts and concluded that the law, like the Ten Commandments, was graven in stone to exist for all time. They had forgotten that the law, like every other institution, is the creature of those who create it.

But lawyers and journalists trained in the law were not deluded. In an authoritative commentary, Professor E. Douglas Hamilton, a lawyer, and Robert H. Phelps, an editor, pointed out: "Since this liberal rule [the New York *Times* Rule] gives the press the power to destroy a man, it requires that newsmen exert a degree of responsibility that some have not risen to in the past."[78]

The warning, unfortunately, was not heeded during the brief and shining moment of this journalistic Camelot. Those deemed to be "public officials" or "public figures" lost several appeals on the basis of the New York *Times* Rule.

The high point of the relaxed libel law came in 1971 in Rosenbloom v. Metromedia. A nudist magazine distributor had won a $750,000 judgment against Metromedia radio station WIP in a libel case. But when Metromedia appealed to the Supreme Court, the judgment was reversed because the nudist magazine distributor was held to be a "public fugure," defined by the court as "a private individual [involved] in an event of public or general concern." Therefore, he was required by law to show malice—a reckless disregard of the truth—and he could not do so. The high court held: "A Constitutional rule that deters the press from covering the ideas or activities of the private individual thus conceives the individual's interest too narrowly."

It was the last victory for the stalwarts of the Warren Court, which had lately come under the sway of the more conservative Chief Justice Warren E. Burger. Only three years later, the character of the court had changed to such an extent with President Nixon's new appointments that a decided reaction set in. In Gertz v. Robert Welch, Inc., the high court upheld a libel judgment for a private individual without proof of actual malice. It declared that private persons involved in public affairs were required to

prove only some degree of "fault"—which could mean negligence—by the defendant journalist or his organization.

Justice William J. Brennan, in dissenting, wrote, "Adoption. . .of a reasonable care standard in cases where private individuals are involved in matters of public interest. . .will. . .lead to
self-censorship since publishers will be required carefully to
weigh a myriad of uncertain factors before pubication." The
American Newspaper Publishers Association seemed to concur,
for it issued a warning that journalists "no longer have the protection of the New York *Times* Rule when libel is alleged by a
private individual, involved in matters of public interest, who
seeks to recover actual provable damages."

The benediction was pronounced by one of the concurring
justices, Harry A. Blackmun, who concluded that the development of the defamation law "has to come to rest."[79] If only it had
been true! But unfortunately for the press, there was still worse to
come.

In Time Inc. v. Mary Alice Firestone in 1976, the Supreme
Court knocked down most previously held notions of who may be
considered a "public fugure." As a result, the field of those who
may sue for libel with some hope of collecting damages appeared
to have been considerably broadened. For, under the Firestone
judgment, all a plaintiff now had to do was to show that the news
organization was guilty of "fault" instead of actual malice.
Thereby, journalists were rendered liable for errors of fact if they
were found to be damaging in such cases.

The high court was severe in applying this new standard in
the Firestone case. It had originated when *Time* magazine reported, in its Milestones section, that socially prominent Mary
Alice Firestone had been divorced on grounds of "extreme cruelty and adultery." However, it developed that she had been
found guilty only of "extreme cruelty." In consequence, when
she sued Time, Inc., a Palm Beach jury awarded her $100,000 in
damages for libel.

The magazine then argued before the Supreme Court, on

appeal, that Mrs. Firestone was a public fugure within the meaning of libel law because she was widely known, had had several
press conferences during her divorce trial and had subscribed to a
publicity clipping bureau. The high court demurred. It declared
Mrs. Firestone not to be a public figure who had to prove actual
malice and sent the case back to the lower court for a determination of "fault" by the magazine.[80]

At best, as a survey of lower court decisions concluded after
the Gertz and Firestone decisions, this was confusion twice confounded. Application of the Gertz criterion for "public figures" in
libel cases was found more likely to be "unsettling and inconclusive than settling and definitive." As for Firestone, the survey
declared, "In no post-Gertz case is application of the new fault
standard more confusing than in litigation involving the divorce of
Mary Alice Firestone."[81]

There were some who took a much graver view. Alan U.
Schwartz, for example, wrote:

> The issues in the Firestone case are crucial to the survival of the
> free press in this country. . . . If the Supreme Court cannot agree in any
> consistent fashion as to who is a public figure, journalists who attempt to
> make use of this "qualified privilege" to comment (short of actual mal-
> ice) on behavior, do so at their peril. . . . If those reporting on judicial
> proceedings are held to a standard which requires a knowledge of legal
> niceties and judicial obscurantism which even most lawyers don't have,
> such proceedings will be reported only reluctantly—and sketchily—by
> newsmen, and in many cases articles of great importance will have to be
> read by batteries of lawyers before they are allowed to reach the public
> eye.[82]

There will be many who will say, "Well, what difference
does it make? If a newspaper can't get its facts straight, and somebody is hurt, it ought to pay. And the same is even more true of
radio and television because of their wider national audience."
This is the attitude that has led to the bedevilment of the British
press. It not only is strapped in a straitjacket of libel law, but also
is plagued increasingly by libel suits from every imaginable quarter. And the courts in Britain, most of them notoriously unsympa-

thetic to the press, do not hesitate to award severe judgments. The result is an inhibited press that cannot, except in rare instances, fulfill its responsibilities as a watchdog against wrongdoing by either governmental or private institutions.

We are not yet threatened with such an untenable position for our own press, but we are headed in that direction. Where courts try to strip journalists of protection for their confidential sources and hold them to an unreasonable standard in their examination of conduct of public officials and public figures, there is no doubt that the freedom of the press in effect is compromised.

The Supreme Court wisely held in New York *Times* v. Sullivan:

> A rule compelling the critic of official conduct to guarantee the truth of all his factual assertions. . .leads to. . .self-censorship. . .[W]ould-be critics of official conduct may be deterred from voicing their criticism, even though it is believed to be true and even though it is in fact true, because of doubt whether it can be proved in court or fear of the expense of having to do so.[83]

The chief critic of the high court in this case, a rather symbolic critic as matters turned out, was President Nixon, who declared in a nationwide broadcast:

> Some libel lawyers have interpreted recent Supreme Court decisions, particularly the outcome of Sullivan v. New York *Times*, as being virtually a license to lie where a political candidate, a member of his family, or one of his supporters or friends is involved. This is wrong. It is necessary that a change be made.[84]

Counter to this was an opinion by an eminent legal authority, Professor Harry Kalven Jr., who wrote that the New York *Times* case "may prove to be the best and most important it [the Supreme Court] has ever produced in the realm of freedom of speech."[85]

The court, however, has altered course today and the press has reason to heed the storm warnings that have been hoisted in the Gertz and Firestone cases. Libel law, after all, has now become what the judges say it is and the accumulated evidence indicates that the judges aren't sure themselves where they will come out from one case to the next. It is not a situation from which any responsible journalist can derive much comfort.

For those who are looking for additional weapons to use against the press, the development of the privacy law in the United States has become a potent item in an already formidable armory. On the basis of his extensive experience in First Amendment cases, Floyd Abrams, the New York lawyer, calls it "the single most ominous threat to the First Amendment's guarantee of press freedom." This was his reasoning:

> One threat involves the possible substitution of an official governmental view—of legislators or judges—for the judgment of editors as to what is "newsworthy." Another is that the more privacy cases are decided against the press, the more the press will be inhibited in gathering the news; as a consequence, much important news-gathering may become all but impossible.[86]

Abrams cites the case of two *Life* magazine reporters who on Sept. 20, 1963, entered the home of a disabled war veteran, A. A. Dietemann, in search of evidence that he was practicing medicine without a license. While one reporter pretended to be a patient, the other took pictures of Dietemann's office without his knowledge or permission. Subsequently, on the basis of evidence the reporters produced, Dietemann was arrested on the charge of practicing medicine without a license and pleaded no contest. But, on the basis of an article *Life* magazine ran about the case entitled, "Crackdown on Quackery," he sued for invasion of privacy and won a $1,000 verdict for injury to his "feelings and peace of mind" in 1971.

In upholding the verdict, the United States Court of Appeals ruled that he could "reasonably expect to exclude eavesdropping newsmen" from his office. The Appeals Court added sharply: "The First Amendment has never been construed to accord newsmen immunity from torts (civil wrongs) or crimes committed during the course of news-gathering."[87]

Thus, the invasion of privacy becomes decidedly risky for the news media. But far more serious consequences also may be in store for news organizations. The United States Supreme Court already has signaled that it could reject truth—an absolute defense under libel law—as a defense in case of privacy. In a Georgia case, the high court agreed that the press could publish "true information. . .in court documents open to public inspection" but it reserved the right to decide at a later time "the broader question whether truthful publications may ever be subjected to criminal liability."[88] If that happens, the press will be in a bad way in the United States.

The Supreme Court indicated its concern with truth as a defense in privacy litigation on the basis of a tragic case that was decided in 1975. A 17-year-old Georgia girl had died after being raped by six teen-age boys; and an Atlanta television station, owned by the Cox Broadcasting Corporation, had identified her by name in a newscast. The girl's father sued under a Georgia law making it a misdemeanor to identify a rape victim. He contended that the family's privacy had been disrupted, causing the Georgia courts to return a verdict in his favor.

Even though the Supreme Court overturned the judgment on the ground that the Georgia law was unconstitutional, the decision set no precedent in the use of truth as a defense. In fact, the high court cautioned that its judgment was confined to the narrow issue "between press and privacy" rather than the actual use of truth as a defense in privacy cases. The result was that Georgia broadcasters and editors have been extremely cautious ever since about identifying rape victims because there is no certainty how long truth will continue to be a proper defense in privacy cases.[89] Journalists, quite rightly, have therefore become increasingly apprehensive over the manner in which the law of privacy may be applied against them.

There are now 47 states that have laws permitting persons to sue for invasion of privacy. Only Nebraska, Rhode Island, and Wisconsin have no such statutes. Considering that the principles of the privacy law were first set down in 1890, this marks perhaps the fastest and most dangerous accumulation of laws involving the press in American history. The authors were Louis D. Brandeis, who later became celebrated as an Associate Justice of the Supreme Court, and a wealthy coworker, Samuel D. Warren of Boston, who had become angered by the depredations of what was then called the "yellow press." In the *Harvard Law Review*, they set down this basic right for the first time:

> The principle which protects personal writings and other productions of the intellect or of the emotions is the right of privacy and the law has no new principle to formulate when it extends this protection to personal appearances, sayings, acts and to personal relations, domestic and otherwise.

What Brandeis and Warren sought was the sanction of the courts to permit individuals to recover damages from publications that overstepped the bounds of "propriety and decency" and served only "idle or prurient curiosity" instead of the public interest. They were particularly critical of gossip that injured individuals. And they advocated the adoption of criminal statutes to provide adequate punishment for invasion of privacy.

Nothing in particular happened to gratify the wishes of the authors for well-nigh a generation. Almost forty years later, as a member of the nation's highest court, Brandeis still was sufficiently interested in the subject to define the right of privacy as "the right to be let alone." This is his phrasing:

> The makers of our Constitution undertook to secure conditions favorable to the pursuit of happiness. They recognized the significance of man's spiritual nature, of his feeling and of his intellect. . . . They sought to protect Americans in their beliefs, their thoughts, their emotions and their sensations. They conferred, as against the Government, the right to be let alone—the most comprehensive of rights and the right most valued by civilized men.

Most privacy cases, however, were not handled by so elevated a standard of law and human conduct for almost another forty years. Instead, the courts did little to differentiate privacy

cases from the ordinary run of libel cases until the appeal in
Time, Inc. v. Hill in 1967. The distinction that had often been
applied by judges to claims of invasion of privacy was whether
the matter involved was "newsworthy." Usually, if the test of
"newsworthiness" was met, there were no grounds for a finding
of invasion of privacy; however, if it was not met and if people of
ordinary sensibilities could take offense over the matter, the privacy action was generally upheld. The trouble with this thesis was
that most judges had a different idea of what was "newsworthy."And so did juries.[90]

In Time, Inc. v. Hill, Richard M. Nixon represented a family
that sued *Life* magazine alleging invasion of privacy. The action
alleged that members of the family had been identified as those
who had been held captive in 1952 by three escaped convicts.
The family—Mr. and Mrs. James Hill, their son and daughter—
had indeed been hostages to convicts for 19 hours but they had
not been harmed. However, a novel and play called *The Desperate Hours* later dealt with the incident in fictionalized form without mentioning the Hills and put the fictitious family through all
manner of tortures. When *Life* magazine directly identified the
Hill family and their experience as the basis for the play, Hill sued
under the privacy statute. He charged that his wife had become
emotionally ill over the *Life* article and that it also was false
because it attributed fictional experiences to his family. A lower
court jury awarded the family $30,000, but the Supreme Court
reversed the judgment.

The basis was the application of the New York *Times* Rule to
privacy cases—that the Hills had not been able to prove actual
malice on the part of *Life* magazine, meaning a knowing lie or a
reckless disregard of whether the matter was true or not. But
beyond that, the high court arrived at what at least six of the
justices considered an adequate use of the term "newsworthiness" in judging privacy cases. This, in substance, was the reasoning of the majority decision:

—The First Amendment barred privacy judgments in the

cases of truthful accounts of "newsworthy" persons and events.

—Privacy actions could be upheld in cases that were not newsworthy if they involved disclosures "so intimate and unwarranted. . .as to outrage the community's notion of decency."

—Only if actual malice was shown could there be a judgment in a privacy case for the plaintiff if the publication or broadcast was "newsworthy" but not true.

When this formula was applied in 1974 to a widow's suit against the Cleveland *Plain Dealer* on the ground that she had been the victim of "calculated falsehoods," a $60,000 judgment for invasion of privacy was upheld by the Supreme Court. The plaintiff, Margaret Mae Cantrell, widow of a man who died in a West Virginia bridge collapse, complained that she had never been interviewed by the paper, that a reporter for the paper had visited her home in her absence and interviewed her children, and then written an article that depicted them as living in abject poverty. Moreover, Mrs. Cantrell pointed out, the article created the impression that she had seen the reporter because it said she "will talk neither about what happened nor about how they were doing" and "wears the same mask of nonexpression she wore at the funeral."

Accordingly, the Supreme Court decided that Mrs. Cantrell had been the victim of "significant misrepresentations," "calculated falsehoods," and had been portrayed "in false light through knowing or reckless untruth." Thus, a private citizen was upheld in a privacy suit because she was depicted in a "false light."

The New York *Times* commented, "The decision appeared likely to create new pressure for caution on the part of publishers in printing accounts of the personal circumstances of private citizens and to make suits on invasion of privacy a more serious threat to the press."[91]

The threat is bound to be intensified with the further development of the privacy law and any additional limitations on the use of the New York *Times* Rule. In the seven years between Time, Inc. v. Hill and the Cantrell case, the Supreme Court

moved to hold the press to an increasingly strict standard of conduct. It may be argued that the error in the former case was not
as serious as the error in the latter, but the fact is that the court
overlooked one mistake but not the other. Thus, the high court
went into the business of making editorial judgments in privacy
cases and, in logical progression, warned in the 1975 Cox Broadcasting case that it might in the end even reject the truth itself as
a defense.

This uncertainty puts the press in an impossible position. One
may say to editors, "Be sure your reporters do not make mistakes
of fact—at least, not serious mistakes." But what good is that if
there is no certainty that a completely accurate report may not be
held to have violated someone's privacy? If the state of libel law
is confused, that of the privacy law is chaotic, and there seems to
be little likelihood of early clarification.

In the judicial arena, no less than in the executive and legislative branches of the Federal government, the press is on trial. Nor
is the situation remarkably different in the several States. Regardless of the purity of the motives of bench and bar, the result is to
tighten the enforcement of the Sixth Amendment at the expense
of the First and to place the press at a disadvantage in the administration of applicable laws. How perfectly outrageous it is for the
courts to hold the press responsible for observing court orders
until they are found to be illegal by the courts themselves, as in
the Dickinson case! Any common gambler may break the law, but
will pay no penalty if the law is found to be unconstitutional.
Why should journalists be treated differently? Yet, not only the
judiciary but also Congress itself—in its contemplated recodifica-
tion of the Federal criminal code—seeks to impose a most peculiar and prejudicial double standard on the press.

It will not do; otherwise the First Amendment will mean
nothing more than mere words on paper in the manner of the
Soviet Constitution's pious and illusory declarations of freedom.
In any prolonged contest between the courts and the press, the

courts are bound to have the advantage. The judge on the bench has demonstrated that he can—and often will—gag, fine, and jail journalists who offend him and hand down wildly conflicting opinions concerning some of the laws that affect the press. To oppose this formidable power, the editor has only his pen and an often indifferent public opinion.

By any standard, it is an unequal match. And if the government's tightening grip on television is any foretaste of the future—a circumstance that will be discussed in the final section of this book—then the press's difficulties will inevitably be intensified.

In the Nebraska gag order case, the Supreme Court declared:

> The authors of the Bill of Rights did not undertake to assign priorities between the First Amendment and Sixth Amendment rights ranking one superior to the other. In this case, the petitioners would have us declare the right of an accused subordinate to their right to publish under all circumstances. But if the authors of these guarantees, fully aware of the potential conflicts between them, were unwilling or unable to resolve the issue by assigning to one priority over the other, it is not for us to rewrite the Constitution by undertaking what they declined.[92]

The burden of proof of these minimal good intentions rests with the courts.

FOUR

THE DECLINE OF FREEDOM

1. Television and Federal Regulation

ON A QUIET November evening in 1977, Walter Cronkite temporarily leveled the barriers between Egypt and Israel in the 30-year Middle East war. Switching quickly from Cairo to Jerusalem on the CBS Evening News with prerecorded material, he obtained the interviews that clinched a historic agreement by Egyptian President Anwar el Sadat for a peace mission to Israel and his reception by Israeli Prime Minister Menachem Begin. Luck and the miracle of television made it possible.

On Sunday, Nov. 20, 1977, the seemingly impossible dream was realized. The Egyptian president pledged no more war before the Israeli Knesset, its parliament, and recognized Israel's right to exist within secure borders. The Israeli government applauded him. That night, as his reward, Cronkite interviewed Messrs. Sadat and Begin, who sat together for CBS News cameras. One wonders what President Carter and Leonid Brezhnev thought of the *chutzpah* of their journalistic competitor.

True, the great event could have happened eventually without Cronkite's benign guidance. It had evidently been in Sadat's mind for a long time. True, also, one of Cronkite's TV competitors might have beaten him to the American TV audience with the coup, for all were trying to do it. But the fact is that he *did* it and thereby demonstrated once again the power of television as a medium of communication.

Scant wonder, then, that all governments—including the gov-

223

ernment of the United States—make the use and regulation of television their first priority in communicating with their people. Yet, despite all the fine words of the past few administrations in Washington, the available evidence indicates that television has suffered more than any other medium of communication from a decline of freedom in this country. Under law, through political pressure, and by acquiescence, television news has let its independence decline. Its appeals to be placed on the same footing as the press under the First Amendment have been brushed aside by the courts, and it has been obliged to fight its battles almost alone.

The broadcast media, of course, knew from the very beginning that they would receive special scrutiny because they use a public facility, the airwaves, the ether, or whatever name the courts at the moment prefer. Moreover, the number of channels available for use by the broadcast media has, until recently, been severely limited. Thus, government licensing applies to them but not to the print media. As Justice Byron White wrote for the Supreme Court majority in the *Red Lion* case decision, "It is idle to posit an unbridgeable First Amendment right to broadcast comparable to the right of every individual to speak, write, and publish. . . . No one has a First Amendment right to a license or to monopolize a radio frequency."[1]

However, the doctrine of scarcity has since been weakened by the development of cablevision. As a result, in 1978, the Supreme Court did not even refer to the scarcity theory as a basis for government TV regulation in the case of the "seven dirty words." Instead, in upholding the right of the FCC to reprimand station WBAI-FM in New York City for broadcasting words that are "patently offensive," the high court ruled 5-4 that government regulation of broadcasting rested on its "uniquely pervasive presence in the lives of all Americans." If that doctrine is expanded, it could mean much more trouble for freedom of expression on the air.

Indeed, such reasoning might well apply to some actions

through which efforts are being made to regulate the press. Advocates of such measures are using the courts and Congress and appealing both to the regulatory agencies and executive authority. They argue for a "right of access" to the press similar to that which binds the broadcast media. They also seek to invoke antitrust action from time to time. And occasionally, someone will go to the length of speculating that the press should be treated like a public utility and regulated accordingly. No matter how far-fetched some of these assumptions may be, they must be taken seriously. One cannot assume that the government will back away forever from a confrontation with a powerful and well-entrenched press.

The broadcast media are powerful, too. Television and radio between them gross over $10 billion annually in advertising revenues and they blanket 99 percent of American homes, plus 60 million automobiles and 11 million public places. There are about 1,000 television stations transmitting to nearly 100 million sets, 70 percent in color. And radio's 8,000 transmitters service 425 million receivers. Cable TV, born only recently, has 12 million subscribers and expects that to double soon.[2]

There are more than 600 powerful and wealthy advertisers in this country who do battle with each other for the precious TV network prime time, which now goes for $120,000 a minute at choicest viewing hours and soared to $288,000 a minute for the professional football Superbowl of 1978.

News programs, far from being a drag on TV, have become big earners in local markets and the networks are doing well enough at exploiting the news to sink in excess of $200 million a year into their combined news budgets. The *Wall Street Journal* has estimated that as much as 60 percent of an individual station's profits could be derived from a highly rated local news program. "In a traditionally high cash-flow business, broadcasters' cups are running over," *Broadcasting* magazine reported.

As for the ailing Public Broadcasting System, President Carter has announced that he favors a federal government subsidy of almost $1 billion for the group by 1982, but there is considerable doubt that he will get it.

Group ownership is dominant in American commercial television, although, with the exception of the three major networks, the broadcast chains are not as large as those of the press. The FCC's rules limit the three major networks to five owned and operated TV stations each, but permit smaller groups to own up to seven TV stations. After the three networks' stations, the largest TV groups judged by net weekly audiences include Metromedia, RKO-General, Westinghouse, WGN (Chicago), Continental, Kaiser, Capital Cities, and Storer. Such newspaper chains as Post-Newsweek, Scripps-Howard, Hearst, Newhouse, and Cox are also important in the broadcast industry.

This structure, however, is scarcely as solid as the newspaper chains. For within the forseeable future, commercial television is likely to find that its monopoly on viewing in the American home has been gravely weakened. Already, there has been a 3 to 5 percent decline for prime time evening viewing, and somewhere between 6 and 11 percent for daytime viewing. This is likely to increase for these reasons:

1. Cablevision now reaches 12 million American homes, a 17 percent penetration of the television audience, and a Young & Rubicam survey indicates that this proportion could go as high as 30 percent by 1981. In addition, pay TV (or Home Box Office TV) now has more than a million subscribers and expects to boost that total to 5 million within a few years.

2. The cassette industry, which enables viewers to record programs in their absence and build up a TV library, is showing increasing signs of growth. At least a million units may be in use by 1981, and there may be more if the price comes down from its current range of more than $1,000 per unit. For every cassette that is sold, commercial TV must count the partial loss of a family's viewing.

3. The tube is now being used for video games—electronic devices that turn the TV screen into a playing field for everything

from football and baseball to tic-tac-toe. Naturally, if the screen is being used for games, it will not be showing "Laverne and Shirley" or "Happy Days."[3]

It is difficult to determine what this will mean for TV news, with its network audience of anywhere from 30 to 45 million or more viewers. Despite the inroads of goverment bodies, the broadcasters do maintain substantial editorial controls over their news operations, which will soon go above $200 million a year. However, as long as the government controls licenses, its influence is bound to be felt in many ways. Broadcasters, often more oriented to entertainment than news at top management level, aren't likely to endanger annual profits of 15 to 20 percent by being too defiant of the government.

While ratings influence much television programming, broadcasters are well aware that the government, too, is looking over their shoulders. And although the Federal Communications Commission has often been criticized for being too lenient with the broadcast industry, its powers are very real and potentially damaging. Broadcasters are never allowed to forget that the United States is the only major world power that does not have its own broadcasting facilities and permits private ownership and private profit in the field. Some day, that could change.

Government licensing of radio was established under the Federal Radio Act of 1927 and spelled out in the Federal Communications Act of 1934, still the basis for broadcast regulation. Through the FCC, the 1934 law authorized the granting of three-year renewable broadcast licenses to serve the "public interest, convenience or necessity." Accordingly, the FCC adopted what became known as the "Fairness Doctrine" to obligate broadcasters to give fair coverage to public issues and reflect opposing views. In addition, Section 315 made provision for political candidates to receive equal time on the air. The "Fairness Doctrine" became law in 1959, when Congress amended Section 315 to provide that broadcasters would "operate in the public interest

and. . .afford reasonable opportunity for the discussion of conflicting views on issues of public importance."[4]

The controls adopted by the government sought to regulate
the character of broadcasting ownership to insure independence
and diversity, maintain variety and relevance in programming,
and provide access to broadcast facilities under the equal time
rule and "Fairness Doctrine." In response to challenges that these
regulations violated the First Amendment, the Supreme Court in
1943 upheld the FCC's position, with Justice Felix Frankfurter
concluding the majority decision as follows:

> The licensing system established by Congress in the Communica-
> tions Act of 1934 was a proper exercise of its power over commerce.
> The standard it provided for the licensing of stations was the "public
> interest, convenience, and necessity." Denial of a station license on that
> ground, if valid under the Act, is not a denial of free speech.[5]

The Supreme Court in effect also underlined the FCC's basic
concept of the broadcaster as a "public trustee," the broadcast
license as a trust, and the public as the beneficiary. For more than
25 years thereafter, the FCC proceeded to elaborate on the fairness obligations of broadcasters in a series of rulings that culmi-
nated in the Red Lion case.

The issue was posed in 1964 when a free-lance writer, Fred J.
Cook, charged he had been unfairly attacked over a small radio
station owned by the Red Lion Broadcasting Company. He demanded the right to reply under the "Fairness Doctrine." When
the Red Lion station asked Cook to pay $7 for reply time, he took
the case to the FCC, which promptly ordered the station to permit the writer to go on the air with his response.

It soon developed that this was no ordinary case and Cook
was no ordinary complainant. He had written an article in the
Nation called "Hate Clubs of the Air," in which he attacked a
fundamentalist preacher, Billy James Hargis. Cook had also written a book that was critical of Senator Barry Goldwater, the Republican Presidential nominee in 1964. Hargis, who conducted

his "Christian Crusade" over the Red Lion station, struck back at Cook.

When the lower courts sustained the FCC order, and the Red Lion station still held out against Cook, the case finally reached the Supreme Court in 1969. The legality of the "Fairness Doctrine" was at stake. Equally important, it was the first time since 1943 that the high court had been enabled to rule on the FCC regulations for broadcasters in general.

The outcome was a triumph for the FCC and government regulation of the broadcast media, as well as vindication for Cook. With Justice White writing the decision, the high court's majority ruled as follows:

> A license permits broadcasting, but the licensee has no constitutional right to be the one who holds the license or to monopolize a radio frequency to the exclusion of his fellow citizens.
>
> There is nothing in the First Amendment which prevents this government from requiring a licensee to share his frequency with others and to conduct himself as a proxy or fiduciary with obligations to present those views and voices which are representative of his community and which would otherwise, by necessity, be barred from the airwaves.
>
> This is not to say that the First Amendment is irrelevant to public broadcasting. . . . But the people as a whole retain their interest in free speech by radio and their collective right to have the medium function consistently with the ends and purposes of the First Amendment. It is the right of the viewers and listeners, not the right of the broadcasters, which is paramount. . . . It is the purpose of the First Amendment to preserve an uninhibited marketplace of ideas in which truth will ultimately prevail, rather than to countenance a monopolization of that market, whether it be by the government itself or a private licensee.[6]

Nothing quite so sweeping had been anticipated by the broadcast industry, which was shocked by the severity of the court's decision. The FCC's rules for replies to personal attacks and editorializing on the air were upheld as an intrinsic part of the "Fairness Doctrine." Henceforth, except for the exigencies of Presidential debates and other extraordinary circumstances, the broadcast media were tightly held in a regulatory vise of the government's making. In many cases involving personal attacks or

political opposition to declared candidates, broadcasters not only
were obligated to provide copies of what was said to those directly involved but also had to offer them time to reply. In effect,
editorial judgment was suspended in such cases and the government's rules had to be followed.

Justice White also concluded for the court majority that the
broadcasters should not be given the same rights as the press
under the First Amendment, saying: "Nothing in this record, or in
our own researches, convinces us that the resource [radio-TV] is
no longer one for which there are more immediate and potential
uses than can be accommodated and for which wise planning is
essential."[7]

Soon the broadcast industry was obliged to accept coun-
tercommercials—advertisements that criticized other advertisements. For example, the antismoking commercials survived even
after cigarette advertising was barred from the air. And in an
excess of enthusiasm, the Federal Trade Commission requested
the FCC to oblige broadcast media to offer time to consumer
groups and others to oppose commercial advertisements not involving public issues. The FCC rejected the proposal.

Such a failure was far from discouraging to the various public
interest groups that had begun to use the authority of the government to regulate the broadcast industry and break up concentra-
tions of media power through press-broadcast cross-ownerships.
Through actions before the courts and the FCC, literally hundreds of challenges to license renewals and cross-ownerships
were filed. It was the beginning of a disturbing new era in govern-
ment-media relationships.

The basis for public intervention in license renewal cases was
laid in 1966 in a ruling involving WLBT-TV of Jackson, Miss.
Two years before, civil rights leaders and the United Church of
Christ had asked the FCC not to renew the station's license,
charging its programming discriminated against black citizens.

When the FCC tossed the case aside, the plaintiffs went to the Court of Appeals of the District of Columbia.

There, they had better luck. Warren E. Burger, later the Chief Justice of the United States, ruled that responsible citizens had a perfect right to challenge license renewals and ordered the FCC to hold hearings on the WLBT-TV case. He wrote: "We can see no reason to exclude those with such an obvious and acute concern as the listening audience."[8]

That opened the door to wholesale challenges of license renewals by almost any group that had a grievance against the broadcast media. If the FCC was sparing in its rejection of such renewals, that did not remove complications for the industry nor reduce the expense of defending such actions. In addition, now and then, there was a suspicion of taint in some of these public interest cases, as witness the challenges to the two Washington *Post* stations in Florida at the time the paper was digging into the Watergate scandal.

Newspapers that owned television stations soon were drawn deeper into the network of government regulation, for in 1970 the FCC opened a major inquiry into cross-ownership of broadcast facilities and newspapers in the same community. The question the government asked was whether such cross-ownerships were in the public interest.

After five years of study and the accumulation of massive documentation, the FCC came up with an answer. It was no. However, one major exception was granted in the ruling filed in January 1975, which promptly became known as the "grandfather clause." It enabled most of the existing cross-ownerships within news media to continue—a boon to the approximately 160 news organizations affected.[*]

---

[*]This affected newspaper-television cross-ownerships in about 50 cities and newspaper-radio ties in more than 120. Of 7,000 American radio stations, the newspapers—chains or individual—own about 300. Of 728 commercial TV stations, newspapers own about 100.

If there was jubilation over this fortuitous circumstance, it was quickly muted. For a formidable challenge was mounted almost immediately before the U. S. Court of Appeals for the District of Columbia. Technically, the plaintiff was a public interest organization called the National Citizens Committee for Broadcasting. But the real challenger was a small public interest legal group known as the Citizens Communications Center, of Washington, D. C., which represented the Citizens Committee.

The principal business of the Citizens Communication Center, supported in part by grants from the Ford Foundation and other philanthropic enterprises, had been to campaign for reform in broadcasting, and its eight-year history had been studded with success. But no case it had handled (it never boasted of more than five lawyers at any one time) approached the divestiture challenge in importance.

What Citizens did, in effect, was to ask the court to kill the FCC's "grandfather clause" and break up existing press-broadcast combines as well as to bar new ones. On March 1, 1977, this is exactly what the Court of Appeals decided to do. It held that "nothing can be more important than insuring that there is a free flow of information from as many divergent sources as possible."

The only exception granted in the decision was for cases where evidence clearly disclosed that "cross-ownership is in the public interest." As for the charge that cross-ownership harms a community, the decision said merely, "After years of study, the record was essentially inconclusive."

The Supreme Court in 1978 settled the matter by barring newspapers henceforth from acquiring radio or television stations in their own communities. However, the high court permitted existing cross-ownerships to continue except in 16 smaller cities where the only newspaper in town also owns the only broadcast property. Both decisions were taken by unanimous vote. Once again, the court refused to permit broadcasters to be covered by the same First Amendment rights as those given to newspapers.[9]

As a practical matter, divestiture was therefore limited to Albany, Ga.; Anniston, Ala.; Arkansas City, Kansas; Bluefield, W. Va.; Dubois, Pa.; Effingham, Ill.; Findlay, O.; Hope, Ark.; Janesville, Wis.; Macomb, Ill.; Meridian, Miss.; Norfolk, Neb.; Owosso, Mich.; Mason City, Iowa; Texarkana, Texas; and Watertown, N.Y. The high court in effect let most current beneficiaries keep the "grandfather clause."

One of them, the Quincy (Ill.) *Herald-Whig*, an evening paper with a TV station and two radio stations in the same city, took a philosophical attitude toward the matter. In reviewing its 30-year efforts in a city of 45,000, it reported:

> We have provided to the area AM radio, FM radio, and televison at a financial sacrifice during the 12 years that it took us to finally achieve a break-even position. We were responsible in a great measure for bringing cablevision to Quincy, which provided six additional cablevision signals in competition with our own.
>
> We have funneled substantial sums of money back into the community which would not have been possible if it had not been for our multiple operation. . . . Our company has also steadfastly contributed 5 percent of its gross before taxes, the maximum allowable, for charitable and philanthropic purposes.
>
> Perhaps the best and most important contribution that we have made to the public interest through our cross-ownership, however, has been our ability to provide the necessary investment, equipment, and people to print what we feel is a superior newspaper and operate superior broadcasting stations in a community where the economic viability of the market did not completely justify it, especially at the outset.

As for increasing the diversity of voices in Quincy through divestiture, the *Herald-Whig* pointed out that a UHF channel allocated to Quincy had never been used although it could have been made available to the ABC-TV network.[10]

Since most television stations are more profitable than newspapers, press-broadcast combinations are vital in some instances to the survival of newspapers. This may not necessarily be so in Quincy, a well-managed small news organization with interests outside its own community. But it was fatal to the Boston *Herald-Traveler*, which had to suspend publication in 1972 when the

FCC took away its license to operate WHDH-TV in Boston and assigned it to a rival applicant.

Even before the Supreme Court's decision barring future cross-ownerships, it was clear that the crusading public interest groups were winning out. Mainly as a result of their pressure, the share of TV channels controlled by newspapers dropped from 40 percent in 1950 to 14 percent in 1969 and 10 percent in 1975.

There have been other side-effects. Joe L. Allbritton, the Texas millionaire who bought the Washington *Star* in 1974 and sold it four years later to Time, Inc., stepped down as the *Star's* publisher because he said his ownership of WJLA, the ABC-TV outlet in Washington, was in conflict with FCC rules. Moreover, he canceled his proposed swap of that station for KOCO-TV in Oklahoma City and $55 million. Thus, he remained in broadcasting, got out of the newspaper business, and also solved a personnel problem for Time, Inc.

There is one other major consequence of the emergence of public interest groups as a factor in the application of government regulation of the media. Through threats and pressure, they are obliging at least a part of the broadcast media to comply with their demands where license renewals are at stake and stations are vulnerable. For example, once the FCC had denied a license renewal application to WLBT in Jackson, Miss., after that station had been accused of discriminating against blacks, stations in Atlanta and Texarkana, Texas, promptly acceded to demands made by civil rights groups. These ranged from the employment of two black reporters by KTAL-TV in Texarkana, to broader service to minorities by 28 stations in Atlanta.

In Lancaster, Pa., under pressure from the Citizens Communication Center and a women's group, Feminists for Media Rights, the owners of the Lancaster *Intelligencer-Journal* and *New Era* sold their radio stations, WGAL-AM and FM. Soon afterward, they carried out a pledge to sell WGAL-TV in Lancaster. The purchaser was the Pulitzer Publishing Company, which owns the St. Louis *Post-Dispatch* and the Arizona *Star* of Tucson. Pulitzer also acquired the other Lancaster-owned station, WTEV-TV in Providence–New Bedford, Mass. FCC approval was required, however, for the transfer of station licenses.

There was one final point in the Lancaster confrontation. During the final seven months of its ownership of WGAL-TV, the Lancaster interests agreed to have more women's programs and said they would contribute $150,000 to create a women's news service. What they asked for in return was assurance that the challenge before the FCC would be withdrawn.

The broadcasters' principal hope for the easing of these pressures, and a relaxation of the FCC's supervisory role, lies in the passage of a proposed new Federal Communications Act during the 1980s. The bill has been drafted by a Congressional committee working with its chief sponsor, Rep. Lionel Van Deerlin, a California Democrat and former broadcaster. Revision is certain.

What Van Deerlin proposes is a recognition of the realities— that broadcasting has changed dramatically since 1934 when the current law was enacted, that regulation by the government has failed for a number of reasons, and that diversity on the airwaves is now assured by the growth of Cable TV, Home Box Office, and their offshoots.

The Van Deerlin bill would sharply reduce government regulation of broadcasting and leave the problems of programming to the marketplace. Moreover, radio and TV would be treated in different ways with radio licenses being awarded for an indefinite period and TV licenses being given unlimited tenure after ten years' study. As an additional bonus, the "Fairness Doctrine" and "equal time" requirements would be relaxed or abandoned in some cases.

Just about the only thing that broadcasters would be asked to do in the current Van Deerlin draft would be to pay for their licenses to help finance public radio and TV as well as a new, mini-type FCC.[11]

Alas for the dreams of broadcasters, the government is not likely to retreat gracefully from the scene, genuflecting to the tube as it goes, and permitting broadcast owners to pile on the profits in any manner they choose. By the time Congress gets done with the new Federal Communications Act, it is scarcely likely to resemble the liberal Van Deerlin draft. Unless there is a miraculous change in government philosophy, controls over the most powerful of all the media of public communications are likely to be greater, not more relaxed. And tough new laws are probable.

It is not an easy situation for the press to contemplate, whether or not it has strong links to broadcasting. For if government regulation and pressure tactics succeed in one area of the communications field, as they have against the broadcast media currently, then it is certain they will be applied in every area. The press is far from immune.

During the period of civil rights demonstrations that swept the country in the late 1960s, minority groups and scholars began agitating for greater access to all communications media. While they concentrated on the broadcast media, television being most important to their designs, the press also was to become deeply involved.

One of the theorists who argued the necessity for a right of greater access to the press was Jerome Barron, a professor of law at George Washington University. What he advocated, in brief, was a new interpretation of the First Amendment by the courts that would oblige the press to give space to interests that were not sufficiently represented in its columns. He demanded that newspapers be put under "constitutional restrictions which quasi-public status invites."[12] This was the burden of his argument:

There is an anomaly in our constitutional law. While we protect expression once it has come to the fore, our law is indifferent to creating opportunities for expression. Our constitutional theory is in the grip of a romantic conception of free expression, a belief that the "marketplace of ideas" is freely accessible. But if there ever were a self-operating marketplace of ideas, it has long ceased to exist. The mass media's development of an antipathy to ideas requires legal intervention if novel and unpopular ideas are to be assured a forum.[13]

There was no concern here over which ideas would be given representation and which would be rejected, how many contributors would be permitted to use the newspaper's columns on any given day and where these presumably unedited and unrestricted articles (as to both length and content) would be published, or in what manner newspapers with limited space and funds would be assured that such mandatory publications would not crowd out necessary news and advertising. Such mundane details seemed to be of no interest to those who sought to force newspapers to give up the right to decide what was to be printed.

The discussion continued for some years in aimless fashion but attracted relatively little attention outside legal circles. Then, quite by chance, a 1913 Florida statute providing for a "Right of Reply" to the press became the issue for a landmark decision by the U. S. Supreme Court.

The challenge originated in 1972 in almost routine fashion, as so many free press actions do. In two editorials preceding a primary election that was to be held on Oct. 3, 1972, the Miami *Herald* attacked the candidacy of Pat L. Tornillo, Jr., the head of the Dade County (Miami) Classroom Teachers Association. Tornillo was running for the Democratic nomination for the Florida House of Representatives, but the *Herald* assailed him as unqualified because of allegedly illegal acts during a teachers' strike. He formally demanded the right of reply; however, the *Herald* refused to publish the statement he submitted.

With Barron as his lawyer, Tornillo promptly sued under the Florida law that provided for a right of reply by political candidates who were attacked by a newspaper and obligated the newspaper to provide free space for them. The *Herald* called the law unconstitutional, pointing out that it had not been used against a newspaper in almost 60 years. A lower court found for the *Her-*

ald, but the Florida Supreme Court in 1973 reversed that judgment. It argued that there was no "incursion upon First Amendment rights or a prior restraint, since no specified newspaper content is excluded."[14]

It was tortured reasoning, to say the least. The *Herald* carried the case to the U. S. Supreme Court, which ruled in favor of the newspaper in 1974 by a vote of 9-0. This was the crux of the opinion written by Chief Justice Burger:

> The choice of material to go into a newspaper, and the decision made as to limitations on the size of the paper, and content, and treatment of public issues and public officials—whether fair or unfair—constitutes the exercise of editorial control and judgment. It has yet to be demonstrated how governmental regulation of this crucial process can be exercised consistent with First Amendment guarantees of a free press as they have evolved to this time.[15]

Burger then elaborated on this theme by showing how chilling an effect the Florida law, if enforced, would have on editorial decision-making by newspapers:

> Faced with the penalties that would accrue to any newspaper that published news or commentary arguably within the reach of the right-of-access statute, editors might well conclude that the safe course is to avoid controversy. Therefore, under the operation of the Florida statute, political and electoral coverage would be blunted or reduced. Government-enforced right of access inescapably "dampens the vigor and limits the variety of public debate. . ."
>
> Even if a newspaper would face no additional costs to comply with a compulsory access law and would not be forced to forgo publication of news or opinion by the inclusion of a reply, the Florida statute fails to clear the barriers of the First Amendment because of its intrusion into the function of editors.[16]

Considering the essentially conservative character of the Burger court, there are several ways of looking at the Miami *Herald* decision within the context of the law of the press. The least plausible is the notion, touched off by newspaper jubilation over the verdict, that the rights of editors to run their papers have been affirmed for all time. It is much more logical to consider the matter at face value—that a particular law, the Florida "Right of Reply" statute, was stricken down as blatantly unconstitutional. Certainly, in libel cases, newspapers must still publish retractions if they intend to show good faith and escape a finding by the courts of "actual malice." They must publish statements of ownership and circulation periodically by law. And they must comply with obscenity statutes and various phases of criminal law, all of which circumscribe what may or may not be printed.

The narrow view of the effect of the Tornillo case was supported by concurring opinions from the leading liberal of the court, Justice Brennan, and the leading conservative, Justice Rehnquist. They both emphasized that the decision "addresses only 'Right of Reply' statutes and implies no view upon the constitutionality of 'retraction' statutes."[17] This is, of course, in line with the high court's traditional procedure of avoiding a decision on any broad constitutional issue if a case can be decided on narrower grounds.

There is no doubt that Professor Barron's theory of forced public access to the press was an incidental casualty of the Tornillo case, since he was Tornillo's counsel.[18] However, it would be a mistake to consider the Tornillo case to be the last word in safeguarding the First Amendment rights of the press. If the Florida "Right of Reply" law was fatally deficient from its inception, and even Florida legal authorities are inclined to think so, this does not mean that other states will not come up with similar statutes that are more carefully drafted. Almost every rule in law has its exceptions, particularly in this unruly era, and that includes the body of law governing access to the media.

A careful study of the Red Lion and Tornillo decisions makes it reasonably clear that the broadcast media, for the time being, are likely to have to go it alone in fighting for greater freedom under the First Amendment. For although a number of newspapers may oppose the "Fairness Doctrine" and Section 315 in principle, very few would link the printed press's fortunes irretrievably with the broadcast media. They argue that the "all for one and one for all" approach to he First Amendment may be good romance but it is neither good law nor good judgment.

This is because the Supreme Court, under current conditions, views the broadcast media and the printed press in an entirely different light as far as the right of access is concerned. The Red Lion decision was predicated on the fact that the airwaves are under public ownership. Thus, the court held that the right of reply under the "Fairness Doctrine" was obligatory on the broadcast media and refused to countenance "monopolization of that market [-place of ideas], whether it be by the government itself or a private licensee." But in the Tornillo case, the court maintained the historic position against limiting the printed press and therefore the right of reply under Florida law was rejected.

It follows that the press still has a superior position over the broadcast media in the high court's interpretation of the First Amendment, and few newspapers are therefore likely to do much more than render lip service to the broadcast cause. What will happen when communications conglomerates achieve more of a balance between their ownership of broadcast and print properties can only be conjectured now. But it could make a difference in the way the law looks at the rights of both.

The challenge to freedom of the press, far from being limited to newspapers and the broadcast media, pops up in unexpected ways across the whole range of modern mass communications. In Miller v. California in 1973, the Supreme Court held that "community standards" would be the guiding rule in determining whether obscenity statutes were violated.[19] And since the obscenity statutes have always been held by the high court to be outside the First Amendment's shelter, the decision in the Miller case poses a threat to publications of all kinds.

The most immediately affected were the "skins," the medium-to-hard-core pornographic magazines, and pornographic films. But the adoption of "community standards" as a rule for determining pornography troubled a substantial part of the press, as well. Many an editor of an older generation remembered that H. L. Mencken had been arrested in Boston for publicly selling his American Mercury with a relatively innocuous piece about a prostitute, at least by today's standards, called "Hatrack." And as late as 1947, the Supreme Court, by a 4-4 vote, let stand a New York Court of Appeals decision that found Edmund Wilson's "Memoirs of Hecate County" to be obscene.[20]

Clearly, the problem of obscenity could not be confined to the ruthless publishers and filmmakers who blatantly tried to pick up a fast buck by appealing to the more salacious elements in American society. The danger always existed that art and literature, and perhaps the press itself, might suffer in the wake of any ill-informed public movement to suppress anything obscene by "community standards."

The most prominent case to arise under Miller v. California was the conviction of Larry Flynt, publisher of *Hustler* magazine, in 1977 for "pandering" to obscenity. He was found guilty in Cincinnati, where "community standards" were invoked against his rather extreme publication. But such was the concern over the extension of the obscenity law that leading writers, editors, and artists all joined in support of his appeal.

To many others, it was abhorrent to let a First Amendment case be rooted in a magazine of such execrable taste.

Lewis Lapham, the editor of *Harper's* magazine, signed a petition favoring Flynt but withdrew it after looking at a copy of *Hustler.* "I'm not sure," he said, "that *Hustler* was what Jefferson had in mind." To which Nora Ephron, a critic of the news media, added, "Most journalists believe in the absolute application of the First Amendment and then something like this comes along. For those of us who believe *Hustler* is a truly obscene magazine, it is a difficult moment."

The New York *Times*'s response was to use this headline over the discussion:

HAS THE FIRST AMENDMENT MET ITS MATCH?[21]

The First Amendment, more than politics, makes strange bedfellows. It is ironic that an important segment of the newspaper and periodical press felt obliged to make common cause with *Hustler* magazine, which deserved no consideration, while keeping a safe distance from the broadcast media, which deserved something better. But this was typical of the confusion over the obscenity issue that arose from the failure of the Supreme Court to chart a clear course.

Justice Hugo L. Black, following a series of particularly obscure decisions on obscenity cases in 1966, wrote in a wrathful dissent:

My conclusion is that certainly after the fourteen separate opinions handed down in these three cases today no person, not even the most learned judge, much less a layman, is capable of knowing in advance of an ultimate decision in his particular case by this Court whether certain material comes within the area of "obscenity" as that term is confused by the court today.[22]

With the "community standards" decision handed down by the high court in Miller v. California, it has piled Pelion upon Ossa and created mountains of confusion over the obscenity statutes. Unless some clarification is attempted, there will eventually be as many different standards of law in the land as there are between the life-styles of New York City and Puyallup, Wash., or Ten Sleep, Wyo.

Indeed, the manner in which the obscenity law has been handled by the Supreme Court is indicative of the confusion that has arisen over many of its judgments in the whole field of the First Amendment. The erratic course of the high court, as noted by Justice Black, is not by any means confined to the obscenity issue. And this is what has generated such uncertainty within the press over what may be expected in future First Amendment cases. The grand sweep of opinion from the liberalism of the Warren Court to the conservatism of the Burger Court may be soberly accepted as inevitable by legal scholars; yet, it will arouse the greatest foreboding among those who are likely to be the most affected by the justices' decisions.

If there were more confidence in the high court, if it had been able to set clear and understandable standards by which the news media could regulate their affairs, there would be less of a rebellious spirit in the press against the courts. The way things are, the press too often can have little confidence in what the Supreme Court and many of the lower courts will do in First Amendment cases. No one should be surprised, therefore, that combativeness and, on some occasions, outright defiance are among the end results of decisions that go against the press.

2. Manipulating the News

Five Croatian terrorists seized a TWA jetliner with 92 persons aboard on Sept. 10, 1976, and demanded that five major newspapers publish their manifesto calling for independence from Yugoslavia. One of the bombs they allegedly had placed in a locker in New York's Grand Central Terminal already had gone off, killing a policeman. They threatened that another one would be detonated "somewhere in the United States" if their demands were not met by the newspapers.

The New York *Times*, the Washington *Post*, the Los Angeles *Times* and the Chicago *Tribune* did exactly what the terrorists had required that night, starting the story on Page 1. The fifth paper, the *International Herald Tribune*, published in Paris, already had completed its press run for the next day's paper and couldn't do so.

William F. Thomas, editor of the Los Angeles *Times*, said, "Anybody hates to print with a gun at his head, but it wasn't a very difficult decision. They'd already killed one guy. I wasn't going to have any other deaths on my conscience."

Ben Bradlee, the executive editor of the Washington *Post*, agreed in essence with this statement of the position, saying, "In these situations, there sure as hell isn't any rule you can make at editors' school. . . . If the President of the United States demanded we print something, we'd be hard put, I think, to find a reason to comply—unless he said there was a crazy man with his finger on the button."[23]

The Croats surrendered to French police at Paris's Charles deGaulle Airport on Sept. 12 and were brought back to the United States for punishment. Had it not been for their success in forcing some of the greatest papers in the land to publish under threat what they could have achieved in no other way, they would have vanished quickly from public consciousness. But their case was of a piece with so many other acts of terrorism, which had been elaborately displayed by the news media, that it was remembered.

There is no doubt that this was damaging. For soon, other irrational instances of terrorism dominated the news and the public became increasingly critical. Consider such cases as these:

—An Indianapolis man, angry at a mortgage company there, wired a sawed-off shotgun to the head of one of the firm's officers and for more than 60 hours detailed his grievances to a nationwide audience through the news media.

—A black Vietnam War veteran demanded for two days that President Carter publicly apologize for the wrongs done to black people, all the while holding a gun at the head of a police officer in Warrensville Heights, Ohio. Once the President had telephoned, however briefly, the terrorist gave up.

It became increasingly clear that people were becoming angry over the amount of news space and air time that was being given to terrorists. From polls and from individual reactions of subscribers, editors learned soon enough of the sharply divided public reaction to such news accounts. To some, people seemed almost as indignant as they had been when Lynette (Squeaky) Fromme pointed a pistol at President Ford in Sacramento on September 5, 1975, and, after being disarmed, was fetchingly portrayed, in her clown's cap, on news magazine covers. Many thought this was a glorification of a particularly stupid crime. Rightly or wrongly, various newspapers and broadcasters were accused of trying to sensationalize terrorism in order to sell more papers and win ever large broadcast audiences.

Then came the attack by the Hanafi Muslims on March 9, 1977, in Washington, D. C. It was a terrifying outrage—three buildings seized, a radio reporter killed, 19 bystanders wounded, and 115 hostages taken, who were threatened with beheading. The leader of the band, Hamaas Abdul Khaalis, demanded that the government give him the convicted slayers of his wife and five of his children, even though the culprits were serving life sentences.

Once again, the terrorists had captured nationwide attention by playing on the essential weakness of the news media in such situations. For two days, there was an air of near-hysteria in the nation's capital. No other story received much prominence from the news media; even one of Jimmy Carter's Presidential news conferences had been downplayed. Then, answering the pleas of Muslim ambassadors from Iran, Pakistan, and Egypt, Khaalis released his hostages on condition that he would be permitted to go home without putting up bail, a demand with which the authorities meekly complied. Later, he was arrested with his followers and brought to justice, but the recriminations that followed took little account of the Hanafis' punishment.

The issue this time was clearly drawn: Were the news media going in too heavily for the coverage of terrorism? Did that kind of saturation coverage actually encourage more terrorism? Should the news media be put under some kind of control in the future?

Ronald Reagan, the ex-governor of California and leader of the conservative Republicans, demanded that broadcasters in particular give up live coverage of terrorism, saying:

If the nation's television assignment editors and radio news directors would take a collective deep breath and declare a moratorium on live coverage of terrorist events during their commission of the crime, they would be cutting off the source of inspiration for an untold number of loose nuts who harbor similarly crazy ideas.

Nor was this proposal confined to those who were essentially conservative in their approach to the news. The National News Council, under the chairmanship of Norman E. Isaacs, issued a proposal for self-restraint in which it asked "all news media to consider the dangers in the practice of live coverage which precludes full context or judicious editing."

However, many editors shot down a proposal by Robert McCord, executive editor of the Arkansas *Democrat*, for a solid front by the American press against the publication of any further terrorist demands. A. M. Rosenthal, executive editor of the New York *Times*, replied, "The last thing in the world I want is guidelines. I don't want guidelines from the government and I don't want any from professional organizations or anyone else. . . . You have to weigh the human dangers and journalistic values of each case as it comes up."[24]

It remained for the Gallup organization to show that the public's anxiety over the presentation of terrorism in the press was very real. A total of 64 percent of the respondents in a Gallup Poll in 1977 expressed the belief that intense coverage of terrorism does encourage similar acts, which was Ambassador Young's position. Only 27 percent thought the depth of coverage didn't matter. And only half of those polled thought such coverage was necessary. Almost as many, 47 percent, believed it to be overemphasized. It is worth noting that nonwhites, by 67 to 24 percent (with 9 percent having no opinion), insisted on the fullest coverage of terrorism, while whites, by 50 to 48 percent (with 2 percent having no opinion), thought it was overdone.[25]

There is no doubt that a considerable part of the press and broadcast media were shaken by the public reaction. Eventually, a few news organizations—the Columbia Broadcasting System and United Press International among them—announced mild precautionary measures on the coverage of news involving hostages and other terrorist situations. But these were, in the main, cosmetic changes and didn't really affect the central issue of whether the press could continue to be trusted to cover the news in its own way, and through its own methods, without any interference.

While there is no conclusive scientific evidence to prove that news of sensational crimes begets other crimes, every experienced reporter knows that shocking stories of this kind tend to move in cycles. The first time I became aware of this phenomenon was in 1937 while I was covering the Beekman Hill murders in New York City, for which a so-called "mad sculptor," Robert Irwin, was committed for life to a State institution for the criminally insane. The sex angles of these slayings of a model, her mother, and a man who boarded with them in their apartment, were heavily played by the sensational New York newspapers, which featured a lot of seminude pictures of the principal victim, the model. Within the next few months, several other sex murders also were committed in the New York metropolitan area, all by persons who were mentally deranged.

More recently, Southerners often blamed the news media for spreading civil rights turmoil by overcoverage of demonstrations by militant blacks. And in the North, when the burning of the inner cities began in the 1960s, critics charged the press and broadcast media with responsibility for the spread of rioting in such cities as Los Angeles, Detroit, Chicago, and Newark.

The attack on the press was continued with such vigor that news organizations in several cities were obliged to adopt some forms of self-regulation. This was the era of the Chicago plan, under which the press pledged itself not to report a disturbance for a relatively brief time until it was certain that it was a matter worth detailed coverage and not a mere flurry. Similar practices were instituted in St. Louis and New York City and among several of the larger news organizations to insure that the public was spared false reports of "race riots."

The voluntary adoption of such precautions, always sound journalistic practice, is, however, not the issue. Nor is there much point in going through the perennial ceremonial of journalistic penitence by denouncing sensationalism in the news media. The founding fathers, in framing the Bill of Rights, recognized that a free press, untrammeled by regulations or censorship, would in its diversity best protect the public interest and serve the nation. That is still the position, although it has become increasingly diffi- cult to maintain.

In an outburst against "yellow journalism" at the time the Charles A. Lindberghs fled to Britain in 1935 to escape undue attention by the press, Walter Lippmann wrote:

> Undoubtedly it is the truth that the only certain answer to yellow journalism is the example and the effective competition of honest jour- nalism. But that example would be greatly fortified if at last the people who are now so horrified and humiliated could continue to be angry long enough to make it dangerously unprofitable to prostitute the liber- ties of the press.[26]

Unfortunately, there is a Gresham's Law of journalism that interferes too often with Lippmann's suggestion that an angry public should not continue to patronize the sensational malefac- tors among newspapers and the broadcast media. With not too many exceptions—William Randolph Hearst's tabloid New York *Mirror* and Bernarr Macfadden's tabloid New York *Graphic* among them—it usually doesn't work out that way.

Instead of singling out the culprits, a censorious public or a beleaguered government often seems more determined to attack the very best and most responsible elements of the news media instead of the worst. In any event, it is one of the sorry truths of our time that a newspaper of considerable quality, the *National Observer*, had to suspend publication while a shoddy one, the *National Enquirer*, still appeals to millions of readers at the checkout counter. The notion of selective punishment through the public may be poetic, but it is impractical.

Still, one has a right to ask, I think, whether downplaying the news of terrorism or violent demonstrations or sex crimes will have any effect whatever on the incidence of such outbreaks. The evidence scarcely indicates that this is even a reasonable possibility today. Is it logical to suppose that abandonment of live TV coverage would have persuaded the Hanafis not to go through with their desperate raid? Or that smaller headlines over terrorist demands would have caused the Croats to give up their pitch for world attention?

It will not do to pile the onus for terrorism on the press for faithfully reporting that it exists. In the cases of the Hanafis and the Croats, the testimony indicated that these were resolute if ill-advised people who were determined to risk their lives for a cause. The size of a headline or the delay of a few minutes of air time would not have been likely to deter them or any others who enlist under the tattered black banners of terrorism.

Just how ridiculous it is to try to contain terrorism by holding down the news of terrorist acts becomes evident when one considers the career of the supreme terrorist of this century, Adolf Hitler. Because his outrages against the Jews of Germany were fully reported during his rise to power, alarm spread on both sides of the Atlantic; had it not been for the supine cowardice of European statesmen, he could have been checked when he marched into the Rhineland. The American press, in this case, did its duty fully and honorably. No sensible person would have contended at the time, and none would maintain now, that it ever would have been possible to play down Hitler.

Where downplaying did occur in the early day of the Vietnam War, the result was an American tragedy. Through ignorance and ennui, compounded by false governmental claims of victory over the Vietcong terrorists, much of the American press failed to give the alert in time to forestall escalation of the conflict. But when the nation understood it had become involved in a peculiar war that American arms could not win, a hundred college campuses became battlegrounds. Then, once again, the cry went up for less media coverage of a national movement that already had burst all restraint.

It was like blaming the historian for the catalogue of human misery, failure, and degradation that it is his duty to record. The futility of the notion of downplaying the student protest movement became self-evident once four students had been shot and killed by National Guard bullets at Kent State University on May 4, 1970. There could never have been a coverup for the picture of a weeping teen-age girl, bent over one of the victims, that became an overnight symbol of national shame. One might as well have tried to hide the anguish of the national conscience.

Thus, all human experience in an open society argues powerfully against trying to control or otherwise contain news that affects the public interest, no matter how repugnant or shocking such intelligence may be. The penalty for suppression, in whole or in part, is far more serious than a loss of credibility by the nation's press and broadcast news organizations. It is entirely likely, if continued for any length of time, to foreshadow the collapse of the democratic system itself.

Admittedly, overplaying the news leads to a serious distortion of values in the opposite direction and the merchants of sensation, who inevitably circle over the course of events like hungry vultures, can outrage public opinion even more than the would-be censors. There are those who contend, with upcast eyes and virtuous mien, that yellow journalism is a thing of the past. But doubts would arise amont those who witnessed the deplorable antics of the New York City press in the "Son of Sam" arrest and the hippodrome that was made of Elvis Presley's funeral by some of the Southern news media.

It is an oversimplification of the problem to say that such crass spectacles are created by fast-buck publishers and unprincipled editors whose reporters operate on the theory that "anything goes if it sells." Such people, unfortunately, are always with us, as

Walter Lippmann observed long ago. And all they care about is the unholy trinity of journalism, "blood, money, and broads."

But sometimes, in the coverage of dramatic events that have seized the public fancy, a kind of mass hysteria develops over the whole range of journalism. It takes possession of the best elements as well as the worst. The usually respectable evening news programs on television then seem caught up in a kind of frenzy. And even our best newspapers devote their largest headlines, and acres of newsprint, to the detailed examination of the most sordid and inhuman acts. Even the sedate news magazines reflect this wave of catch-penny madness when they slap the grinning faces of terrorists and killers on their covers for all the world to see.

Ordinarily grave and responsible journalists, in such situations, can find themselves caught up in a mob of pushing, heaving, shoving, and yelling news people and photographers who have circled some instant celebrity—a young woman with eight husbands or an abdicated king, an absconding banker brought to justice or the mistress of a bishop, the author of a fake biography or an actress who has revealed a love affair with a President.

Even in the normal course of events, pressures develop over the coverage of breaking news that cause journalists to lose control of themselves. I have seen a door to the White House Oval Office literally ripped from its hinges in a reportorial stampede to get out an important and unexpected Presidential announcement. In the rush to spread the word of Japan's surrender in World War II, able-bodied men were bowled over and trampled because everybody wanted to be the first with the news. Nothing is likely to change this instinctive scramble for the wire, the telephone, or the camera and microphone when the news does not break directly on television itself.

This is the least defensible and most detestable form of journalism—the journalism of the herd. It occurs whenever big news develops suddenly and with dramatic impact, drawing herds of aggressive news people and their equipment to a single spot to focus on a single person or group. When the authorities give in to this kind of mob, almost anything can happen—as witness the murder of Lee Harvey Oswald on camera.

To try to explain this phenomenon is not to condone it. No responsible person defends "herd journalism" or its results. But it is also true that no one, in or out of authority, has ever found a satisfactory way of dealing with its excessess and still maintaining the basic principles of the First Amendment. Many a President, particularly after an assassination or an attempted assassination, has reflected on the problem without changing anything. And solemn committees of journalists have conducted inquiries and recommended greater self-discipline, but that has been the extent of their accomplishment. As the Prince of Condé exclaimed when hordes of professional newsmongers infested the public places of Paris in the 16th century, dispensing rumors for a few sous, "The evil is without a remedy!"[27]

Consider the "Son of Sam" case in New York City. Here was another horrifying situation. A fiendish killer had stalked the greatest city in the land for a whole year, hunting down couples in parked automobiles, seemingly at random. He had killed seven of these unfortunate young persons and wounded seven others. The Mayor and Police Commissioner of the city had been making loud noises, particularly the former, who was up for reelection, but seemingly there wasn't a clue to the identity of the slayer. What the authorities had to go on was a letter he had written, in rambling and confused fashion, to a columnist for the New York *Daily News*, Jimmy Breslin, in which he had signed himself, "Son of Sam."

Quite legitimately, Breslin had written an open letter to the killer, suitably displayed with blockbuster Page 1 headlines, appealing to him to give up. Such a strategem had actually worked in the case of another killer, New York's so-called "Mad Bomber" of the 1950s, when Edward A. Mahar of the New York *Journal-American* decided to try such a public appeal. It made good sense and it turned out to be good journalism. But when it failed in the case of the "Son of Sam," both Breslin and the *News* were accused, quite wrongly, of trying to cash in on human misery.

At another time, shortly before the arrest was made that broke the "Son of Sam" case, the police learned to their consternation that both the New York *Times* and the *Daily News* knew the authorities had the killer's fingerprints. However, in response to an appeal, both newspapers withheld publication of this crucial bit of news. So far, except for the follies of the New York *Post* under its new Australian owner, Rupert Murdoch, the press in New York had acquitted itself with a reasonable degree of professionalism and competence.

Then, with dramatic suddenness, the police surrounded a drab Yonkers flat on a steaming August night in 1977 and arrested a 24-year-old postal clerk and former anxiliary policeman, David Berkowitz, charging him with being the "Son of Sam." And Berkowitz was quoted by the authorities that night of August 10 as saying with a smile, "Okay, you got me." Much more incriminating evidence was then released by the New York officials, who threw off all restraint. And a large section of the news media, well aware of the intense public interest in the case, gave way to the hysteria of the moment. One editor was quoted: "It was one of the most nauseating, disgusting displays I've ever seen in my life."

The story was so hyped up that it attracted nationwide and world wide attention. ABC gave it 20 minutes on the August 11 evening news, and NBC and CBS both used eight minutes, which amounted to saturation television coverage. The New York *Daily News* boosted its circulation by 350,000 with the news of the arrest, going to 2.2 million for the day. And the shameless New York *Post* almost doubled its normal circulation, selling more than a million papers.[28] A *Post* reporter was quoted, "I'm supposed to come up with something new on Sam tonight. I don't know where I'll start. I'm sick of the whole story. I feel pretty slimy."[29]

The New York *Times*, which had been criticized by Rupert Murdoch for underplaying the story during the search for the killer, came through as it nearly does with a solid Page 1 account and a somewhat larger than normal set of headlines. On the day of the arrest, the Times extended its press run 90 minutes and sold an extra 50,000 copies, not much, given the circumstances.°

Days later, *Newsweek* came out with a picture of Berkowitz on its cover together with a story captioned, "The Sick World of Son of Sam," and apologetically added this explanation in its press section: "After the enormous play already given to this story by the most respectable papers and television networks, it's hard to believe that a cover story adds appreciably to Son of Sam's fame. *Newsweek* put this on the cover because it is a national story of compelling interest."[30]

Surveying the disordered scene, the *New Yorker* quietly observed that "just about everything done by the press here. . .has made a bad situation worse for the citizens of New York." But then, the *New Yorker* always was above the battle because it seldom descended into the brawling arena to cover the news, only commented on it.

At a distance, one could reflect that it had been a lot worse in the Bronx County Court House more than 40 years before, when Bruno Richard Hauptmann was brought in and accused of the murder of the Lindbergh baby. The wages of sensation, then as now, are a matter of private doubt within the profession—and public disgust.

Although the overplaying of major news is deplorable by any standard of judgment, it is not always a bad thing. Throughout much of the 1960s and early 1970s, there was a national uproar over aircraft hijackings. As is customary, the massive attention given to these spectacular events by the news media led to an avalanche of criticism and threats of regulation.

Indeed, reading the letters columns on many an editorial page after a hijacking, one would have thought that the editor— and not some hapless desperado—was the culprit. Still, the press

---

°Berkowitz pleaded guilty in a Brooklyn courtroom nine months later.

persisted in blanket coverage every time a hijacking occurred. And television cameras brought all manner of shocking scenes into the nation's living rooms. No citizen, in short, was able to remain unaware for very long of the continual threat to the nation's air transport system and to the many millions of passengers who use it each year.

For awhile, most of the airlines tried to get away with business-as-usual. Some officials thought it would be impossible to develop a system for checking all passengers that would not interfere with normal boarding procedures and normal air schedules. They predicted chaos if anybody tried it. Instead, one of the favorite remedies proposed by many well-meaning people was for newspapers and the broadcast media to play down or ignore the hijackers on the theory that others might not then try to emulate them.

The news media, as usual, paid no attention to such nonsense. Eventually, under the pressure of events and saturation coverage, an adequate passenger checking system *was* developed that discouraged most hijackers. Guards *did* move into air terminals with loaded sidearms. The government also managed to obtain an agreement from Fidel Castro's Cuba not to harbor future hijackers.

It was not long before hijackings began to decline within the United States. And when that happened, the news media turned to something else for their daily fare. The passengers became so accustomed to the efficient air lines' inspection of their persons and baggage that what had once seemed impossible now became a matter of routine. It was at least one case in which sensationalism in the news media actually helped expedite the solution of vexing national problem.

The news media would have fewer crises and a larger measure of public respect if all their adventures in mass coverage worked out as well as it did in the case of hijackings. But the urgent business of keeping up with the breaking news is far more chancy than the American public has been led to believe. Nor are the gathering and distribution of the news as simple and automatic as they seem to be. In journalism, in particular, Kelly's Law is generally the determining factor where there is some doubt about coverage, to wit: "If something can go wrong, it will go wrong."

While he was president of NBC News, Richard C. Wald made this comment on the criticism of the way the Hanafi Muslims' story was handled:

> I am, too, a citizen of this country, of this culture we live in. So, I'm torn. I want to report, but I don't want to help to overdramatize. . . . It's a terrible tightrope to walk but if you don't try walking it, you'll lose everything you've got.
> I don't know any really good rules to guide us in these situations, but what we do is: we try to hire sensible people, promote smart bosses, tell them to be careful, and generally it works. They wind up being sensible and smart and they don't do terrible things and it works out okay. Every once in awhile it doesn't. It's the price we pay for the system we have.[31]

It makes no sense, finally, to put a watchman atop the city gates to give warning of approaching danger and then instruct him to blow his trumpet softly—or take it away altogether because, at one time or another, he has been disorderly. Actually, it is worse than having no watchman at all, because the people of the sleeping city are under the illusion that they are being protected. And in reality, they have no protection at all.

3. Togetherness and the Press

Unlike the European journalist, a familiar and sometimes a dominant figure in the social and political life of the continent, the American journalist has generally gone his own solitary way. In the beginning, this was not his choice. It was forced upon him by the conditions of his employment and the doubts of the rest of society about his competence, his good faith, and his intentions.

During the Great Depression of the 1930s, I remember quite well that we reporters were invariably thrown into our own company because few others wanted anything to do with us. We were poorly paid, worked long hours, had no particular social status, and were inclined not make much of our college backgrounds (if we had any), because we were not in a business that then placed any particular value on a college education.

There was an additional factor that separated us from the public at large. On the papers for which I worked, and I know that it was also true of others, there were strict rules forbidding us to seek public office, to serve private organizations in any capacity, to help such worthy institutions as the American Red Cross and the Salvation Army, or to occupy ourselves in community work for school boards or social organizations.

What this amounted to was the acceptance of an enforced status as second-class citizens.

The intent of this journalistic ghetto, into which we were thrust, was perfectly high-minded on the surface. By remaining placidly within its bounds, we were insulated from conflicts of interest in our work as reporters, writers, and editors. Not being involved with school boards, we could not be accused of undue friendship with or hostility to the educational process. Not being a part of any organized campaign for the benefit of worthy charities or civic organizations, we could be trusted to report on them impartially.

Politics had to be approached differently. Since nobody could forbid us to belong to a political party, a rigid objectivity was the rule for all political copy because it was common knowledge that —except for a house Republican here and there—we people on news staffs were mainly Democrats or independents. Until the great Depression, the relatively few Communists in our ranks remained underground.

Carried to its extreme, this frenzy to guard against the prejudices of poorly paid and often suspect journalists produced some peculiar results. One of the largest papers in the country had an inviolate rule against permitting Catholic reporters to write about Catholic events and Jewish reporters to be assigned to Jewish events. The WASPS on the staff were thus overworked; for some reason nobody seemed to worry very much if Protestant reporters covered Protestant events.

As for the possibility of undue favoritism for labor and allied liberal causes, editors simply picked the "right" people for such assignments. It wasn't much of a problem in the early years of the century because we journalists had such a lofty idea of our own importance that we looked down on labor unions. The result was that the printers, in their black holes, laughed at us as improbable dreamers because their pay was considerably higher than ours. But we thought of ourselves as the *gentlemen* of the press.

Looking back over the panorama of more than fifty years, it occurs to me that we contributed considerably to our own social ostracism. We were rather smugly content to be the Doolittles of our time, the "undeserving poor" in Bernard Shaw's phrase; being thoroughly enamored of Sinclair Lewis's prejudices in *Main Street* and *Babbitt* we ridiculed the prentensions of middle class. Far from aspiring to some form of upward mobility, we in New York gravitated to Greenwich Village and its fairly free (for that era) sexual mores. We tolerated works like Maxwell Bodenheim's *Naked on Roller Skates*, but not Booth Tarkington's *The Magnificent Ambersons*.

We knew quite well all the while that our publishers, our directing editors, and some of our commentators—the "safe" ones—were regularly associated with the broader societies of the community and nation. But far from envying their freedom to indulge in their middle-class and, more rarely, their upper-class associations, we ridiculed them. In our lowly drinking resorts, the speakeasies that became neighborhood saloons after prohibition conked out, there was a lot of sardonic talk about country club publishers and golf course editors. We relished our role as the Eternal Outsider, not being able to change it for anything better.

It was the calamity of the great Depression that stirred us out of our torpor. First came a drastic reduction in the number of newspapers, including such great ones as the New York *World*, which cost so many of our fellow-journalists their jobs and condemned them to the relief rolls. Then, our own pay was sharply cut, in many instances, when desperate managements sought to keep themselves from going under. The shock of it made us, for the first time, pay some attention to the drum-beating of the self-appointed American proletariat—the small coterie of radical thinkers who had gathered about the unkempt father figure of Heywood Broun, as implausible a savior as any the Depression produced. We listened to him when he urged us to join him in forming the Newspaper Guild, but few of us could subscribe to his enthusiastic creed: "Now we have a labor union and by God I like it!" We fell in with him because we were frightened and had nowhere else to turn in the big cities of the land, and a lot of the smaller ones as well.

I cannot say precisely how long we editorial people struggled to build a protective editorial union, which was soon swallowed up by the larger commercial and business department contingent that joined us. In my own case, it was four years; then, I simply had to give up because I saw that my union work was dominating my life and I preferred reporting to organizing. And so the professionals emerged to take charge of our union, replacing those of us who were admittedly amateurs.

After a sharp struggle for control, these career union people succeeded in removing the relatively few Communists who had maneuvered themselves into positions of influence. The union grew and prospered. But improvements in our lot came at a dreadfully laggard pace, despite all the strikes and boycotts and secondary picketing of advertisers that unionism entailed.

There is no doubt that the Guild contributed to the betterment of the journalists' position in the United States. Certainly it improved the security of those employed by newspapers that managed to survive the Depression. Yet, in 1946, just after World

War II, the average minimum wage of reporters in all Guild contracts was only $61.67, and my own, as diplomatic correspondent of the New York *Post*, was a princely $115 a week. True, the five-day, 40-hour week applied to us by law, as it did to most others in the labor force, and we had severance pay, sick leave, and other security benefits. But our social outlook had changed very little. Upward mobility still existed only for our superiors. And even the printers still lorded it over us with their superior pay and working conditions.

Twenty years later, the average weekly wage of a reporter based on all Guild contracts was only $151.59 as of April 1, 1966.* Then, something happened. For as inflation took hold, we saw the upstart television newsmen achieving spectacular gains in pay and working conditions without benefit of a lot of tough union activity. At the same time, the consolidation process among newspapers had attained such momentum that the chains now dominated daily print journalism. Profits were escalating; for all forms of journalism, an era of unparalleled prosperity had begun. It was scarcely unreasonable of us to want to share in it.

One other factor of importance developed in the mid-1960s. The 60 or so accredited schools of journalism, few of which had ever been very highly regarded in the profession, suddenly began to be inundated with students. Advanced thinkers argued that the idealistic youth of the nation had at last recognized the superior merits of journalism as a profession and as the "cutting edge of social change," as an unsung phrasemaker of the time put it. A more likely attraction, in all probability, was the emergence of a new and sparkling image of the journalist as the dashing adventurer or the all-knowing, highly paid seer of television. Whatever the reason, journalism enrollments increased tenfold in a decade and we began feeling uncomfortable competitive pressures from the new generation of journalists as well as our contemporaries.

---

*Guild contracts provide for minimum wages. The pay quoted here is the *average weekly minimum wage* of all Guild contracts.

What happened to us in the 1970s signaled a dramatic change in both our economic and our social status. Between 1966 and August 1, 1977, the average weekly minimum wage of a reporter in all Guild contracts more than doubled, going to $335.16, with all other categories taking a similar leap. On the Washington *Post*, the reportorial minimum wage went to $529.50 a week; the New York *Times*, $486.27; the Minneapolis *Star & Tribune*, $422; the Sacramento *Union*, $391.79; the Memphis *Commercial Appeal* and *Press Scimitar*, $350.90. Even a small paper like the Pawtucket (R. I.) *Times* was paying $325.25[32] Among those with personal service contracts, the rewards became almost commensurate with those of television and the industrial world outside of journalism.

At the top level, the newspaper directorate—with few exceptions—still lagged behind the bumper yields of the television barons. Arthur Ochs Sulzberger, publisher of the New York *Times*, was reputed to have earned $210,000, plus $75,000 bonus in 1976, while the paper's managing editor, A. M. Rosenthal, was said to have received $120,000 in the same year.[33] Katharine Graham, as chairman of the Washington Post Company, received $260,500 in 1976. By contrast, the 1976 earnings of television executives included $747,077 for Leonard H. Goldenson, chairman of ABC Inc.; $500,577 for William S. Paley in his final year as chief executive of CBS Inc.; $377,050 for Edgar H. Griffiths, president of RCA; and $301,825 for Thomas S. Murphy, chairman of Capital Cities Communication, Inc.[34]

Regardless of the distance that separated the newspaper publisher from the staff in terms of rewards, everybody recognized that the newspaper business at last had changed completely. The old raffish characteristics of the journalist very largely disappeared; with the exception of a few eccentrics here and there, the alcoholics also vanished from the newsrooms of the better papers. Reporters seldom shot craps in the morgue, the newspaper's library, after hours. They went home to their families and their mortgages. Nor did many copyreaders stop off for a convivial evening in the corner saloon; they, too, lived regular lives, for the most part. Soon, those of us who had survived the era of Heywood Broun were dumped unceremoniously into the era of Woodward and Bernstein.

If we were momentarily dazzled by the somewhat hesitant decision of our peers in society to accept us at what we regarded as our true worth, there was some excuse for us. For with the recognition of the broadened power that inherently resided within the news media, and the renewed attention that was paid to communications of all kinds, we found that an enhanced sense of status had been thrust upon us. Whether we like it or not, we were no longer the Eternal Outcast, the undeserving poor. In place of such romantic notions, we had to accept the blunt truth that we were unabashedly middle- to upper-middle-class in a nation that was still, for better or worse, dominated by middle-class values.

The times, in short, had caught us up in their unruly embrace and whirled us into a lopsided social orbit that we were ill prepared to negotiate. Our publishers, editors, and commentators, plus a few selected Washington or foreign correspondents, were effusively welcomed by the great foundations and national societies into studies dealing with the nature of the press. Freely translated into nondiplomatic language, this meant that the national power structure felt moved to try to flatter the press into a greater measure of self-restraint toward government and the private sector. Moreover, most of the great universities annually presented approved journalists with honorary degrees—the pale white badges of merit.

The difference in status was just as marked at the working level of the press. Ordinary journalists were importuned to participate weekly in panel discussions on public affairs, or in simulated news conferences with distinguished figures on television. Nor was this only at the local and regional level. National news shows featuring working news people became common on network television as well, particularly in the cultural never-never

land to which the public is admitted only during the Sunday
daytime hours. It followed that those in journalism who displayed
a reasonable talent for discussion and could be minimally articu-
late were also welcomed to university platforms as lecturers,
teachers, or both.

Thus the journalist, at long last, had been given a seat near
the mighty and the powerful at the table presided over by the
National Establishment. Unlike Eugene O'Neill's "Hairy Ape,"
the journalist now belonged.

The era of Togetherness spawned so many conferences, conventions, study groups, and allied endeavors that editors soon
found that they could be away from their desks every week of the
year, if they were foolish enough to do so. They were now People
of Consequence. So were their reporters and writers. And when
great events dominated the tube and the front page, a bemused
public was accorded the privilege sometimes of watching and
listening to journalists interviewing each other instead of the
sources of the news. It should be observed that in the time of
Hildy Johnson such incestuous goings-on took place in the corner
saloon instead of in full view of millions of television viewers.

But strangely enough, the stringent newspaper rules against
belonging to, or working for, outside organizations were not relaxed by the vast majority of editors and publishers. Thus, the old
journalistic ghetto became gilded but it was still a ghetto. For if
some privileged journalists were given permission to belong to the
Council on Foreign Relations, which did not allow coverage of its
meetings, others who were less privileged could not even join
their local PTAs. Indeed, one nationally known newspaper of
liberal inclinations was reputed to have made an effort to prevent
the *wives* of reporters from belonging to the PTA! It was enough
to give the average journalist a paranoid view of his relations with
the world outside his own profession. Accordingly, he remained
essentially ingrown—with few exceptions—and continued to associate mainly with fellow journalists.

The journalist's innate suspicion of outsiders accounted for the difficulties of such innovations as press councils and other devices to give the public a sense of greater participation in the news media.

The idea of a press council as a kind of halfway house between the public and the news media originated in Britain in 1949. Because of the opposition of the press all over the United Kingdom, the original model had little acceptance until 1964, despite the praise of two Royal Commissions. What it tried to do was to investigate complaints by the public against the press and make a judgment on them; however, it had no power and could not oblige a guilty newspaper to publish its findings, much less mend its ways, unless it agreed to accept the council's verdict. Few, however, did so in the first 15 years.

Then, in 1964, the British made a monumental change in the structure of their press council by adding a number of nonjournalistic members representing various segments of the public and subordinating journalistic membership. A distinguished former judge of Britain's highest court was persuaded to become chairman. The result was salutary. Many of the news organizations that had opposed the British Press Council now became its most enthusiastic supporters. They even put up the money to keep it in business, an unexpected vote of confidence. Do not suppose, however, that these hard-bitten press lords had seen a vision of the Holy Grail, a battered Fleet Street version thereof, and come forward on their knees as repentant sinners. The reality, it turned out, was something less than inspiring.

It developed that one provision of the Council's procedure obliged all complainants to sign a paper agreeing not to take their claims to court and to abide by the Council's decision. Since the press in Britain had been bedeviled by law suits, many of which had gone against the defendant newspapers, almost any promise of relief, no matter how slender a hope it represented, was welcome. In addition, Fleet Street had seen its press freedoms so hedged in and circumscribed by censorious courts and a fearful government that it conceived of the Council as a medium of self-defense. And that is the way it turned out.

Before long, American foundations and societies interested in some form of press restraint began experimenting with the consultative movement in this country. At first, it was hard going. Only one or two newspapers were willing to contribute funds— and these were pitifully small. Most editors believed that the notion of the public looking over their shoulders was just another poorly concealed effort at censorship in sugar-coated form.

Eventually, in the mid-1960s, local press councils began functioning in places like Bend, Oregon; Riverside, California; and Sparta, Illinois. Larger ones were set up as experiments in Seattle and Honolulu. And at length, the first regional press council was established in Minnesota in 1971 with the cooperation and financial support of the John Cowles newspaper and television interests, the dominant news media in the area. Despite a lot of professional skepticism, Minnesota kept going while smaller councils like those in Bend and Riverside folded up for lack of interest and lack of funds.

In 1972, the Twentieth Century Fund created a task force of public-spirited citizens to examine the problem of operating a consultative organization in journalism at the national level. The result was a recommendation that led to the establishment in the following year of the National News Council in New York City. It was set up as an independent and private organization, financed by the Twentieth Century Fund and the John and Mary Markle Foundation, "to receive, examine, and report on complaints concerning the accuracy and fairness of news reporting in the United States, as well as to initiate studies and report on issues involving the freedom of the press."

This was a monumental undertaking, considering the size and extent of the American engine of information. There could be little hope of financial support from the news media at the outset.

Nor was there much assurance of cooperation, particularly after the New York *Times* and several other major organizations registered the firmest opposition to the whole notion.

Arthur Ochs Sulzberger, publisher of the New York *Times*, said he feared the Council "would encourage an atmosphere of regulation in which government intervention might gain public acceptance." To which Executive Editor A. M. Rosenthal added, after watching the Council's first three years, "I have a strong feeling that the kind of thinking that led to the creation of news councils is the kind of thinking that leads to the creation of guidelines; a desire to sit in judgment on the press and individual editors and tell them what they may do and what they may not do."[35]

The American news media, at that juncture, simply saw no need to entrust their affairs, much less their defense, to a new and rather weak organization with little public visibility. There also was no reason, at that time, to fear that the courts would overpower the news media, making recourse to private arbitration more attractive. In consequence, the National News Council staggered along for the better part of four years, shuffling its personnel, changing its leadership and experimenting with various courses of action. It almost went under for lack of funds.

In 1977, under the chairmanship of Norman E. Isaacs, it took out a new lease on life. William B. Arthur, former editor of *Look* magazine, continued as executive director with a small staff, but the board membership was expanded to 18, about half of them from the news media. With grants from the Gannett Newspaper Foundation and other media sources, sufficient funds were assured for a few more years of modest operation. But instead of confining the council to complaints, about 400 of which had been received in the first four years, the ebullient Isaacs changed course. "We'll still receive and study complaints about coverage but that will only be a part of our job," he said. "We feel we can do an immense service in spotting and calling attention to threats to press freedom across the country."

It was what one might have expected from a dedicated newspaperman. Before long, the former executive editor of the Louisville *Courier-Journal* and *Times* was cheered by an endorsement from one of the leaders of broadcast journalism, William S. Paley, then about to retire as chairman of the board of CBS. He wrote:

CBS has come to recognize the evidence of the National News Council's ability to strengthen the growth of a free and responsible press in America. Therefore, CBS not only pledges its cooperation with the Council, including reporting by CBS of any Council findings adverse to CBS News, but also affirms its support of the aims and procedures of the Council.[36]

However, much of the opposition remained unmoved and unconvinced. Ben Bradlee, executive editor of the Washington *Post*, said, "There's a lot wrong with the newspaper business that the Council never gets around to." And John P. McGoff, president of Panax Corporation, a Michigan-based newspaper chain, called for the disbanding of the Council and the resignation of its top executives after a split Council decision that condemned Panax's editorial policy. At issue was the chain's use of two articles attacking the Carter administration, which brought about the separations of two Panax editors. "There ought to be no self-appointed organization to police us," McGoff said.

Nevertheless, the embattled organization tried the best it could to follow a steady, if uncharted, course. In the early years of the century, when the credo of the poorly paid journalist amounted to an exercise in philosophical anarchism, the Council would not have lasted six months. That it was able to survive five years amounted to a triumph of hope in what was, as nearly all professionals agreed, an unlikely and unpopular cause.[37]

Another move to provide the public with greater access to newspapers was the revived notion of appointing a staff public defender to receive and act upon complaints by readers. Among the first to decide on the experiment was the management of the Louisville *Courier-Journal* and *Times*, then under the leadership of the able and talented Barry Bingham, Sr. In 1967, he agreed to the establishment of the post of Ombudsman for the two newspapers and concurred in the appointment of a working newspaperman, Robert Schulman, to handle what appeared to be a thankless job.

The term, which is Swedish, orginally applied to someone who dealt with an individual's complaints against the government, serving as a kind of intermediary. What Schulman was assigned to do was to listen to the public's complaints about news coverage in Louisville and do something about it, but not in print.

The idea, in itself, wasn't new. I remember that Joseph Pulitzer's New York *World* and *Evening World* had a similar operation at about the time I became a New York newspaperman in 1924. Then, the Ombudsman, only he wasn't called that, had a small office near the entrance to the *World*'s awesome city room, where the city editor sat on a raised dais and surveyed his realm like a little king. It was obvious that the city editor had power, the Ombudsman did not. But he tried.

Whenever anybody wrote, telephoned, or appeared in person to complain about the *World* newspapers, the case immediately was shunted to the genteel functionary in the small, little-noticed outer office. He was, as *World* staff people recalled, an elderly gentleman, quietly and conservatively dressed, who received callers with exquisite courtesy. He would listen gravely, take notes, and give assurance that "something would be done." But that early Ombudsman's corrective actions were rare. He served mainly as a buffer and was not encouraged to be an activist. The columnist F. P. A. (Franklin Pierce Adams) was much more to be feared. In his daily Conning Tower on the Op-Ed page he would sometimes scold his fellow staff members for errors of fact, judgment, and good taste.

In Louisville, the Ombudsman was encouraged to be a public defender in every sense of that much-abused term. Schulman handled as many as 3,000 complaints a year. He sought corrections, when necessary, from staff members of the newspapers. Each day he issued a memo to management and staff, which had to be taken seriously. He also maintained correspondence with complainants until they were satisfied or wore out their welcome with unreasonable demands. Nobody was wildly excited about the innovation, least of all the reporters who were constantly in the line of fire. But the management persisted. After six years of service, Schulman's performance was adjudged so worthy that he was given the additional responsibility of media critic and a decent amount of news space for his opinions.

This was Togetherness with a vengeance. What it meant was that the Louisville newspapers, which had no local press competition, were committed to criticizing their own performance in print as well as that of the national news media. It was not a principle to which many other news organizations adhered. To be sure, *Time* and *Newsweek* had press sections but they did not criticize themselves in their own pages. Nor did the occasional broadcast critics of the press turn their attention to the shortcomings of their own medium as a regular part of their duties.

A few hard-bitten journalists had set themselves up as press critics. However, all but one or two lacked a showcase for their wares until the *Columbia Journalism Review* was founded, with he support of the Ford Foundation and like-minded organizations, at Columbia University. For a while, regional critical reviews of the press and broadcast media were popular but most of them ran out of funds. A few hung on somewhat longer but none enjoyed particular prosperity. Media criticism, like the Ombudsman's task as a public defender, was not destined to achieve wide popularity.

What happened was that a few outstanding newspapers established the combined post of Ombudsman and media critic, emulating the Louisville papers. The only two who operated in a major city for any length of time, however, were Charles B. Seib of the Washington *Post* and George Beveridge of the Washington *Star*. Like Schulman and Joe Liebling, the *New Yorker*'s occasional press critic until his death, both were seasoned newspapermen who were widely respected within the profession. Seib had been a managing editor of the Washington *Star*. Beveridge had won a Pulitzer Prize as a reporter for the Washington *Star*.°

Answering the criticism of John S. Knight that an Ombudsman merely did the work that an editor should do, Beveridge once observed, "Knight missed a big point. Nothing I do involves delegation or usurpation of the editor's responsibilities. Mine is the power to complain, and that I can do without restraint, publicly or privately."[38]

Of this small and motley group, it was Seib who established himself as the most authoritative voice. When he complained about the degradation of the English language in the columns of the nation's newspapers, including his own, his article was widely reprinted, discussed, and dissected. He also had the temerity to reproach the news media for its coverage of the uprising of the Hanafi Muslims in the nation's capital, calling it a "Media Event." Quoting the Washington *Post*'s lead that the Hanafis had "terrorized" the city, Seib commented:

> Allowing for journalistic hyperbole, that was essentially true. But it was true only because the media made it true.
>
> A community can be truly terrorized only if the terrorists have real power—if they can cripple the machinery of law and order. That clearly didn't happen in Washington.
>
> What did happen was that the media, with its capacity for instant and massive communication, spread the word. Only that made it possible for a handful of men holding 100-plus hostages in three buildings to "terrorize" a city of a million. The news business did what it always does when it deals with violence, bloodshed, and suspense; it covered it excessively.[39]

Seib was modest about both his role in journalism and his influence. "Self-monitoring," he once said, "is the same as saying let Congress monitor itself or let the White House monitor itself. But it's better than nothing." All of which caused a press critic, Edwin Diamond, to mourn his lot as follows: "Why is it that only the better papers and the better broadcast groups that need it

---

°At best, there were only about 20 full-time Ombudsmen on American dailies of more than 50,000 circulation.

least have media critics? Why not the worst? How can we (as critics) break through to the general reader/viewer and not just to the other elite?"[40]

The answer is, unfortunaltely, that the general reader/viewer is not very often aware that the press does exercise, to a limited degree, the necessary function of self-criticism. Nor does the general reader/viewer know much about the National News Council, the labors of the Ombudsmen, or any other facet of the movement to induce the journalist to abandon his posture of isolation and become more responsive to change.

The press, in short, is set apart from most of the other motivating forces in American society because it chooses to be. The position is more than a convenience. Given the press's commitment to the adversary principle, it is a strategic necessity. There is little likelihood, in consequence, that either pressure or persuasion by well-meaning people or public-spirited organizations will cause the press to seek a greater accommodation with the government or the resentful part of the private sector in the forseeable future. Togetherness is not a theme that most journalists habitually practice or even understand. There's not much news in a society that is based on self-congratulation. Nor much hope, either.

4. The Case for a Free Press

In the five centuries since Johann Gutenberg demonstrated the art of printing on his converted wine press in Mainz, a truly free press has been a rarity in the world. And so it remains today.

Many great and ancient lands now suffer under dictatorships. Being unable to maintain an open society, their peoples are cruelly and sometimes brutally denied the right to print what is in their minds and speak what is in their hearts. Worse still, there are rulers who exercise power by deception and guile and proclaim their press to be free when it is in reality so stifled by laws and regulations that its supposed independence is a mere mockery.

Of the 149 members of the United Nations who pledged themselves to seek peace and a better world, little more than a score—exclusive of ministates—permit freedom of speech and of the press.[41] The United States is by far the largest of these. It is also the most powerful and the most generous in its exercise of those human rights that are the most precious to free peoples and the most sought after by those who struggle against terror and repression.

The American impulse is to try to change the world and make it over in the American image, but Chile, Cuba, and Vietnam prove that doesn't work. Instead, authoritarian regimes dominate the continents of Asia, Africa, and South America, and are advancing across Europe from the East.

There is no assurance of permanent safety for Western civilization in general, and the United States in particular, because of the schism between Moscow and its rival Communist power center in Peking. Changes in either regime could bring a reversal of policy that would confront the West with the most formidable challenge in its history. Even now, despite their divergent aims, the Soviet Union and China follow parallel courses in their denial of the most fundamental of human rights—freedom of speech and freedom of the press being the first and most important.

As George Beebe of the Miami *Herald* stated the position when he accepted the chairmanship of the World Press Freedom Committee, "Many proposals before the United Nations Educational, Scientific, and Cultural Organization seek to spread the Russian school of press control into the Third World. This is not a Red Scare. This is a Red Reality."[42]

So it turned out. At the 19th general conference of UNESCO in Nairobi, a Russian-supported resolution was introduced that would have bestowed international approval on state control of all activities "in the international sphere of all mass media under their jurisdiciton." What this meant was that Third World countries would have been given the right to oversee all information about themselves that originates within their borders, in addition to controlling their own news media. It would have constituted intolerable interference with all foreign correspondence.

While the measure was stalled by an implied threat of the United States to quit UNESCO if it passed, it came back two years later in aggravated form to haunt the West. In the Soviet Union, the principle of controlling the work of correspondents was put into practice when two Americans, Craig R. Whitney of the New York *Times* and Harold D. Piper of the Baltimore *Sun*, were convicted in a Moscow court of libeling Soviet TV employees. Both had written that a faked confession from a Soviet dissident had been broadcast by Soviet TV and they stood by their stories. They were told to publish retractions, which they refused to do, and to pay court costs. The Soviet move was an obvious bid to harass and intimidate foreign correspondents in the spirit of the Nairobi resolution.

There was no doubt that the measure, in one form or another, would come before a renewed UNESCO general conference. Clayton Kirkpatrick of the Chicago *Tribune* said, "We now face a heavy responsibility in protecting our interests."[43]

Many of the Third World countries that wanted to impose some kind of censorship on foreign news at Nairobi have gone ahead and done it anyway. Some acted in the Soviet manner, others were even tougher. After a survey of the overseas bureaus of the Los Angeles *Times* in the year following Nairobi, Otis Chandler, the publisher of the newspaper, said the "two most distressing problems" for the press were these:

—The intensifying hostility of many Third World nations toward the Western media and the barriers some of these nations are erecting against the legitimate process of reporting the news.
—The continuing restrictions on U. S. correspondents in the Soviet Union and the continuing total exclusion of U. S. resident correspondents from the People's Republic of China.

Chandler observed that some Third World countries were patterning their information policies after those of Moscow and

Peking, which is scarcely a surprise under the circumstances. He noted, too, that a few African, Arab, and Asian states have gone farther than Josef Stalin "to isolate their societies from outside scrutiny." Thus, unspeakable horrors can be committed by brutalizing regimes in Communist Cambodia and Idi Amin's Uganda without significant notice in the outside world. It is almost as if Buchenwald, Bergen-Belsen, and all other murder camps in Nazi Germany had never existed, as if Aleksandr Solzhenitsyn had never written about Stalin's Gulag Archipelago.

This is something that could deeply affect the United States, for it is no mere technical matter. There is much more to it than censorship, with which journalists can cope if need be. What it comes down to, as Chandler and others have reported, is a denial of information, a closing of sources, a refusal to grant access to any correspondent whom a regime mistrusts for any reason.

Given the aggravating nature of the energy crisis and its effect on the average American, plus the driving necessity for a broad accommodation between the United States and the dominant Arab bloc in the Third World, the process of news blackouts abroad could have unacceptable consequence at home. Chandler raised the issue with these questions:

> . . .How can the [American] government formulate—and the public pass judgment on—a sensible policy toward countries about which we know little or nothing beyond information supplied by the government's own agencies?
> If it is deemed to be in the national interest of the United States to cooperate in building a new international economic system to assist the Third World, another question must be asked: Can the American taxpayer be expected to support policies benign toward nations secluding themselves behind malignant walls of secrecy?[44]

There is also in this context a question to be asked of news managers, and it is posed by David Ottaway, who was for six years a Washington *Post* correspondent in Africa. Summing up his own experiences, and those of many of his fellow-correspondents in Third World countries, he wrote:

The blatant—and many subtler—ways of suppressing and controlling the news have resulted in a tremendous amount of self-censorship and self-restraint. But even more disturbing, particularly to many individual correspondents working for news agencies, is the growing acceptance by management in London, Paris, and New York of the outright suppression of controversial news for the protection of existing contracts and the better pursuit of new ones.

There is a real dilemma here: Should the whole truth as best we correspondents can determine it be sacrificed so that at least some of the truth gets through to the outside world?[45]

I append my own question: "If serious restrictions are to be imposed on the free press of the United States, how can we hope to knock down the wall of secrecy that is being erected about us by totalitarian regimes?"

It is not easy to reply to any of these questions because there are no pat answers. Those who are searching for a certified method of trying to limit the performance of the press to suit their own notions, and still appear before the nation as the champions of American liberty, are perpetrating an unconscionable fraud on the public. This country cannot exist as a democracy for very long with a press that is partly controlled and partly free.

It will not help us with world opinion if our statesmen denounce the Soviet Union for violating the Helsinki accords on arms control and human rights, and still permit judges to sent American journalists to jail because they refuse to disclose their sources, which would mean placing those sources at the mercy of vengeful public officials.

It will not insure tranquility at home if our government falsely raises the cry of national security, as it has done in the past, to excuse or protect wrongdoing and grievous error in high places.

It will not insure respect for law, much less public order, if new statutes are continually proposed in the Congress to prevent the press from publishing harsh and difficult truths that the public is entitled to read, to hear and to discuss.

We either are an open society or we are not. We shall either go forward together with trust in ourselves and respect for those who differ with us or we shall never be able to retain the Bill of Rights intact. It is one thing to proclaim our inalienable right to life, liberty, and the pursuit of happiness, a pleasant national custom every Fourth of July. It is quite another to keep them.

If we have learned anything from the national traumas of the past decade, it is the truth of Joseph Pulitzer's observation that "our Republic and its press will rise or fall together."[46] For, contrary to popular mythology, a newspaper—or any other news organization for that matter—does not make huge profits out of a revelation of a national calamity. Except for a brief time at the height of the Watergate expose, the adoption of an adversary position against the government in the current era has not halted the downward drift the the press in the public opinion polls.

This places both government and press in a cruel dilemma: The lessons of history show that the press cannot be elevated to a higher degree of public favor unless public confidence and trust are restored first to the government. But it is scarcely likely that the government can recover public confidence as long as the press continues to disclose its shortcomings.

It is one of the quirks of American life that this should be so at a time when the American government is the richest and most powerful in the world and the American press, even with its independence called into question, is stronger and more prosperous than it has been at any other time in its history. Still, if the public continues to mistrust both, the system at best rests on a shaky foundation.

This is not to say that we are trembling on the brink of another great Depression or that revolution is just around the corner; however, the gaping holes that have been ripped in our social fabric to date are serious and they will not easily be mended as long as press and government maintain an attitude of mutual mistrust and mutual suspicion.

The unthinking will say, "Why doesn't the press cooperate

with the government to the benefit of both?" It would make just as much sense for the Democrats to cooperate with Republicans, for the prosecution to cooperate with the defense, for creditors to cooperate with debtors. Such thing do happen, but only when the price of noncooperation means disaster for all concerned. And then, sometimes, the more powerful of the antagonists is able to impose his will on the weaker. It is not a very satisfactory way of maintaining a democratic ideal.

Rivals, probing for soft spots, often advance the notion of mutual cooperation. I remember, just after World War II, a *Pravda* correspondent walked into my office at Lake Success, flashed a gold-toothed smile, warmly pumped my hand after introducing himself and said, "We have no differences, you and I. We are journalists. We are interested only in news. Between journalists there should be a nonaggression pact."

Ah, if it were only so! I explained to my visitor, regardless of my estimate of the sincerity of his intentions, that the history of nonaggression pacts shows that they are broken when they become inconvenient. Moreover, I went on, such an agreement would scarcely be approved by either my newspaper or my countrymen, the cold war already having set in. Again, the gold-toothed smile. More pumping of the hand. A bow, and my visitor returned to the *Pravda* cubbyhole. Nothing ventured, nothing gained.

No thoughtful American, journalist or not, would argue with my decision. But many would ask, as editors have found out for themselves in recent times, why it also is not the patriotic duty of the journalist to cooperate with his government. It is an ingenuous question, but it is much in the minds of the conservative factions in this country, and requires an answer. Bluntly put, the assumption of a universal policy of press cooperation with the government means that our newspapers and broadcast media eventually would be reduced to the level of parrotlike spokesmen for the government. They would utter whatever the government wished to distribute to the people in its unexamined and less than infinite wisdom. For cooperation between press and government, however reasonable it may seem on the surface, usually leads in only one direction—the convenience of the government. Granted the vagaries of human nature in high office, it could not be otherwise, whether power is exerted by an Idi Amin, an Indira Gandhi, or a Richard Nixon.

In the years to come, if the external dangers to the United States should increase and the clamor for national security should rise to a frenzied pitch, it may well be that the press could be obliged to abandon its adversary position and yield to the pressure for conformity. It has happened to many newspapers within this generation. No one who covered Senator Joseph R. McCarthy, Jr., can forget that when he created national hysteria over the supposed presence of Communists in government, he dominated the headlines on many a first page and heard his voice echo from many an editorial page. It could happen again.

The question therefore must be asked: "Can the free press survive in the United State?" Much depends on the public's attitude toward the press. In its currently passive state, public opinion tolerates the covert hostility of the executive branch toward the press and remains unmoved by restrictive gestures affecting all the news media in the federal and state legislative branches and the courts. There is, indeed, some tendency on the part of the public to applaud some of those who make it their business to attack the privileges of the press. As Clark Thomas of the Pittsburgh *Post-Gazette* put it when he was president of the National Conference of Editorial Writers:

> The American public is always inclined to turn against a concentration of power. This has been the case with big business, big labor, big government. Now it is the turn of the big press. It is entirely likely that people think we've gotten too big for our britches and want us taken down a bit.[47]

This in turn poses other questions: "Is the press hurting itself? Do people believe it is abusing its freedom?" The most responsible segment of public opinion is obviously restive because of the continued concentration of power over the news media in relatively few corporate entities. The growth of conglomerates, which make news a part of their general business, does not tend to increase public confidence in the integrity of the public intelligence that is offered in print and on the air. Nor are the great newspaper chains, in themselves, accepted as public benefactors.

It is all very well to say that the consolidation of ownership of the news media has gone on for most of this century, that it was inevitable, and that it has given the country a much stronger base for its engines of public information. All this is true, to a degree, but there does come a time when an aroused public cries, "Halt!" It has happened in industries with greater concentrated power and wealth than the news media, where divestiture was forced by the government. In consequence, if there is a continued flaunting of power by the news media in the years to come, the First Amendment is not likely to prove a great barrier to antitrust action.

True, not many publishers have expressed concern so far. But one who does, Katharine Graham of the Washington *Post*, says nobody really knows the full extent of the chains' absorption of our remaining independent newspapers. "Will the public care if one person owns them all?" she asks. "Obviously it would and then. . .would the public care if six people owned them all? Yes. . . You have an irreversible trend going and nothing can stop it short of government intervention and then, at that point, we all choke. . . I really don't know the answer."[48]

Not many others are confident that they know the answer, either. All of which means that Rep. Morris Udall's proposal of antitrust studies in the news media field is likely to continue to attract attention. Moreover, Senator Edward M. Kennedy, the leading liberal Democrat in the Congress today, has a watchful Senate subcommittee on antitrust and monopoly legislation. "If and when needed," he says, antitrust laws "are ready and fully able to promote a diverse and competitive press."[49] This is not so much a threat as a statement of fact.

In other respects, the press also may not be helping its own cause very much with the public. Most newspaper people have protested, from sheer instinct, the current tendency on the part of numerous papers to drift away from the rigorous presentation of the news and load up the news hole with a lot of soggy features. The excuse for the rise of such fare, including everything from idle gossip to recipes, is that television now covers the news, a half-truth at best.

But at the end of a massive survey of public opinion, Leo Bogart gave his views to the Newspaper Advertising Bureau: "News remains the most important component of a newspaper, even for the infrequent readers who are most attracted to features. Even in today's intensely competitive media environment, we will be most successful if we continue to do very well our traditional job of reporting the news."[50]

It remains to be seen whether Bogart's thesis will win acceptance in the newspaper newsrooms of the nation. On the New York *Times*, it is a sour joke among reporters who work on the 5-day-a-week special feature sections that a new one is about to be started called, "News." Surely, if the public can get only bulletin news from television's evening news programs and more features than news from its newspapers, it is a weary truism that people will not obtain sufficient information to make the judgments required of a democratic society. The news magazines, for all their excellence, come out a week late and cannot cover the entire market.

Neither the receding glories of the Watergate investigation nor the current tub-thumping for feature papers can conceal the inadequacies of the media's news presentation. For, during the past 30 or 40 years, the press has been surprised too often by news that it should have covered, but didn't. There was, for example, the massive movement of blacks from the rural South to Northern cities in the 1940s, the wholesale migration of Puerto Ricans to New York City shortly afterward, the rotting decay of

our inner cities, the flight of the middle class whites to the suburbs—vast population movements that everybody knew about
but few reported on until the riotous explosions of the 1960s.

There were, as well, other social problems that were not
covered in depth until they blew up—the voting rights campaigns
of the remaining blacks in the South, the lack of school integration in Northern cities, the festering evil in the poor ghettos of
many a metropolitan community today. Yes, reporters were accurate with street addresses and middle initials, but the larger truths
eluded them at home (and I was one of them for 25 years).
Abroad, the position was even worse, for it is scarcely a secret
that a substantial part of the press defended the Vietnam War
until very late in the Johnson administration; to be explicit, the
Tet offensive in 1968.

The press was also late in recognizing the strength of the
women's movement, later with the campaign to protect the environment, and it still lags in the coverage of consumer affairs in
many parts of the nation. Many young readers find little in news
pages to attract them to the press, and polls indicate that they
make a poor showing as viewers of TV news, as well.

Politically, there has been some progress and a greater degree of sophistication both in the news columns and editorial
pages. We do not now have the violently partisan press that existed in the first half of this century, notably the anti-New Deal
press. And yet, there is still a heavy editorial bias in favor of
Republican candidates, representing a party that can claim only
20 percent of American voters. In the 1976 election, President
Ford had the support of more than three times as many papers as
Jimmy Carter.

All these things are bound to affect the credibility of the
press. When they are added to the rising costs of newspapers,
which now range from 15 to 25 cents a copy, and the difficulties
of home delivery in apartment complexes and condominiums that
are guarded like fortresses in crime-prone communities, it is no
wonder that the press is in trouble in spite of its record profits.

The deficiencies of the press in providing information are compounded by the inefficiency, the negligence, and sometimes the deliberate intent of government at every level to withhold the kind of news that should be public property. It amounts to a national scandal that public bodies throughout the land, in defiance of open meeting laws, still do much of their work in secret by adopting such devices as executive sessions, private telephone conferences, and unannounced meetings at odd hours in the early morning or late at night. It is often quite expensive and time-consuming to force disclosure of necessary information through the Freedom of Information Act at the national level. And the various "Sunshine Laws" in the states usually operate under a heavy cloud cover.

Roger Mudd of CBS reported that the Carter administration was doing a bit better than its predecessors. "The government is more open than before," he said, "but not as open as we thought."[51]

Under these circumstances, it would seem that it would be somewhat more important for the government to cooperate with the press in the dissemination of necessary information than to try, by devious means, to oblige the press to give greater cooperation to the government.

There is, of course, a species of government cooperation with the press that is very important to the maintenace of this republic. It is the familiar process of leaking news and most government officials denounce it as an affront to decency and a threat to the survival of the nation. Yet, if it were not for the willingness of some in government to give a certain amount of supposedly confidential information to the press, the citizens of this land would know a lot less than they should. Some officials leak on principle, some out of partisanship, and many for personal or agency advantage; but, whatever the reason, the practice of leaking information is well established and no law is likely to do away with it.

After all, sometimes the government deliberately leaks a story at the highest level for its own advantage.

It is rare, however, for anybody in government at any level to support an impartial outside investigation that is conducted in the public interest. When it happens, it can be beneficial. There was the case of a lanky, tough-looking kid named Ed May, an investigative reporter for the Buffalo *Evening News*, who entertained the suspicion that the adminstration of public welfare in the State of New York constituted a major scandal. That wasn't yesterday. It happened in 1960.

May sold his city editor on the proposition and asked for a three-month leave of absence to become a caseworker for the New York State Department of Public Welfare. He received permission, got right on the job and soon found his suspicions justified. At the end of three months, he wrote a series called "Our Costly Dilemma," which the Buffalo *Evening News* published in some 20 installments. It showed specifically where public welfare was costing the taxpayers much more money than was necessary. It disclosed terrible inefficiency and demonstrated that archaic procedures often actually took money away from the very people it was supposed to help and wasted it on paper work. At the conclusion of the series, May demonstrated from his own experience how millions of dollars could be saved with benefit to the recipients of welfare.

For that piece of investigative reporting, May won a Pulitzer Prize for Local Reporting in 1961. But the significant part of the story is that he was nominated for the prize by the very official whom he investigated—the Commissioner of Public Welfare in the State of New York.

On the basis of 22 years of experience as the Administrator of the Pulitzer Prizes, I know of very few other instances in which a government official recognized the constructive work of an investigative reporter in such a spectacular way.

True, a lot of governors, mayors, and DA's have nominated

newspapers, editors, and reporters, but usually it is for work that exposed their political opponents, not themselves. There is no record, for example, of anybody in the Nixon administration being overcome by admiration for the press and nominating a reporter for a Pulitzer. And to date, for that matter, there seems to be little enthusiasm for the press's investigative work in the Carter administration, but the Bert Lance affair may have something to do with that.

There is at least one other case of government support for an investigation that turned out well—an inquiry into Medicaid frauds in New York City by Bill Sherman, a young investigative reporter for the New York *Daily News*. With the cooperation of the city's Health Department, which gave him a Medicaid card and helped him find out why taxpayers were being robbed of millions of dollars by unscrupulous doctors and others, he also won a Pulitzer Prize in Reporting, this one in 1974.

The May and Sherman awards are rare examples of formal government-press cooperation in investigations of government affairs. There may be others, of which I have no knowledge, but in any event there are not many, as every reporter knows all too well. The usual governmental stance, in the face of an investigation, is to deny all, stonewall like mad, blame everything on the press, and hope for the best. When officials do cooperate, it generally happens in the manner of Daniel Ellsberg in the Pentagon Papers case and "Deep Throat" in the Watergate investigation.

It strikes me that journalists have only themselves to blame when government gets away with a stonewall defense, whether or not there is any basis for it. Because so many of them have adopted a stand-offish attitude toward the public at large, they have been successfully depicted as grasping self-seekers who attack established institutions for whatever personal benefits they can gain. And so we find, as a result, that newspapers are often accused of forcing unnecessary inquiries into the conduct of pure, selfless, high-minded public servants in order to boost their circulations. This kind of nonsense emanated sotto voce from Carter administration sources in the Bert Lance case and a lot of people actually believed it.

The press's mistake is that such slanders are seldom answered. Both editors and reporters have heard this response so often during the course of an investigation that they usually do not bother with a denial unless they are taken into court. And sometimes, that is too late.

We know from experience that a vigorous, competent, and dedicated free press is never going to have an easy time investigating the ills of popular government, because it is in the very nature of government to defend itself at all costs. To admit fault under pressure is the most damning of official crimes, as far as officialdom itself is concerned. It follows that tension is bound to be created if the press tries to penetrate government secrecy in the course of a proper investigation.

Does this mean, then, that the press is alway to blame for the existence of tension with government and for the maintenance of an adversary relationship? I do not think so. Sometimes, in fact, quite the opposite is the case. Who created the tension over the Pentagon Papers—the New York *Times* or the Nixon administration that tried to suppress publication? Who created the tension over Watergate—the Washington *Post* or President Nixon, with his policy of stonewalling the investigation? And who created tension over Bert Lance—the newspapers that checked his background after a Senate committee twice had approved him as budget director, or President Carter with a last ditch effort to defend his friend?

I believe the answers are obvious. I do not mean to equate the positions of the Nixon and Carter administrations here. Nixon had to face up to impeachment charges and was forced out of office. Carter's fault, like that of his Democratic predecessor in the White House, Lyndon Baines Johnson, was to persist stubbornly in a course of conduct and policy that eventually proved to be damaging to the credibility of his administration.

In most instances with which I am familiar, it is precisely this defensive attitude that accounts for most of the tension between government and press. It leads to a denial of access to meetings, to public records, to accountable public officials, and to documents wrongly withheld in the name of national security. These things did not occur in the cases of Ed May and Bill Sherman, because government, in both instances, was receptive to reforms and improvements suggested by an honest, thorough, decent, and necessary investigation. There was no coverup.

I am not so unrealistic as to suggest that we can expect more examples, that we no longer have to look for government leaks to force necessary disclosures, or that any government agency that "welcomes an investigation" actually means it. With rare exceptions, this just isn't going to happen, no matter how desirable it may be. It would go against human nature.

In my own active career as a newspaper reporter, I can remember any number of leaks from sympathetic officials, but just one on-the-record instance in which the chairman of a legislative committee actually helped me—once in 25 years! Yet, it is clear enough that if there were more formal cooperation between public officials and the press, there would be less tension and greater public benefit.

So it is difficult to accept the general thesis that the press, no matter how grievous its faults, is primarily responsible for the existence of an adversary relationship with government in a democratic society. A wrong-headed and needlessly defensive attitude on the part of government can be just as damaging, sometimes more so. But the proclamation of this self-evident truth is not going to change anything.

The impartial investigation of official conduct remains the principal way for a democratic society to defend itself from abuse. If properly elected or appointed government representatives can do this job, well and good; but if they fail, then the task falls by default to the press. And it would be a worthless, irresponsible, and supine press that did not accept this responsibility.

As for the executive branch, the tendency to use "national security" as a pretext for unnecessary secrecy did not end with the downfall of Richard M. Nixon. The nation now knows that "national security" has been used since at high levels of government to try to persuade the press not to print material that the public is entitled to know.

Here again, it is the spirit—much more even than the deed—that is alarming. For despite all disclaimers, reporters and editors and broadcasters are well aware of the persistently critical attitude at the White House and the Department of Justice in the last three administrations.

All too often, the atmosphere in the capital is charged with tension between government and press. What it means is that this government has embarked on a collision course with its press. To be sure, it breaks off and makes a few concessions, apologies, and assurances when it must. But all too soon, it veers back on its hazardous course.

This is, therefore, a difficult and dangerous time in the history of this republic. For if government and press should smash into each other in such a way as to force the nation to choose between them, the outcome could be disastrous not only for the free press but for all the other rights contained in the First Amendment.

NOTES

I. A Question of Confidence

1. New York *Times*, May 5, 1976, p. 41.
2. *Saturday Review*, Editor's Page, Nov. 12, 1977, p. 4.
3. It happened April 1, 1977, at a regional meeting in Knoxville, Tenn., of the Society of Professional Journalists/Sigma Delta Chi.
4. *The Bulletin of the American Society of Newspaper Editors*, September 1976, pp. 9-13.
5. New York *Times*, Dec. 10, 1976, Op-Ed page.
6. Mahoney on the Op-Ed Page of the New York *Times*, July 7, 1977; West, McNaughton, and Powell quoted in the *Quill*, April 1977, pp. 15-18.
7. Ibid.
8. Connally in the New York *Times*, May 2, 1977, p. 31; Phillips in *Harper's* magazine, July 1977, p. 24; Udall quoted in the *Guild Reporter*, April 22, 1977, p. 3. Kilpatrick in the *Quill*, December 1976, pp.10-11.
9. The SEC report on Exxon and other American business firms is in the Associated Press file for Sept. 27, 1977; the Lance case is summarized in *Time*, Oct. 3, 1977, p. 15 et seq., and *Newsweek*, Oct. 3, 1977, p. 22 et seq.
10. Harris poll released Jan. 5, 1978. Dr. Roshco's analysis was based on an earlier Harris poll in 1977.
11. Roper poll released January 1978.
12. Roper poll released in April 1977, by TV Information Office.
13. The Gallup survey was conducted in Spring 1976.
14. Letter to me from Dr. Gallup, April 27, 1977.
15. "Trust and Confidence in the American System," by Francis E. Rourke, Lloyd A. Free, and William Watts. (Washington, D. C.: Potomac Associates, 1976), pp. 10-16.
16. Ibid., p. 26.
17. Ibid., pp. 12-13 and 27.
18. Lazarsfeld expounds this theory at some length in his book, *The People's Choice* (New York: Columbia U. Press, 1968).
19. Rourke, Free, and Watts, "Trust and Confidence."
20 Harris poll released Jan. 5, 1978.
21. The NORC poll was in March and April 1976.
22. The Roper poll was in January 1978.
23. The Gallup poll was part of a document on "The Credibility of the Press" in December 1973, and was prepared for newspaper editors.
24. Later Gallup poll, *ASNE Bulletin*, May-June, 1978, p. 21.
25. Gallup polls in 1973 and 1978.
26. Curt Matthews, "Public Esteem of Press Appears to Have Eroded," St. Louis *Post-Dispatch*, June 13, 1976.
27. "20% Found Opposed to Press in Survey," UPI dispatch in the New York *Times*, Dec. 16, 1974.

28. "A National Study of Public Attitudes," by Marquis Childs, the *Quill*, February, 1976, p. 8.

29. Walter Lippmann, *Liberty and the News* (New York: Harcourt, Brace & Howe, 1920), p. 76.

30. Alexis de Tocqueville, *Democracy in America*, I, 92 (New York: Vintage, 1945).

31. Harris poll published Sept. 9, 1976, in the Knoxville *Journal*.

32. *Writings of Thomas Jefferson*, edited by P. L. Ford (New York: G. P. Putnam's Sons, 1892-99) IV, 359-60. Letter to Edward Carrington, January 16, 1787.

33. Ibid., VIII, 218-19. Letter to Gov. Thomas McKean, Feb. 19, 1803.

34. Frank Luther Mott, *American Journalism*, 3rd ed. (New York: Macmillan, 1962). The story of the Baltimore *Federal American*, p. 174; the murder of Lovejoy, an antislavery editor, p. 307.

35. John Hohenberg, *Between Two Worlds* (New York: Praeger, for the Council on Foreign Relations, 1967), pp. 292-93.

36. Warren H. Phillips, "A Free Press—If You Can Keep It," lecture at the University of California, Riverside, March 8, 1976.

37. Kilpatrick in the *Quill*, December 1976, pp. 10-11; Gallagher in APME Red Book, 1975, p. 123; Carter press policy and court rulings in New York *Times*, June 26, p. A-19, July 6, p. 1, and July 12, p. A-12, all 1978; also *Editor & Publisher*, June 24, 1978, p. 7.

II. The Adversaries

1. The complete Learned Hand quotation is: "The First Amendment presupposes that right conclusions are more likely to be gathered out of a multitude of tongues than through any kind of authoritative selection. To many this is, and always will be, folly; but we have staked upon it our all." (U. S. *v.* Associated Press, 52 F. Supp. 362)

2. *New York* magazine, Dec. 20, 1976, p. 112.

3. Transcript of excerpt of "Today" program for January 21, 1977, beginning at 8:40 *a. m.* over NBC-TV network, recorded by Radio-Tv Reports Inc., 41 E. 42d St., New York, N. Y., 10017, and made available to me through the courtesy of NBC.

4. On the NBC "Today" show, May 5, 1977.

5. Acheson reproduced the statement, originally made in January 1953, in a letter to me dated April 6, 1965.

6. The New York *Times*, June 17, 1977, p. B-5, cols. 6 and 7.

7. Vermont Royster, "The American Press and the Revolutionary Tradition" (Washington, D. C.: American Enterprise Institute, 1974), p. 2.

8. The statement is in the New York *Times* entry for John L. Hess, a reporter, in the Pulitzer Prize competition in January 1975.

9. Sources for the Hussein story: Washington *Post*, Feb. 18, 19, 20, 1977. *Newsweek*, March 7, 1977, p. 16, and March 14, 1977, p. 40; *Time*, March 14, 1977, p. 80. Sources for follow-up action: Mondale interview, Washington *Post*, March 5, 1977, p. 1.; text of Presidential news conference, March 9, 1977, pp. 7-8; draft text, executive order on National Security Information, September 1977, pp. 23 and 30-31; Dole text and State Department cable, Topeka (Kansas) *Daily Capital*, Oct. 6, 1977, p. 1.

10. Senator Muskie wrote to me on Sept. 21, 1977, that he had no recollection of the substance of his talk with Carter. Muskie came out against the censorship provisions of Senate bill S-1 in 1975, but said he was for a bill that would protect legitimate national secrets without threatening the news media with prosecution. In four months of correspondence with the White House, I obtained no further clarification of Carter's views.

11. Text of NBC's "Meet the Press" program July 11, 1976.

12. Curtis Wilkie of the Boston *Globe*, in the *Quill*, January 1977, p. 15.

13. David Wise, "Friendship Can Be Dangerous," *TV Guide*, May 21, 1977, p. 5.

14. The New York *Times*, Nov. 6, 1976, pp. 1 and 8.

15. The *Quill*, December 1976, p. 12.

16. *New Republic*, Jan. 22, 1977, pp. 25-26.

17. *Newsweek*, Nov. 22, 1976, p. 82.

18. In a letter to me, Jan. 27, 1977.

19. *Newsweek* (May 2, 1977, p. 32) reported that a Harris poll immediately after Carter assumed office gave him a 75 percent popularity rating. The New York *Times* (May 27, 1977, p. 17) ran a Gallup Poll with a 66 percent popularity rating and later (June 16, 1977, p. A-17) an additional Gallup Poll with a 64 percent rating.

20. New York *Times*, April 24, 1977, Op-Ed Page.

21. *Time*, March 28, 1977, p. 57.

22. Ibid.

23. I have consulted many sources for this account of the Lance case, including some of the correspondents and other figures who were directly involved. The printed material is voluminous. The New York *Times* and Washington *Post* are required reading from Sept. 6 through Sept. 22, 1977. Carter's news conferences on the networks in this period were of particular importance and the texts were scrutinized. *Time* and *Newsweek*, from Sept. 5 through Oct. 3, gave both news summaries and comment that were enlightening. The Associated Press file, too, was useful, particularly the Aug. 26 PM report and the AP poll in the AM report of Sept. 20. Individual reporters whose work I consulted included Martin Schram of *Newsday* for a brilliant summary on Sept. 21, and Dolph Simons, Jr., for his Saturday column in the Lawrence (Kansas) *Journal-World*, Sept. 17.

The Carter polls are summarized in *Newsweek*, Mar. 20, 1978, p. 23; AP day report for Mar. 29, 1978; Walter Mears's column and AP day report for May 5, 1978. The Washington *Post*, Sept. 22, 1977, carried Carter's farewell to Lance, and, on Apr. 13, 1978, Lance's warning of press censorship. The columnists' opinion of the Carter presidency are summarized in Thomas Griffith, "Newswatch" in *Time*, Nov. 7, 1977, p. 100, and Charles Mohr, New York *Times*, Oct. 23, 1977, p. 1. Frank Cormier's AP piece about the Helms case was in the PM report for Nov. 9, 1977. Attorney General Bell's plea to the press was carried under a Boca Raton, Fla., dateline on the AP's AM report on Novermber 16, 1977. The Marston affair was carried in a *Newsweek* summary, Jan. 30, 1978, p. 34; Carter's responses in his news conference in the New York *Times*, Jan. 30, 1978. The New York *Times*-CBS News poll on Carter was released June 30, 1978.

24. The Pulitzer paper in St. Louis, the *Post-Dispatch*, survived.

25. W. A. Swanberg, *Pulitzer* (New York: Charles Scribner's Sons, 1967) pp. 417-18. The standard history of the *World*, from which the Pulitzer principles are taken, is James W. Barrett, *Joseph Pulitzer and His World* (New York: Vanguard, 1941).

26. New York *Times*, June 19, 1977, p. E-3.

27. Robert E. L. Baker, "The Press Freedom War," *Journalism Educator*, October 1975, pp. 18-21.

28. Carl Bernstein and Bob Woodward, *All the President's Men* (New York: Simon & Schuster, 1974), pp. 105-8, 235.

29. *Newsweek*, July 11, 1977, p. 66; New York *Times*, Feb. 15, 1977, p. 16, *ASNE Bulletin* January 1977, p. 20, carried a statement by A. M. Rosenthal, executive editor of the New York *Times*, that he ran the paper "with my stomach."

30. Speech June 23, 1976, before the Society of Professional Journalists/Sigma Delta Chi, at Albany, Oregon.

31. From text of NBC's "Meet the Press," Jan. 23, 1977.

32. *North American Review*, 102 (April 1866).

33. This is generally credited to Wilbur F. Storey, editor of the Chicago *Times*.

31. It was quietly removed early in 1978 in favor of a less strident ad.

35. Los Angeles *Times*, Nov. 26, 1976.

36. The *Times*'s report showed it earned $69,513,000 in 1976, up 47.1 percent, with a 7.1 percent after-tax margin for Times Mirror and a before-tax earning of 11.4 percent for the newspaper division alone. The Knight-Ridder group, in second place, was up 59.6 percent in earnings with a 7.7 percent profit. The Gannett Company, third largest earner, boosted earnings by 23.9 percent with profits at 11.6 percent. Statistics are from company

documents as published in *Editor & Publisher, Guild Reporter, Time, Newsweek, Fortune,* and by the American Newspaper Publishers Association. *Guild Reporter* headline in issue of June 10, 1977.

37. New York *Times*, Aoirl 15, 1976, p. 19; also, Feb. 4, 1978, p. 1; *Editor & Publisher,* Feb. 11, 1978, pp. 9-10, and Jan. 28, 1978, p. 13. John S. Knight's column in Miami *Herald,* Feb. 8, 1978, p. 6A.

38. "Facts About Newspapers, 1978," published by the American Newspaper Publishers Association, Reston, Va. See also the Washington *Post* series, "The Newspaper Business," 12 articles published on consecutive days in business section beginning July 24, 1977.

39. *Editor &Publisher Yearbooks*, 1970-76, for comparative circulations. Other statistics from the ANPA's "Facts About Newspapers, 1977." Readership Project from the *ASNE Bulletin*, October 1977, pp. 22-23.

40. New York *Times* statistics from *Editor & Publisher*, Feb. 25, 1978, p. 18; others from *Editor & Publisher*, Feb. 18, pp. 17-19, and May 13, 1978, p. 91; also Colin, Hochstin & Co., the *Guild Reporter*, Sept. 23, 1977, p. 1.

41. *Columbia Journalism Review*, March/April 1977, p. 19. For reports of newspaper changes, see *Editor & Publisher*, Jan. 7, 1978, p. 40; New York *Times*, Feb. 4, 1978, p. 1; *Wall Street Journal*, Jan. 31, 1978, p. 1, and *Editor & Publisher*, Feb. 11, 1978, pp. 9-10, and AP night report May 9, 1978, for Gannett merger proposal.

42. Transcript of discussion before 1977 convention of the American Society of Newspaper Editors in Honolulu, p. 218.

43. Washington *Post*, July 24, 1977, Business Section. The statistics are from "1977 End-of-Year Data, U. S. Newspaper Groups," compiled by Professor Paul Jess of the University of Kansas.

44. Transcript of a question and answer exchange between Lee Hills and me, July 11, 1977.

45. Transcript of the ASNE meeting in Honolulu, 1977, pp. 226-27.

46. Ibid., pp. 232, 233.

47. Ibid., pp. 228, 232.

48. The incident occurred a few years before Lork Thomson's death. I was the visitor.

49. Transcript of exchange between Lee Hills and me, July 11, 1977.

50. Patterson's remarks are from the transcript of the ASNE convention in Honolulu, 1977, p. 229. Ghiglione's position is taken from his article in the *ASNE Bulletin*, "Does More Mean Merrier?" October 1977, pp. 3-5. The estimate of 400 independent dailies in the U.S. is from the New York *Times*, Feb. 4, 1978, p. 1.

51. Clinton Rossiter & James Lare, eds., *The Essential Lippmann*, (New York: Random House, 1963), p. 410.

52. Quoted in Jonathan Daniels, *They Will Be Heard*, (New York: McGraw-Hill, 1965), p. 18.

53.A. M. Schlesinger, *Prelude to Independence*, (New York: Knopf, 1957), p. 46.

54. Glyndon G. Van Deusen, *Horace Greeley*, (Philadelphia: U. of Pennsylvania Press, 1953), p. 51.

55. Quoted in Daniels, p. 107.

56. Meyer Berger, *The Story of the New York Times* (New York: Simon & Schuster, 1951), pp. 107-8.

57. Ralph McGill, *The South and the Southerner* (Boston: Little, Brown, and Company, 1959, 1963), pp. 232-33.

58. *In Search of Light: The Broadcasts of Edward R. Murrow* (New York: Knopf, 1967), p. 355.

59. Quoted in John Hohenberg, *Free Press/Free People* (New York: Columbia University Press, 1971), pp. 317-18.

60. Carl Van Doren, *Benjamin Franklin*, (New York: Viking Press, 1938), p. 32.

61. Upton Sinclair, *The Brass Check*, published by the author (Pasadena, Calif., 1920).

62. Miller won two Pulitzer Prizes for his work, the first in 1967, the second in 1976. Benno C. Schmidt, Jr., *Freedom of the Press vs. Public Access* (New York: Praeger, 1976), p. 58.

63. *In Search of Light*, pp. 247-48.

64. Quoted in Edwin Emery and Henry Ladd Smith, *The Press in America* p. 715. (Englewood Cliffs, N. J.: Prentice-Hall, 1962)

65. David Wise and Thomas B. Ross, *The U-2 Affair* (New York: Random House, 1962) pp. 168-72.

66. Quoted in Schmidt, p. 59.

67. There are many sources for this material. The basic source is the New York *Times*, April 8-20, 1961. See also Arthur Meier Schlesinger, Jr., *A Thousand Days* (Boston: Houghton Mifflin, 1965), pp. 260-61; Ben H. Bagdikian, "Independence and the Cuban Crisis," *Columbia Journalism Review*, Winter 1963, pp. 9-11; Kennedy's admission was quoted by Clifton Daniel in the *Times*, June 2, 1966; the *Times*'s editorial was published May 10, 1961.

68. This is personal testimony. I interviewed nearly all the resident correspondents and stringers in 1964 for a Council on Foreign Relations book about Asian-American relations, *Between Two Worlds* (New York: Praeger, 1967).

69. Editorial in New York *Times*, June 16, 1971.

70. John Hohenberg, *The Pulitzer Prizes* (Columbia U. Press, 1974), p. 308.

71. My own recollection of the Board meeting, March 9, 1972.

72. *The Pulitzer Prizes*, pp. 310-11.

73. Daniel Patrick Moynihan, "The Presidency & the Press," *Commentary*, March 1971.

74. Quoted in Ithiel De Sola Pool, "Newsmen and Statesmen, Adversaries or Cronies?" in Aspen Notebook on Government and the Media, 1973.

75. UPI Reporter, July 14, 1977, and Jan. 12, 1978.

76. AP Log, Oct. 31, 1977. All these papers won citations from the Associated PRess Managing Editors organization.

III. The Press at Bay

1. I once heard the eminent lawyer, Louis Nizer, hold forth on the subject for two hours with the greatest enthusiasm before a Columbia Law School audience. It is typical of the view of the American bench and bar.

2. Charles Wintour, *Pressures on the Press: An Editor Looks at Fleet Street* (London: Andre Deutsch, 1972), pp. 131-32. The case of the alleged "human vampire" was that of John George Haigh, who was convicted in 1949 of murdering Mrs. Olive Durand-Deacon.

3. Albert G. Pickerell, "No 'Night Lawyers' in U. S. Newsrooms—Yet," *ASNE Bulletin*, October 1976, pp. 14-15.

4. Anthony Lewis's comment is in "Libel Suits, Britain's Indoor Sport," New York *Times*, Aug. 8, 1976, p. E-16. Wintour, *Pressures on the Press*, describes the Official Secrets Acts, pp. 140-53. The government description of the Official Secrets Acts is from a pamphlet, "The British Press," published by the British Information Services, July, 1968, pp. 38-40.

5. Harold M. Evans, "Is the Press Too Powerful?" *Columbia Journalism Review*, January/February 1972, p. 13.

6. Ibid., p. 16.

7. I am indebted to British Information Services for this research; the letter of transmittal from W. E. H. Whyte, the director, is dated December 10, 1975.

8. The Fortas case was reported in *Life* magazine, May 4, 1969, and in the New York *Times*, May 5, 1969. Citations for Pulitzer Prizes are from the Pulitzer Prize records, 1917-1977, at Columbia University.

9. Henry Fairlie, "Profit Without Honor," *New Republic*, May 7, 1977, p. 16.

10. The best biography is Sir Edward Cook's *Delane of the Times* (London, 1916). See

also Rupert Furneaux, *The First War Correspondent: William Howard Russell of the "Times"* (London: Cassell and Co., 1945).

11. Judge Medina was senior judge on the U. S. Court of Appeals for the Second Circuit when he wrote his essay on "Omnibus 'Gag' Rulings" for the New York *Times*, which published it on November 13, 1975, p. E-13.

12. New York *Times*, May 11, 1961.

13. Quoted in J. R. Wiggins, *Freedom or Secrecy*, rev. ed. (New York: Oxford U. Press, 1964), p. 14. *Editor & Publisher*, Dec. 15, 1962, p. 14.

14. Louis M. Starr, *Bohemian Brigade*, (New York: Knopf, 1954), p. 170.

15. *Memoirs by Harry S Truman* (New York: Doubleday, 1956), II, p. 2.

16. These provisions are in Section 10 (2) of the Atomic Energy Act of 1946.

17. I actually saw such a message once and it was shamelessly labeled classified information.

18. Edwin Emery, *The Press and America* (Englewood Cliffs, N. J.: Prentice-Hall, 1962), 2nd ed., p. 606.

19. Ibid., p. 617.

20. Letter to me dated May 23, 1977. Used with permission.

21. Quoted in an editorial in the New York *Times*, June 20, 1971.

22. New York *Times*, March 20, 1975, p. 31; Oct. 31, 1977, p. 29.

23. Letter to me dated July 28, 1977.

24. James Reston, *The Artillery of the Press* (New York: Harper & Row, 1966) p. 64.

25. Ibid., p. 20.

26. John Hohenberg, *The Professional Journalist* (New York: Holt, Rinehart & Winston, 1973), 3rd ed., p. 532.

27. Bob Woodward and Carl Bernstein, *All the President's Men* (New York: Simon and Schuster, 1974), p. 114.

28. This requires no demonstration of press virtue. Space shots are seldom big news any more.

29. New York *Times*, May 2, 1957.

30. Having been one of them for five years at the New York *Post*, I hope that my prejudices may be excused.

31. New York *Times*, July 7, 1977, p. A-11. the Carter deep backgrounders described here were held July 1 and 6, 1977, at the White House.

32. David Mazzarella, "The Press and Shuttle Diplomacy," *ASNE Bulletin*, November/December 1976, pp. 3-5.

33. Boston *Globe*, August 15, 1976.

34. Ibid.

35. AP Log, August 11, 1975.

36. Leslie H. Gelb, "The Kissinger Legacy," *New York Times Magazine*, October 31, 1976, p. 13, et. seq.

37. AP Log, June 6, 1977.

38. New York *Times*, July 16, 1978, p. 1; *Newsweek*, July 11, 1977, p. 9.

39. Senate Select Committee on Intelligence report in the New York *Times*, April 27, 1976; related articles in the New York*Times*, April 29, 1976; the *Times*'s CIA investigation, Dec. 25, 26, 27, 1977; Colby testimony, Dec. 28, and related articles on subsequent dates until Dec. 31; Karnow article, Dec. 18, 1977, p. E-19; Carl Bernstein report in *Rolling Stone*, Oct. 4, 1977; Charleston *Gazette* report in New York *Times*, Nov. 28, 1976, p. 44; Louisville *Courier-Journal* and *Times* report in the *Courier-Journal*, p. 1., Jan. 9, 1977; ten-year report on U. S. Information Law in New York *Times*, Aug. 8, 1977, p. 1. Additional material on CIA and the media in the *Quill*, February 1976, p. 6.

40. See the Senate Intelligence Committee's report on alleged U. S. involvement in assassination plots against foreign leaders, released Nov. 20, 1975, and associated documents.

41. See the editorial, "The Limits of Loyal Dissent," New York *Times*, August 2, 1977.

42. Material on the Schorr case is taken from his book, published in 1977 by Houghton Mifflin, Boston; his comment before the House in *Newsweek*, Oct. 11, 1976, p. 17; his testimony in AP report for Sept. 15, 1976; House committee decision, AP report, Sept. 22, and Schorr-CBS settlement, AP report, Sept. 28; see also Charles W. Whalen Jr., "The Schorr Follies," New York *Times*, Aug. 29, 1976, p. E-17, and Anthony Lewis's column, New York *Times*, Sept. 19, p. E-1. Comment on Schorr's book in Newswatch by Thomas Griffith, *Time*, Dec. 5, 1977, p. 114.

43. James M. Perry, the *National Observer*, June 20, 1977. Rep. Obey's comments on the press were made during a speech before the Western Wisconsin Press Association in Eau Claire earlier in the year.

44. Quotation on the Eastland inquiry in Gay Talese, *The Kingdom and the Power* (New York: New American Library, 1966), pp. 243-44; quotation by Miller, New York *Times*, March 15, 1976, p. 23.

45. Transcript of discussion before 1977 convention of the American Society of Newspaper Editors, p. 244.

46. From the text of Udall's speech before the National Press Club, April 5, 1977.

47. Lee Hills statement dated July 11, 1977, in response to question from me. Udall's Independent Local Newspaper Act in *Editor & Publisher*, Dec. 31, 1977, p. 10.

48. From a roundup of comment in the transcript of the 1977 convention of the American Society of Newspaper Editors and another in *Air Force Magazine*, June 1977, p. 10.

49. TV profits statistics from *Broadcasting* magazine, Feb. 13, 1978, pp. 100-1 and 104, and Jan. 23, 1978, p. 32. See also "The Media Goliath," *Harper's*, July 1977, pp. 28-29. Other profit statements from the Associated Press report for May 9, 1977.

50. Kevin Phillips, "Busting the Media Trusts," *Harper's* magazine, July 1977, p. 23.

51. Anthony Lewis article distributed by New York *Times* News Service for publication Sept. 23, 1976.

52. Admiral Stansfield Turner's testimony before a Senate committee, Aug. 3, 1977, commented upon in the New York *Times*, Aug. 5, p. A-10. Gannett deal in *Wall Street Journal*, Jan. 31. 1978, p. 1.

53. *Time*, August 8, 1977, p. 42.

54. Most of this discussion is based on documentation supporting the position of the Reporters Committee for Freedom of the Press before the Senate Judicary Subcommittee, submitted June 21, 1977, and subsequently.

55. *Editor & Publisher*, Nov. 22, 1975, p. 44.

56. The *Quill*, July/August 1977, p. 6.

57. From press release of the Reporters Committee for Freedom of the Press, Oct. 28, 1977, and Feb. 1, 1978, plus reports for those dates in the Washington *Post* and New York *Times*. Anthony Day's analysis in the *ASNE Bulletin*, Feb. 1978, p. 16. President Ford also threatened the press with executive and legislative sanctions but nothing came of it. See New York *Times*, Feb. 20, 1976, p. 55.

58. New York *Times*, July 1, 1971, p. 1 et seq. Includes text of decision.

59. Miami *Herald*, July 4, 1971, p. 6A.

60. Blackstone's *Commentaries on the Laws of England*, Vol. 4, pp. 151-52. This quotation is taken from the 1941 edition edited by Bernard C. Gavit and published in Washington, D. C., by the Washington Law Book Co. The earliest American edition of Blackstone (1765-1769 in England) was edited by St. George Ticker and published in Philadelphia in 1803 by Birch and Small.

61. Near v. Minnesota, 283 U. S. 715-16.

62. Thomas I. Emerson, *The System of Freedom of Expression* (New York: Random House, 1970), p. 506.

63. Televised trials were undergoing testing in the courts of Florida and the State of Washington in 1977, regardless of the high court's action.

64. New York *Times*, June 7, 1966, p. 1.

65. Quoted in Benno C. Schmidt, Jr., "The Nebraska Decision," *Columbia Journalism Review*, November/December 1976, p. 53.

66. Ibid., p. 53.

67. Letter by Floyd Abrams in *New York Law Journal*, Aug. 17, 1977, with explanatory letter to me Sept. 13, 1977, and text of testimony before Senate Judiciary Subcommittee by Reporters Committee on June 21, 1977.

68. Sulzberger speech before Judicial Conference of Second Circuit, New York, Sept. 12, 1975.

69. Testimony of Reporters Committee for Freedom of the Press before Senate Judiciary Committee, June 21, 1977; *Editor & Publisher*, Jan. 28, 1978, p. 47; UPI Reporter, Feb. 9, 1978. Stanford case, New York *Times*, June 1, 1978, p. 1.

70. *ASNE Bulletin*, February 1978. Claude Sitton: "Can the First Amendment Survive?" p. 17. Stanford case comment, *Editor & Publisher*, June 17, 1978, p. 9.

71. John V. R. Bull in the *ASNE Bulletin* , November 1977, pp. 16-17; see also UPI Reporter, Oct. 6, 1977, on First Amendment Coalition. Kaufman verdict from New York *Times*, Nov. 8, 1977, p. 1. Los Angeles *Times* commentary published Dec. 3, 1975, editorial page. Kerby comment in Bull article.

72. Judge Medina's comment from Bull article. Murphy comment from Los Angeles *Times* editorial, Dec. 3, 1975. Virginia decision from AP File, May 1, 1978.

73. See New York *Times*, p. 1, for a report of the Supreme Court refusal to intervene in Ohio and South Carolina "gag" cases, Jan. 10, 1978, and for a p. 1 story Dec. 26, 1977, on New York Court of Appeals "gag" decision, with editorial comment on p. 22. The Branzburg case is documented in Branzburg v. Hayes, 408 U. S. 665 (1972) and in New York *Times*, June 30, 1972.

74. U. S. v. Dickinson, 465 F. 2d 496 (5th Circuit, 1972), affirmed from bench 476 F. 2d 373, certificate denied 414 U. S. 979 (1973). See E. Barrett Prettyman, Jr., "Press Freedom: Legal Threats," New York *Times*, Jan. 22, 1975, p. 39.

75. On Farr case, see New York *Times*, July 1, 1976. On Fresno Four, see UPI file, dateline Fresno, Sept. 18, 1976. For Shelledy, see New York *Times* and *Wall Street Journal*, Nov. 1, 1977. Criticism of Shelledy in the *Quill*, February 1978, p. 24.

76. Alan U. Schwartz, "Danger: Pendulum Swinging—Using the Courts to Muzzle the Press," *Atlantic*, February 1977, p. 29, et seq.

77. New York *Times* v. Sullivan (376 U. S. 254).

78. E. Douglas Hamilton and Robert H. Phelps, *Libel: Risks, Rights, Responsibilities* (New York: Macmillan, 1966), p. 188.

79. Rosenbloom v. Metromedia, 403 U. S. 29, is discussed in Benno C. Schmidt Jr., *Freedom of the Press vs. Public Access* (New York: Praeger, 1976), pp. 77-79. Gertz v. Robert Welch, Inc., in 418 U. S. 354. See also *Columbia Journalism Review*, May/June 1975, pp. 38-40; *Editor & Publisher*, Aug. 31, 1974, p. 15, and June 12, 1971, p. 9.

80. Time, Inc. v. Firestone, 96 S. Ct. 970. See also Schwartz, "Danger."

81. Harry W. Stonecipher and Robert Trager, "The Impact of Gertz on the Law of Libel," *Journalism Quarterly*, Winter 1976, p. 609 et seq.

82. Schwartz, "Danger."

83. New York *Times* v. Sullivan, 376 U. S. 279.

84. New York *Times*, March 9, 1974, p. 11.

85. Harry Kalven Jr., "The New York Times Case," 1964 Sup. Ct. Rev. 194.

86. Floyd Abrams, "The Press, Privacy, and the Constitution," *New York Times Magazine*, Aug. 21, 1977, p. 11, et seq.

87. Ibid., pp. 65 et seq.

88. New York *Times*, March 6, 1975, p. 12.

89. Ibid.

90. The first paper on the law of privacy by L. D. Brandeis and S. D. Warren was "The Right of Privacy," *Harvard Law Review*, (1890), pp. 193, 195, 205; Justice Brandeis's

definition of "the right to be let alone" in Olmstead v. U. S., 277 U. S. 438, 478 (1928); the analysis of what is "newsworthy" is enlarged upon in Emerson, p. 550.

91. Time Inc. v. Hill, 385 U. S. 383, 384, 385. See also Emerson pp. 550-55, and comment by the New York *Times*, Nov. 19, 1974, p. 39, and by Floyd Abrams in *New York Times Magazine*, August 21, 1977, p. 70.

92. New York *Times*, Aug. 3, 1976, p. 35.

IV. The Decline of Freedom

1. 395 U. S. 388, 389.

2. Statistics from TV Information Office, WBAI case, New York *Times*, July 4, 1978, p. 1.

3. *Time* (Jan. 9, 1978, p. 69) reported that TV viewing declined for the first time in 1977. Nielson's ratings put the prime time drop at 3.1 percent, Arbitron at 5 percent for daytime hours, Nielson gave the decline as 6.4 percent, Arbitron as 11 percent from 9 A. M. to noon. See also New York *Times*, Oct. 30, 1977, p. 35B, and Nov. 13, 1977, p. 1D; *Journalism Quarterly*, Autumn 1976, pp. 399-404; 6th annual du Pont Columbia Survey (New York: Crowell, 1978), pp. 3-11, 113-124 passim.

4. Federal Radio Act of 1927, 44 Stat. 1162 (1927); Federal Communications Act of 1934, 48 Stat. 1064, 47 U. S. C.

5. National Broadcasting Co. v. U. S., 319 U. S., 190, 226-27 (1943).

6. Red Lion Broadcasting Co. v. FCC, 395 U. S. 367, 378-79, 388-90, 393.

7. 395 U. S. 392-93, 399.

8. *New York Times Magazine*, July 31, 1977, p. 22.

9. *Editor & Publisher*, Jan. 28, 1978, p. 47; New York *Times*, June 13, 1978, p. 1.

10. Quincy Newspapers, Inc., "Annual Report to the Shareholders for 1976," dated May 31, 1977.

11. Supreme Court cross-ownership decision in New York *Times*, June 13, 1978, p. 1; *Editor & Publisher*, comment, Dec. 10, 1977, p. 9. Van Deerlin draft, text of Federal Communications Act of 1978, as proposed by a House committee. Commentary in New York *Times*, June 26, 1978, p. A-18. Lancaster case in *Editor & Publisher*, Dec. 10, 1977, p. 9, and *New York Times Magazine*, July 31, 1977. Allbritton in New York *Times*, June 1, 1978, p. B-6.

12. Jerome Barron, "Access to the Press—A New First Amendment Right," *Harvard Law Review*, 80, (1967), p. 1669.

13. Ibid., p. 1641.

14. Tornillo v. Miami Herald Publishing Co., 287 So. 2d 78 (1973).

15. Tornillo v. Miami Herald Publishing Co., 418 U. S. 258 (1974).

16. Ibid., pp. 256-58. Incidentally Tornillo lost the primary election.

17. Ibid, p. 258.

18. Benno C. Schmidt Jr., *Freedom of the Press vs. Public Access* (New York: Praeger, 1976), p. 234, elaborates on Tornillo case.

19. *New York Times Magazine*, March 6, 1977, p. 16.

20. Thomas I. Emerson, *The System of Freedom of Expression* (New York: Random House, 1970), p. 470.

21. *New York Times Magazine*, March 6, 1977, p. 18. Meanwhile Flynt announced his conversion as a "born-again Christian" and professed to hit the sawdust trail pending the outcome of appeals against his conviction. In Cleveland on Nov. 1, 1977 (see Cincinnatti *Enquirer* for that date), a federal judge declared unconstitutional the state obscenity law under which Flynt was convicted. This did not wipe out Flynt's conviction but it aided his chances for appeal to the Supreme Court. While he was a defendant in still another obscenity trial in Lawrenceville, Ga., on March 6, 1978, Flynt was shot and paralyzed from the hips down.

22. Ginzburg v. U. S., 383 U. S. 480-81.

23. David Shaw, "Editors Face Terrorist Demand Dilemma," Los Angeles *Times*, September 15, 1976.

24. Ibid., Shaw in the Los Angeles *Times*; *Time*, March 28, 1977, p. 57; UPI Reporter, May 12, 1977.

25. Gallup Poll press release, April 28, 1977.

26. Clinton Rossiter and James Lare, eds., *The Essential Lippmann* (New York: Random House, 1963) p. 407.

27. John Hohenberg, *Free Press/ Free People* (New York: Columbia University Press, 1971), p. 16.

28. *Newsweek*, August 22, 1977, p. 77.

29. "Media," by Peter W. Kaplan and Paul Slansky, *New Times*, Sept. 2, 1977, p. 6.

30. *Newsweek*, August 22, 1977, p. 79.

31. Richard C. Wald, lecture at the University of California, Riverside, March 21, 1977, pp. 14-15. (Published by the Press-Enterprise Company, Riverside, Calif., 1977.)

32. From the Newspaper Guild's Collective Bargaining Manual, 1977.

33. *Time*, Aug. 15, 1977, footnote, p. 81.

34. *Broadcasting* magazine, May 2, 1977, pp. 28-29.

35. "National News Council Strives for Recognition," Associated Press story in Boston*Globe*, Aug. 29, 1976; see also prospectus of the National News Council, One Lincoln Plaza, New York, N. Y., 10023.

36. Paley's letter dated Jan. 24, 1977, files of the National News Coucil.

37. Bradlee quoted in AP report for AM, Aug. 29, 1977. Panax case in *Editor & Publisher*, Jan. 7, 1978, p. 7, and *Columbia Journalism Review*, January/February 1978, p. 69. Other sources on NNC are *Columbia Journalism Review*, November/December 1975, and *Editor & Publisher*, Jan. 1, 1977, p. 40.

38. The *Quill*, April 1977, pp. 28-29.

39. Washington *Post*, March 18, 1977, p. A-27.

40. The *Quill*, April 1977, pp. 28-29. Diamond, who did press criticism for the Post-Newsweek broadcasting interests, was one of a very small line of electronic critics that began with Don Hollenbeck of CBS radio befor World War II.

41. At the beginning of 1970, Freedom House noted that fewer than 20 percent of the world's peoples lived in countries the organization deemed free. India and Pakistan since have overthrown their authoritarian governments, but their freedom is far from assured.

42. IAPA News, No. 236, October/November, 1976, p. 2.

43. Clayton Kirkpatrick, "We Were Lucky This Time," *ASNE Bulletin*, January 1977, p. 6. At a regional UNESCO conference in Bogota, Colombia, in 1978, another attempt at all-out control of the news flow in Latin American countries nearly succeeded. See *Editor & Publisher*, Jan. 18, 1978, p. 10 and p. 56.

44. Otis Chandler, "Global View," *ASNE Bulletin*, Sept. 1977. p. 7.

45. David Ottaway, "African Experience," *ASNE Bulletin*, Sept. 1977, p. 10.

46. *North American Review*, May 1904.

47. During a lecture at the University of Kansas, Lawrence, Kansas, November 18, 1977.

48. Quoted in the "The Newspaper Business," Washington *Post*, Business Section, July 24, 1977.

49. Ibid.

50. "How the Public Gets its News," by Leo Bogart, speech before AP Managing Editors, New Orleans, Oct. 27, 1977.

51. Roger Mudd on CBS Evening News, April 20, 1977.

INDEX